HARM'S WAY

UNIVERSITY OF
CALGARY
PRESS

Edited by
Anthony Rasporich
and Max Foran

DISASTERS
IN WESTERN CANADA
HARM'S WAY

© 2004 Anthony Rasporich and Max Foran

National Library of Canada Cataloguing in Publication
Harms' way : disasters in Western Canada / edited by Max Foran
and Anthony Rasporich.

Includes bibliographical references and index.
ISBN 1-55238-091-2

1. Disasters--Prairie Provinces--History. I. Foran, Max II. Rasporich, Anthony
W., 1940- III. Title.

FC3209.D58R38 2004   971.2   C2004-901574-5

Published by the University of Calgary Press
2500 University Drive NW, Calgary, Alberta, Canada T2N 1N4
www.uofcpress.com

We acknowledge the financial support of the Government of Canada through
the Book Publishing Industry Development Program (BPIDP) for our publishing
activities. We acknowledge the support of the Alberta Foundation for the Arts for
this published work.

  Canada Council   Conseil des Arts
for the Arts   du Canada

Printed and bound in Canada by Houghton Boston
∞This book is printed on acid free paper
Cover design, page design and typesetting by Mieka West.

CONTENTS

PREFACE

This book of essays began as a conversation between the editors, late in the last century, a series of questions really: had anyone tackled the stories of various disasters that had beset western Canada from the beginnings of settlement? Some work had been done, including a few popular essays by Frank Anderson on the Frank Slide, blizzards in the Rogers Pass, the Regina Tornado, and the Hillcrest mine disaster, and a couple of recent surveys by Faye Holt and Janet Looker on a wide variety of Canadian disasters. In sum, the scholarship on the subject was cursory, and needed some deeper discussion with reference to the prairie West. From there, the genesis, so to speak, began a search for appropriate topics and authors which resulted in the list of articles collected here.

In the meantime, the Red River flooded again and again, the Pine Lake Tornado tore through vacationers' summer idyll in July 2000, hoof and mouth scares once again raised farmers' and ranchers' anxieties, drought began to wreak its cyclical havoc, as grasshoppers chewed their way through grain crops and frightening scenarios of DNA mutations in seed crops revived Rachel Carson's dire warnings in *The Silent Spring* some decades ago. In short, this book seemed more and more relevant as it came together and a Biblical plague of sorts once more stalked the land in the new millennium. What also seemed remarkable was that the human response to recent misfortune and disaster in the West contained many of the codes of response and experience garnered from previous times of troubles. These essays, then, contain a genetic code of sorts, a pioneer legacy of reaction and collective response, and bear repeating in similar times and circumstances. They are not intended, then, as doomsday scenarios for the morbid imagination, but rather as records of the persistence of the human spirit and its adaptability to the challenges served up by nature in western Canada over more than a century of development.

Several votes of thanks must go to the authors' creativity and patience in waiting for this process to unfold, and to the publishers, particularly Walter Hildebrandt and the anonymous readers at the University of Calgary Press, for encouraging the production of this volume. And finally, the editors, who have been living witness to one or two of these events given their relative seniority, must emphasize their wonder at the human spirit as communities cope with a world turned upside down and inside out. In sum, this book is a celebration of that courage and adaptability in the face of dire misfortune.

INTRODUCTION

Anthony Rasporich

Disaster and catastrophe are central to human history, and central to our conception of history itself. Dramatic traumatic events have always fascinated historians, both professional and amateur; indeed, the conception of history itself was something in the order of a catalogue of natural disasters until the nineteenth century and the rise of the professional historian. The eruptions of Mount Vesuvius, the Great Fire of London, and the Lisbon Earthquake were all highlighted in early historical chronicles as spectacular events, often overshadowing the subtler long-term historical developments which shaped human history. These latter forces, which emphasized human evolution through underlying conditions which altered only gradually, highlighted different types of change, such as climatic deterioration, the migration of wildlife, the rise of market economies, and the rise of the nation state and modern capitalism. History in its academic guise favoured the fable of the tortoise over the hare; the slow-moving forces of the decades and centuries won out over the quick bursts of energy summoned by daily events. In fact, a whole school of history, the *annales* in France, prided itself on precisely this distinction, in claiming that the synchronous history of daily events was of rather lesser importance than the deeper changes witnessed over time, particularly the *longue durée* of a century or more.

Yet, a newer country like Canada, with its deeper history of centuries of development through its native peoples as First Nations and a relatively shorter one of European settler culture, has a uniquely dual sense of history set in a large space. Until recently, it has been the latter version which has been the dominant narrative of the last two or three centuries of historical development. In this North American version of settler culture, the daily chronicle of human existence has emphasized the short-term drama of survival, rather than the urbane outlook of older societies that there is indeed nothing new under the sun. The frontier interpretation of history, of human striving against elemental natural forces, is a more youthful North American narrative emerging in the late nineteenth century as a driving myth to dramatize the conquest of a continent. Carried along with it was a sense of conviction, particularly among American historians like Francis Parkman and Frederick Jackson Turner, that a new human type, the frontiersman, the rugged individual, was in the making. Daily events in the drama of human struggle against alien peoples and environments mattered very much in this type of history. In this narrative, disasters, natural and man-made, were everyday tests of the capacity of the human spirit to survive against all odds.

That sense of struggle, of painful discovery and loss of innocence in the face of natural and man-made disasters, is also embedded in Canadian consciousness, albeit in a different collective sense than the American, but nonetheless with a similar sense of urgency. Communities such as the abandoned villages of the Palliser Triangle could and did disappear in the Dust Bowl conditions of the 1920s and 1930s, as, more suddenly, the community at Frank disappeared in a few minutes under the rock slide of 1903. The tragic tale of the Beothuks of Newfoundland or the Mandans of the Dakotas was all too familiar to the native peoples as well: extermination, whether by climate, disease, or the European hand, was always there as an ultimate threat to survival. Also, there was less of a sense of critical human mass to sustain North Americans against the Malthusian threats to human population with anything resembling the confidence of Asian and European cultures that civilization was likely to persist, whatever the challenge.

This book is not to suggest that western Canadians have experienced any more disaster or tragedy than other Canadians, or for that matter, any other peoples, since any such claim would be absurd. Nor is there any premium in establishing a body count related to such disasters, since we omit here one of the heaviest tolls of all for western Canadians, the losses experienced during two world wars in the twentieth century. The annual remembrances of military losses is enough to document the collective grief which Canadians as a whole feel for their war dead every fall. So do the cenotaphs in even the smallest of towns in western Canada attest to the impact of twentieth century wars on this region as a part of the larger nation.

No, the tale here is about human responses, collective and individual, to over two centuries of natural and man-made disasters. There are ten stories here which demonstrate how peoples responded to their world being turned upside down by famine and disease, by flood, fire, and rock slide, by wind and by cold, by dynamite and gas explosions, and even by such seemingly mundane threats as weeds upon crops. In short, it is about what happens at the contingent margins of human existence, when things go wrong, and occasionally very dramatically so. It deals with the human response when confronted by such challenges, heroically individual or collectively resolute, both at the time and circumstance of extreme duress, but also later in the determination to rebuild and protect against future contingencies. As one of our contributors, David Jones, has said of the prairie dryland farmers, they had by the late 1930s become "disaster proof" after being hardened in the crucible of the Great Depression.

Also, how are such disastrous events woven into the folk narrative of experience and mythology of survival in western Canada? Where are our shrines of disaster, grief, and shame, and how do these provide a collective identity of social purpose and regional character? Where does the harsh winter of 1906–7 fit into that narrative, now that James Gray has given us the ultimate Biblical metaphor of famine and pestilence in his twin tales of disaster, *Men Against the Desert* and *The Winter Years*? Or, how does too much water and wind in the form of the Red River floods, or the Regina, Edmonton, and Pine Lake tornadoes fit into the regional narrative of a largely agricultural and dryland history? Then again, by sheer numbers of casualties, none of them compare to the insidious, catastrophic effects of the smallpox epidemics on the native peoples in the eighteenth and nineteenth centuries, or to the influenza epidemic of 1918–19 on the population of western Canada and the nation at large. And perhaps most awesome of all was the loss of animal populations, particularly the disappearance of the buffalo in the 1870s, an event of cataclysmic proportions for the native peoples and Métis of the West. Similar but equally dramatic challenges have been posed to the ranching communities with the winter kills of 1906–7, and bovine tuberculosis and hoof and mouth epidemics through the twentieth century, yet they too have not been so readily absorbed into the mythic narratives of western Canadian history, largely dominated by the ethos of the prairie settler culture.

Yet another question which arises from the combination of fact and myth and their interplay as history has been their interaction on both the regional and the national stage. For example, our national histories have said little of the environmental, social, and cultural history contained here. Look for the record of the Frank Slide, the Regina Cyclone, the Hoof and Mouth outbreak, Atlantic No. 3, and other catastrophes recorded here, and they are largely absent from the official national histories. Perhaps the Halifax Explosion "made it" to the national roll call of human disasters because of the scale of casualties and as a part of the World War I context, and also due to its mythic recounting in Hugh MacLennan's gripping tale, *Barometer Rising.* The Springhill Mine Disaster, and its more recent variant, the Westray explosions, have also become integrated into the national media coverage, yet the earlier western variations on the theme such as the Frank, Bellevue, and Hillcrest disasters in the Rockies have been less prominent nationally. The spectacular Frank Slide was, until the essay presented here, largely relegated to a subplot of amateur historical interest by Frank Anderson, the same writer who wrote about forgotten western outlaws, who also did not fit the mould of the orderly West promulgated in the official national version of western development.

I shall intrude here with a personal reminiscence, which derives from the region of northwestern Ontario, one that is neither east nor west, but exactly in the middle of Canada, and isolated enough to be of little interest. This particular incident, in fact, never made it into a recent and otherwise very comprehensive compilation of Canadian disasters.[1] The author missed it likely because the Canadian media largely missed it in the aftermath of the Hiroshima explosion of the atomic bomb on August 6, 1945. But, the next day, a dust explosion at the Saskatchewan Pool 4A elevator in Port Arthur (since 1970, Thunder Bay) shattered a reinforced concrete structure, likely as sturdy as the last concrete remnant that stood in the middle of the city of Hiroshima. The smaller explosion in Port Arthur only took the lives of only twenty-five workmen, but the shock wave was an intense one felt miles away in the harbour and in the working class suburbs of the community to the west of the grain elevators. Then, again in 1948 and 1952, further grain dust explosions ripped apart the adjacent grain elevators, resulting in further losses of life, some affecting loading crews on the freighters being loaded at the time. Again, no national story or subsequent mythology of heroism developed. Then, in the summer of 1959, another grain elevator in the same vicinity suddenly slipped into the harbour causing a minor tidal wave which caused millions of dollars in damage to the harbour. The point of these stories was that there were no stories, and little collective memory of them. The owners were the prairie wheat pools, and the engineer who built them was C. D. Howe, who virtually ran the Canadian government of the day. While there were studies for improvement in dust control, there were no judicial inquiries and/or royal commissions of the sort that have since become *de rigueur* in such later transportation disasters as the Dryden air crash of 1989, which did attract the attention of national media, by this time national and electronic in character.

To some degree, then, we are faced with the conundrum, "If the tree falls in the uninhabited forest, does it make a noise if none are there to hear it?" A possible response is that it depends on who and how many are listening, and how far away they are from the scene of the disaster. Clearly, the scale of the Hiroshima explosions in wartime dwarfed the losses next day in a smaller Canadian community. Clearly, also, the huge public impact of the air-bombings of the World Trade Center and the Pentagon of September 11, 2001 have been compared to the attacks on Pearl Harbor which brought the United States belatedly into World War II in 1941. Such cataclysmic events can be used to mobilize nations, which cite date, day, and numbers as part of the cry for both mourning and retribution. Such global disasters are clearly more compelling because of their wide impact on the human consciousness globally and their ability to impact on human memory with widely disseminated visual imagery of film and television.

A related issue to the Tolstoyan conundrum is the more practical characterization of the treefall as a benign event (not for the tree) if no one is in the way. Disasters depend upon concentrations of population in the path of natural and man-made destruction, and the higher the density, the more awesome the destruction. A classic case was the huge forest fire of 1825 in the Miramichi region of New Brunswick which consumed one-fifth of the entire colony's timber, but which never drew much public attention beyond that sparsely populated colony of the British Empire. In that sense also, the dispersion of human population across the vast spaces of western Canada as a far flung colony of Great Britain in the late-nineteenth century might be construed as a sound collective strategy of survival. Certainly, the Baron de Hirsch thought so in his philanthropic schemes for the settlement of European Jews as farmers in North and South America, faced by the pogroms in Russia in the late nineteenth century. It could also be said that the selection of the harsh climate of the northern plains by intending settlers was a poor pioneering strategy except for those communal groups with prior experience in adaptation to harsh continental climates in northern and eastern Europe.

Whether false advertising and/or human gullibility brought the intending settlers to the dryland conditions of the Palliser Triangle, or to poor soils in the Pembina Mountain region of southern Manitoba, questions arise about poor strategic choices in the first phase of settlement, leading to vulnerability to disaster in the second phase. Similarly, the choice of coal mining as an occupation in the Crowsnest Pass or the Coal Branch might be viewed as a poor occupational choice given the high rate of industrial accidents in the mining industry. Human choices inevitably often place people in harm's way, with higher risks attached to some locales as opposed to others. Certainly, coal mining beneath Turtle Mountain in 1903 seems to have been a riskier choice than living and working in the city of Regina in 1912, or vacationing on the shores of Pine Lake in July 2000, yet all seem to have been poor spatial choices in retrospect. Similarly, strategic choices of a generational nature over a longer period can be fraught with hazard; indeed, choices to abandon particular locations and to move on rather than to stick it out may prove to be the wisest strategy in the long run. Human agency and the choices people make are a vital part of the story of disasters, since they are active agents in the historical process which brought them to the time and place of the unfolding drama of natural disaster.

* * *

To bring the story directly into focus on western Canada, it is likely that the total of human losses for all disasters other than those caused by disease was likely less than the slow and steady attrition over time in single-fatality industrial and highway accidents. If one compares the loss of life in the Hinton Via Rail crash of 1986, at twenty-three, and the Air Canada crashes at Moose Jaw in 1954 and Chilliwack in 1956, which saw less than a hundred fatalities, they pale by comparison to the steady incidence of traffic deaths in Calgary today, which account for an attrition of nearly two hundred deaths in Calgary in 2001, and over four hundred in Alberta. Thus, if there is a Benthamite calculus possible for disasters, it must be a contingent one, dependent not only on how many are affected and over what period of time.

There is also is the impact which events had upon their times, their impact upon community consciousness, and the resultant will to prevent a recurrence of similar events in future. The quiet, yet steady resolve of Winnipeggers and Manitobans which brought into place the flood plain diversion known as "Duff's ditch" in the 1960s is a classic remedy, as was the piling of earth dikes along the Bow River in Calgary in response to various floods in the twentieth century. Tornadoes and hailstorms are typically less amenable to rational control, yet attempts have been made for earlier warnings and cloud-seeding, and there have been the financial palliatives of hail and crop insurance. These actions accompanied increased government intervention on behalf of drought-stricken farmers such as happened in the creation of the PFRA and other government initiatives of the 1930s and beyond. As to remedies for disease and epidemics such as smallpox, tuberculosis, and influenza, it is instructive to note that all of these diseases generated a great public demand for public health measures to control them in the 1920s and 1930s. The virtual disappearance of smallpox and tuberculosis later in the century spoke well of this vigilance and societal will to eradicate them as threats to the public weal. Similarly, the quite Draconian public health response to hoof and mouth disease spoke equally strongly of the resolve to avoid further outbreak among cattle in the 1950s. And lastly, proof that every cloud had a possible silver lining lay in the response to the oil field disasters of the post-Leduc era in Alberta, where the demand for development was spurred, not curbed, by the Atlantic No. 3 blowout of 1948.

Yet, not all of the papers here contain the message of reaction/response and rational remedy, since each disaster was in its own way unique in its pathology as an historical event. Looked at individually, they reveal the multiplicity of human collective behaviour under stress. In this respect, the first paper by Hugh Dempsey on the devastating effects of smallpox on the plains Indians is an instructive example of this uniqueness. The issue of decimation by simple cultural contact with Europeans leaps from this paper, as the plains tribes were variously exposed to serial infections of measles, scarlet fever, and smallpox throughout the eighteenth and nineteenth centuries. Dempsey explores the devastating ravages of the disease which claimed thousands of lives. He also examines some of the fictions which arose from the epidemics, including the famous one of deliberate infestation by the supplying of "death blanket(s)" infested with the disease to the Blackfeet by a whiskey trader named John "liver eating" Johnson. History as tragedy, it seems, must have its villains, as well as its victims.

The second paper, by Janice Dickin, is a reprint of a pioneering paper she wrote on the subject of the first great influenza epidemic of the modern era, which killed twenty million people worldwide, and 50,000 in Canada, a number equivalent to our total military losses in World War I. Scarcely a family was not touched in some way by this epidemic, yet inexplicably, little was written about it until this article on the Calgary epidemic, and its sequel on Canada as a whole, appeared in the mid-1970s. That such a catastrophic event should be so ignored and forgotten until recently is inexplicable, since it led directly to demands to establish a Department of Health at the federal level and to reforms in public health. Most recently, medical historians and anthropologists have resurrected frozen corpses from northern Canada, and have concluded that the influenza pandemic was the result of a unique fusion of two viruses, one human and one swine, which produced the deadly strain of 1918–19. A vital point to be made here is that western Canada was firmly tied to a global event of monumental proportions and could not escape, even given its widely dispersed population, the ravages of a worldwide epidemic, and speculation is that it would not avoid another particularly virulent strain today should one appear again. The recent appearance of the SARS virus early in 2003 underscores the continuing vulnerability of Canada to international travel and a potential global pandemic of the 1918 scale if unchecked by stringent public health initiatives.

The next paper, by Lorry Felske on the Frank Slide, or more correctly, the Turtle Mountain Slide, is an insightful analysis of a spectacular rock slide that killed seventy-six people, but also deposited eighty million tons of limestone in huge blocks across the valley and buried the town below. Though only the third most devastating mine disaster in the Crowsnest Pass region, it persisted as perhaps the most picturesque and permanent site of mine-related tragedy visible to the eye on the surface. Felske explores the complex relationship of the slide to economic development, as the CPR was anxious to dispel rumours that it might impede coal supplies for western development as well as agricultural settlement and expansion. Yet, in terms of local impact, the trauma was huge, as in the tragic early ends of the owners, Gebo and Frank, and among the population of Frank, Felske records the serendipitous effects of the huge rockfall. As well, he explores the issue of culpability of the mineowners in ignoring evidence of ominous rumblings in the mountain and the firing of all underground supervisory staff just three weeks before the slide occurred. In some ways, it is a mine disaster story like others, yet it is, as the author notes, compellingly unique in its historical legacy.

The story of the grim winter of 1906–7 is, as the author, Joe Cherwinski, points out, a legendary one embedded in western Canadian fiction from Frederick Philip Grove to Wallace Stegner and W. O. Mitchell. Yet historians have been slow to recognize the winter and its impact upon humans as well as livestock, and only recently have begun to address its significance. In his recent article, reprinted here, Cherwinski details the winter and its human impact on settlement in the myths that it immediately generated, including the notable one of "Frozen Englishmen," unable to heat their houses and trapped in their isolated homesteads, slowly starving and freezing to death in the prairie blizzards of November 1906. The first victims were supposedly the Ratcliffe family, recently settled near Weyburn, Saskatchewan, the subjects of a rumour spread by a local farmer who said he had seen the family's bodies frozen in their shack in the Dirt Hills. The Mountie sergeant sent out to check out the story not only found them well, but with two and a half tons of coal and plenty of provisions. The story was, however, even more alive and spreading out in the North American dailies, and proved very difficult to kill in retractions. The frantic attempts by the railways, the government, and the police at damage control underlined once again, as in the Frank Slide story, that such tragedies, real or imagined, were bad for business, and had to be denied quickly and forcefully.

The account of the Regina "Cyclone" of 1912 by Patrick Brennan represents yet another examination of a western story which has not travelled much beyond province and region. Yet it does represent what has become the archetypal wind disaster story of western Canadian summers, followed notably by the Edmonton Tornado of 1987, which claimed twenty-six lives, and the Pine Lake Tornado of 2000, which resulted in thirteen deaths. These sudden cataclysms with very short warning result in total devastation of whatever human habitat lies in their path, and in that sense the Regina Cyclone was no different. It levelled some five hundred homes and businesses, leaving 2,500 homeless out of a city of 30,000, and causing $1.2 million in property damage. Although only twenty-eight lives were lost, over two hundred were left injured, some of these seriously. The classic contest between various levels of government – municipal, provincial, and federal – to avoid the encumbrances of loans for rebuilding are detailed meticulously here, with the end result that the provincial government did not retire its loan share until 1958! Once again, the negative elements of the story had to be gainsaid, and one way to do it was to say that all great cities, such as London, Chicago and San Francisco, had their disasters, and that their adversity was what made them great! Such boosterism and positive promotion were clearly the message needed to promote a "Bigger and Better Regina" and to forget the past as quickly as possible.

The paper by David Breen on the Atlantic No. 3 "Disaster" follows a similar vein in its exploration of the oil well blowout in the Leduc field south of Edmonton in 1948. One might have titled this paper, "The Smell of Prosperity," as the Atlantic well burned as high as 3,600 feet and spewed smoke as high as 9,000 feet, all visible to Edmontonians twenty miles to the north. The intervention of the Alberta government, Imperial Oil, and the Oil Gas and Conservation Board in curbing the blowout was unprecedented, but also necessary in order to allay public fears and assure Imperial of its investment in the field. The blowout was quickly brought under control by September 1948, and all claims settled by early 1949. Not only was the blowout providential in terms of asserting the government's and the Conservation Board's authority, but it was good for business in that it advertised the abundance of the Alberta field internationally at a time of concern about the scarcity of global oil supplies. As Blair Fraser wrote in *Maclean's*, "It certainly put Alberta on the map." Thus, it had in common with the Regina Tornado the common legacy that disaster was an opportunity, at least as seen from a wider economic perspective.

The next paper by Max Foran on the "Hoof and Mouth" disease outbreak of 1952 in Saskatchewan is a highly topical one, given the recurrence of that disease, in combination with others such as "mad-cow" disease, recently in Great Britain and now in western Canada. As he points out, the virus was not new, and the remedy in both Europe and North America was usually swift and efficient, with quarantine first, and destruction of the infected herds to follow. Over 1,700 animals were slaughtered by May 1952, with compensation from the federal government following at a half million dollars to stock owners. While the disease was considered controlled by August 1952, the western Canadian cattle economy was deeply affected in short-term losses of export sales to the United States late in 1952. But a decline in American as well as Mexican beef supply resulted in an unexpected end to restrictions on Canadian beef by early 1953. Once again, a scapegoat was identified, an itinerant agricultural worker, Willi Bruntjen, who supposedly brought the virus in on his clothing. Although this was not proven after eleven days of intensive tests, the syndrome of the subversive outsider carrying plague in his packsack was all too familiar. The latest protocols surrounding the inaccessibility of Saskatchewan farms to Prince Charles gives further credence to such suspicions of outsiders, whatever their rank. And finally, the recent course of the "mad cow" outbreak in the western prairies is chillingly familiar to that of 1952 in the brutally efficient measures to contain and eliminate the disease. Hopefully, the restoration of the American beef market will run a similar pattern to the earlier "hoof and mouth" outbreak described herein.

Clint Evans is the next author to deal with agricultural history in western Canada, from the hitherto unexplored perspective of weed imports and infestation over the entire period of settlement. He notes that early infestations of stinkweed and thistles were observed in the 1880s as serious problems for cultivation, and by the turn of the century, Manitoba was overrun by foreign-sourced weeds. The traditional control of weeds through summer fallowing proved largely ineffective as a long-term solution, and Manitoba wheat was declining in quality as a result, losing an estimated $20 million in value in rejections at the grain elevators in 1905. Similar problems erupted in Saskatchewan and Alberta by 1910, and various remedies in tillage were tried without effective result through the 1930s. Temporary relief was gained with the 2,4-D herbicides in the decade after the war, but latent problems remained, particularly in the form of chemical residues and potentially disastrous genetic transformations now being reported on prairie farms. This particular problem, as its author points out, is not the cataclysmic one-hour event that disrupts lives and destroys property, but is the sort of long-term disaster in the making that has destroyed entire civilizations in the past.

David Jones' extensive writings on the Palliser Triangle have illuminated the catastrophic consequences of climatic change on the dryland region of southeastern Alberta. He delineates here the two images of this region. One, "the garden," was the early promotional product of external boosters, agricultural experts, and town promoters in the region. The second, a product of the dry cycle beginning in 1917 and lasting a decade, was that of "the wasteland," characterized by crop failures and depopulation more severe than in southern Saskatchewan during the Great Depression. He then turns in his last section to the use of this region during and after World War II as a testing facility for gas warfare and munitions research related thereto on the Suffield Block, northeast of Alderson. With the disappearance of wild horse herds in 1994, he bleakly comments on these last survivors of a totally blighted prairie ecology, fit only for small animal mutations. It is a far cry from the utopian garden aspiration of a century past, and an appropriate companion piece to the warning by Evans in the previous paper of the impending grassland disaster that lurks on the Prairies.

Certainly, the persistent nature of drought in this past growing cycle and the catastrophic effects on the cereal crops and hay production confirms the trend toward further farm depopulation in several areas of the Prairies.

The last paper is a survey by J. M. Bumsted on the flooding in the Red River Valley over the past two centuries, which has occurred often although not with any certainty or predictability. The nature of this disaster is that it is not sudden and without warning as in other disasters, but rather gives ample warnings of its approach so that evacuation is orderly and flood dikes can be thrown up in anticipation. And, in modern times, the media is also given ample opportunity to send television crews to report on the rising waters and anticipated damage. Such is not then an ordinary disaster; all that surprises is the height of the water, usually reported on in Grand Forks and then Emerson, giving time for fortification and/or evacuation. Even disaster relief has taken on familiar rhythms, and by the 1950s the fiscal divisions of responsibility were established, with the federal government absorbing 50 per cent of the cost of immediate relief and 75 per cent of the cost of flood fighting. The increased frequency and serious of flooding in 1948, 1950, and 1956 resulted in a political culture of flood control so powerful that plans were made to protect against a flood of the greatest severity, the devastating flood of 1826. In the end, as Bumsted points out, the Red River Floodway project, designed to divert floodwater around Winnipeg, moved more earth during the early 1960s than was moved during construction of the Panama Canal or the St. Lawrence Seaway. The result was an insurance policy against the most serious challenge to come, the 1997 flood which devastated Grand Forks, North Dakota, but missed Winnipeg, with inches to spare. The irony, as he points out, was that urban inner city blight continued to eat away at Portage Avenue and environs, while Grand Forks' core was completely rebuilt. Yet, the history of planning and engineering to solve the flooding problem, manifested a sensibly Canadian response to a chronic problem of disaster relief and control.

This last paper in some ways does address the western Canadian penchant for planned responses to regularly occurring, chronic repetitions of disasters entailing emergency relief. In some cases, it is early warning weather reports on extreme storm developments, as in the most recent experience with the Pine Lake and Edmonton tornadoes. These disasters spurred the development of comprehensive protocols for disaster relief by Alberta Disaster Services, which was mandated under the provincial Disaster Services Act. In other areas it is seen in the development of protocols for Waste and Hazardous Materials Disposal, the development of evacuation plans for sour gas well blowouts – all have been responses to repeated disasters in recent history, and some were actuated by historical experiences such as those detailed above. Even at this writing, emergency procedures and increased construction standards anticipating a major coastal earthquake in the Vancouver area are in place. And, on the one-hundredth anniversary of the Frank Slide in the spring of 1903, the Alberta government announced provisions for the installation of early warning sensors to detect another potential slide on Turtle Mountain. Learning by negative experience has been a longstanding Canadian practice, enforced by an abiding respect for the power of nature to disrupt in every aspect of its domain, and on a regular, if random, basis. At the same time, the resilience of westerners in the face of expected adversity lies in their pragmatic assessment of difficult situations in such phrases as "It could have been much worse." That process of becoming "disaster proof" and striving for positive outcomes in rebuilding and anticipating a better-built future derives from experiences such as those recorded here.

NOTES

1   Janet Looker, *Disaster Canada* (Toronto: Lynx Images, 2000), xvii–xix.

SMALLPOX SCOURGE OF THE PLAINS

Hugh A. Dempsey

Of all the calamities that befell the Indians of the western Canadian Prairies, none were so devastating or far-reaching as the smallpox epidemics that swept through the region between 1736 and 1870. During that period, at least four major epidemics decimated the Blackfoot, Cree, Assiniboine, Kootenay, and other tribes. The contagions resulted in starvation, loss of leadership, dislocation of families and bands, curtailment of hunting territories, and ultimately an inability to resist the relentless western march of European settlement.

The word in Blackfoot for smallpox, or for any skin eruption, is *ap'iksosin*, with the term *o'mukskapiksin* ("big eruption") being used specifically to describe smallpox. Other related terms are *sika'poksin* ("black eruption") for scarlet fever, and *etoksa'poksin* ("red eruption") for measles.[1] All were deadly diseases for which the Indians had no immunity and which resulted in high mortality rates each time they struck. For example, in 1819 a measles epidemic wiped out a third of the Blackfoot, Blood, Peigan, and Gros Ventre tribes, and in 1864 scarlet fever killed 1,100 members of the Blackfoot nation.[2]

Little is known about the earliest smallpox epidemic, as it occurred more than twenty years before the visit of the first European, Anthony Henday, and half a century before fur traders became established in the upper Saskatchewan region. The first documented evidence of the outbreak appears in the journals of Pierre Gaultier La Vérendrye. On March 26, 1736, he states that a group of Crees living along the Winnipeg River had all died of the disease.[3] The epidemic is also described by David Thompson, who, about 1787, interviewed an elderly Cree Indian named Saukamappee. This man had lived with the Peigans most of his life and his recollections date back to about 1730. He remembered that while he was still a young boy the Peigans drove the Shoshoni south of the Stag River (perhaps the Red Deer). Then, he recalled, "death came over us all, and swept away more than half of us by the Small pox, of which we knew nothing until it brought death among us."[4]

A Piegan scouting party found a large Shoshoni village but were surprised when they could not see anyone around it. They also were puzzled by the fact that a herd of buffalo was grazing undisturbed nearby. When the Peigans attacked the following day, their war whoops were silenced by what they saw. "There was no one to fight with but the dead and the dying," said Saukamappee, "each a mass of corruption."[5] After holding a council, the Peigans decided to plunder the camp of anything that was clean and to take the Shoshoni horse herd. A short time later, the pestilence broke out in the Peigan camp but because they had never experienced anything like it before, they did not attribute it to their raid; rather, they were convinced that it was being spread by an evil spirit. "We had no belief that one Man could give it to another, any more than a wounded Man could give his wound to another," said Saukamappee.[6]

This belief persisted for generations, with the result that the Blackfoot often sought relief from the epidemics through the actions of their medicine men. If evil spirits were causing the smallpox, they reasoned, then the holy men might be able to counteract it.

According to Thompson, until the 1730s the Shoshoni had occupied the plains of southern Alberta while the Blackfoot nation was north of the Bow River. As a result of the epidemic, war ceased between the two tribes for a few years and the Shoshoni, who were equally decimated by the smallpox, withdrew across the Rocky Mountains and left the plains open for the Blackfoot to occupy.

Anthropologist Claude Schaeffer found evidence that this same epidemic had infected a band of Kootenay Indians known as the *Tona'xa* who at that time were living in the Alberta foothills.[7] They had attacked a Shoshoni lodge but discovered that its only occupant was dead. Their chief, Charcoal Bull, warned the warriors not to touch the body, but a young man took a pair of moccasins and a short time later he was struck down with the disease. It soon spread to others in the war party and they took the contagion back to their camps in the Crowsnest Pass area. Soon the entire band was affected, and when it was over, only eight people had survived. They took refuge with the Flathead Indians across the mountains and the Blackfoot moved into the foothills area that the band had once occupied.

The next smallpox epidemic to affect the western plains occurred in 1780. It began along the Mississippi River and quickly spread west and north. According to David Thompson,

> This disease was caught by the Chipaways (the forest Indians) and the Sieu (of the Plains) about the same time, in the year 1780, by attacking some families of the white people, who had it, and wearing their clothes. They had no idea of the disease and its dreadful nature. From the Chipaways it extended over all the Indians of the forest to its northward extremity, and by the Sieux over the Indians of the Plains and crossed the Rocky Mountains.[8]

It was first reported in the Alberta region in October 1781, near the Red Deer River and at the North Saskatchewan River in the following month.[9] By this time, there were still no trading posts in what is now Alberta. Thompson encountered the pestilence at the Eagle Hills, where he met some Crees who were recovering from the disease. When the trader went to their camp, he found that most of the inhabitants were dead and there was a "stench most horrid."[10] The survivors had been too weak to flee so they had pitched their tipis only two hundred yards from the tragic scene. "They were in such a stage of despair and despondence," said Thompson, "that they could hardly converse with us.... From what we could learn, three fifths had died under this disease."[11] In December 1781, traders at Cumberland House received word from Hudson House, their most westerly post on the North Saskatchewan River, that "smallpox was raging all around us with great violence, sparing very few that take it."[12] From there the disease spread rapidly upriver, into areas unvisited by European traders and right to the Rocky Mountains and beyond. To the north and east of Hudson House it spread to Cumberland House, The Pas, and York Factory.[13]

Once a person had contracted the disease, he was usually abandoned by his family, for they considered him to be beyond help, so even if he recovered, there was a good chance that he would starve to death. Others tried to find relief from the fever by plunging into cold rivers and lakes, thus hastening their demise.

Nine years after the 1780–81 tragedy, trader Edward Umphreville painted a graphic word picture of the smallpox epidemic:

That epidemical and raging disorder has spread an almost universal mortality throughout the country in the interior parts of Hudson's Bay, extending its destructive effects through every tribe and nation, sparing neither age nor sex.... The distresses of the Indians by this visitation have been truly deplorable, and demand the tribute of pity from every humane person ... at first [they] imagined it to be no more than a simple breaking out on the skin which would disappear of itself; but it was not long before they had every reason to entertain very alarming apprehensions. Numbers began to die on every side; the infection spread rapidly; and hundreds lay expiring together without assistance, without courage, or the least glimmering hopes of recovery....

Without the least medicinal help, or that common aid which their case demanded, a prey to hunger and disease, these forlorn Indians lay in their tents expiring, under the accumulated weight of every scourge which human nature can experience. Wolves and other wild beasts infested and entered their habitations, and dragged them out, while life yet remained, to devour their miserable morbid carcases; even their faithful dogs, worn out with hunger, joined the ferocious wolves in this unnatural depredation. Heads, legs and arms, lay indiscriminately scattered about, as food for the birds of the air and the beasts of the mountains: and as none were buried, the very air became infectious, and tended to waft about the baneful contagion. Such has been the fate of many of the tribes inhabiting these parts, and which has nearly terminated in their extinction.[14]

Most of the victims were men, with far fewer women and children falling prey to the disease. This left an insufficient number of persons to hunt, and many camps were reduced to starvation after their small supplies of dried meat ran out. And as if to punish the survivors, buffalo and deer could not be found at their usual grazing areas, and the lakes seemed to be devoid of swans, geese, and ducks. By the time the epidemic was over, Indians stated that they had lost more than half their total population.[15] Among the Plains Cree alone, an estimated twelve hundred persons died.[16]

During the next few decades, the Blackfoot and Cree tribes suffered more great losses through measles, whooping cough, and scarlet fever. In 1801, the Gros Ventre Indians were victims of a small outbreak of smallpox that came to them from their southern relatives, the Arapahos. At this time, the Gros Ventres occupied an area along the present Alberta-Saskatchewan border and south into Montana. One trader said the disease also had spread to the Blood Indians of southern Alberta,[17] but Peter Fidler refuted this, saying that it had infected only the Gros Ventres and had "cut off 100 principally of Children, & fortunately it did not spread amongst other Indians."[18]

Meanwhile, European scientists had developed a procedure in the early 1700s to immunize people by making a deep incision into their flesh and inserting pus from a pustule of a smallpox patient. This process, known as variolation, was controversial as it sometimes resulted in the death of the patient.[19] In 1797, Dr. Edward Jenner discovered that vaccinating a person with cowpox provided an effective and safe means of immunization. Vaccines developed from cowpox were easily produced and were introduced into North America a short time later. Lewis and Clark expedition were supposed to have taken such vaccine with them in 1803 when they set out on their voyage of exploration, but their supply proved to be defective and was left behind.[20]

In the 1830s, the Hudson's Bay Company sent instructions from its London office that vaccine be distributed to its trading posts in the hopes that smallpox could be eradicated among its Indian customers. However, the traders took little or no interest in the procedure and few Indians were vaccinated. By this time, the British had trading posts at Edmonton House, Rocky Mountain House, Fort Pitt, and Carlton House for the Blackfoot, Cree, Assiniboine, and other tribes, while those along the Upper Missouri were served by the American Fur Company's posts at Fort Union and Fort McKenzie.

The great smallpox epidemic of 1837–38 had its beginning on the Missouri River, the disease breaking out among some white and native passengers on the steamboat *St. Peters* while taking goods to the various trading posts along the river.[21] The captain knew he had smallpox on board, but instead of putting the goods on shore, fumigating them, and shipping them upriver in keel boats, he made his scheduled stops at Fort Pierre and Fort Clark. There the plague was transmitted to the

This Sioux pictograph portraying the winter count for 1837 shows a member of the tribe suffering from smallpox. Source: Alexis Praus, *The Sioux, 1798–1932: A Dakota Winter Count* (Bloomfield Hills, Michigan: Cranbrook Institute of Science, 1962), 15.

The symbol for the 1837 Peigan winter count shows a member of the
Blackfoot tribe with smallpox. Source: Paul Raczka, *Winter Count*
(Brocket, Alberta: Oldman River Culture Centre, 1979), 45.

Arikara, Sioux, and Mandan Indians, virtually wiping out the latter tribe.[22]

When the steamboat left for Fort Union, it still had much of its infected cargo aboard, as well as a sick man, Jacob Halsey, a partner of the Upper Missouri Outfit. This man had been vaccinated earlier and had contracted only a mild case of smallpox, but he was still capable of transmitting it to others. When the boat arrived at the fort on June 24, 1837, there were no Indian camps nearby and the only native inhabitants were about thirty women, wives and residents at the fort. A short time later a woman came down with the ailment and died. There was no cowpox vaccine at the fort so the traders decided to use the variolation process. However, they got it tragically wrong. According to historian Clyde D. Dollar, "This well-intentioned but dangerous step proved fatal to thousands.... Those intended to be protected were *inoculated*, not vaccinated, and this difference put 'Death in their veins.'"[23] All who were inoculated caught the disease and perished. Two weeks later, one of the traders complained "there was such a stench in the fort that it could be smelt at a distance of 300 yards. It was awful – the scene in the fort, where some went crazy, and others were half eaten up by maggots before they died."[24]

During this time, an Assiniboine chief came to trade. He was turned away after being shown one of the patients, but he still contracted the disease and took it back to his tribe, whose camps extended from northern Montana into southern Saskatchewan. They were struck hard by the smallpox, with an estimated 80 per cent of the victims, or one thousand people, dying of the disease.[25] According to trader Edwin Denig, who himself contracted a mild form of smallpox, "A singular characteristic of this disease was that two-thirds or more died before any eruption appeared. This event was always accompanied by hermorrhages from the mouth and ears. Except in some few cases of the distinct kind, the fever always rose to a pitch of frenzy, in which state many committed suicide or died in other horrid forms."[26]

Meanwhile, the American Fur Company's negligence in permitting the spread of the disease continued. In early June, trader Alexander Culbertson had sent a keelboat of furs from Fort McKenzie to meet the steamboat at Fort Union, and to pick up a supply of goods destined for the Blackfoot trade. These were loaded on board, but while the men were rowing upstream toward Fort McKenzie, smallpox broke out among the passengers and crew. The afflicted included a Blood Indian, an American, and two young Métis girls. The officer in charge, Alexander Harvey, halted the boat at the mouth of the Judith River to keep it in isolation until the contagion had passed. However, some five hundred lodges of Bloods and Peigans were waiting impatiently at Fort McKenzie to trade, and when they learned of the boat's location, they demanded that it be brought to the fort, or they would go downstream and seize it. [27]

Feeling that he had no other choice, Culbertson ordered the keel boat to be brought to the fort. This was at the end of June 1837, by which time two of the patients on board had died while the others were recovering. Historian Jack Holterman wonders, "It seems strange that the Blackfeet disregarded the danger so carelessly. Older members of the tribes must have recalled the previous pandemic of smallpox that had swept through their country in 1781–82." [28] Yet Culbertson himself had no doubt why the Blackfoot ignored the threat of an epidemic. As he said, "Their theory of most diseases was that an evil spirit had entered into the body of the sufferer and that a cure could only be effected by its expulsion. For this purpose the charms of the medicine men were believed to have peculiar potency, which procured their almost invariable employment." [29]

One might wonder more about the reaction of Culbertson than that of the Indians. The trader was fully aware of the dangers, yet he brought the boat, its passengers, and its contents to the fort to satisfy the Blackfoot trade. Within a short time, smallpox had broken out among the employees of the trading post, with Culbertson himself coming down with the disease. He tried to vaccinate those in the fort with smallpox using the variolation method, but almost everyone caught the disease and twenty-nine died. As for the Blackfoot tribes, they traded and returned to their hunting grounds.

Culbertson heard nothing from them for two months, so in October he set out to search for them. Near the Three Forks he discovered a camp of sixty Peigan lodges. As related by a man who interviewed Culbertson:

> Not a soul was to be seen and a funereal stillness rested upon it. They approached with anxious hearts and awed by the unwonted quiet, for the vicinity of an Indian village is not

apt to be the scene of an oppressive silence. Soon a stench was observed in the air, that increased as they advanced; and presently the scene in all its horror was before them. Hundreds of decaying forms of human beings, horses and dogs lay scattered everywhere among the lodges.... Two old women, too feeble to travel, were the sole living occupants of the village. All who had not died on the spot had fled in small bands here and there, frantic to escape the pestilence which pursued them at every turn, seizing its victims on the prairie, in the valley, among the mountains, dotting the country with their corrupting bodies, till thousands had perished.[30]

Farther north, the epidemic was so terrible that hundreds of Blood Indians died at the confluence of the St. Mary and Oldman rivers, near the present city of Lethbridge. As a result, the region forever became known as *Akai'niskwi*, or "Many Died."[31]

The Hudson's Bay Company traders at Edmonton House learned of the smallpox epidemic in November 1837, when a party of Sarcees came begging for medicine. By that time, the tribe's population had already been reduced from a thousand to less than 250 souls. John Rowand, chief factor at Edmonton House, reported that

... our principal Chiefs ... informed me that more than half of all the Slave tribes are no more. When I mention the Slave tribes you must understand it includes five different tribes, all the Blackfeet, Blood Indians, Peigan, Circees [Sarcees], and Fall or Gros Ventres.... Accounts we have about the Blood Indians who were first attacked with the Sickness & who were supposed to be about four hundred Tents of them alone, are now also reduced to a very small number. These same Indians I must confess have pillaged and killed many a poor unfortunate white man across the Rocky Mountains and when they found an opportunity. However if the account we have is correct very few of these miserable Indians are living now.[32]

According to Rowand, the sickness began with a dreadful pain in the head, back, and neck, followed by bleeding from the nose, and once a person contracted the disease they died within two or three days.

The British may not have known the details of how the epidemic started, but they were aware that it came from American trading posts on the Missouri River and had spread north to infect the Blackfoot, Cree, Assiniboine, and other tribes that also traded with the British. Sir George Simpson, governor of the Hudson's Bay Company, learned of the epidemic while he was in Montreal and shipped vaccine to York Factory and Moose Factory, and from there to the various posts. At the same time, circulars were sent out, urging the chief factors to immunize everyone within reach, "by force if necessary," to stem the spread of the contagion.[33] However, Edmonton House, which was hit the hardest by the epidemic, had no vaccine, and when some did arrive, it proved to be defective.

Farther east, William Todd, stationed at Fort Pelly, learned about the epidemic in September when three Crees from the Qu'Appelle reported that "some bad disease has got into the American Fort in Consequence of which their gates are kept constantly Shut and no Indian Allowed to enter."[34] Fort Pelly was one of the few posts that had vaccine on hand, and as Todd suspected the outbreak was smallpox, he took immediate steps to immunize the people at the fort and Indians in the area. He also taught a number of Indian chiefs how to administer the vaccine and sent them to their camps to vaccinate others.[35]

The disease moved northward on its relentless path of death, reaching Carlton House in November. There the officer in charge had vaccinated his men, but the vaccine proved ineffective. At the same time, traders at Ile à la Crosse and Fort Chipewyan anxiously clamoured for new vaccine in the event that the epidemic reached their areas. Noted historian Arthur Ray, "The situation was equally desperate at Edmonton House. Rowand, who was in charge of the district, does not appear to have had any vaccine on hand when smallpox reached the area, nor any familiarity with vaccination procedures."[36]

The result was that where the vaccination was successful, many Plains Cree in eastern Alberta, Saskatchewan, and Manitoba were spared, while at the same time the disease ran rampant among the Blackfoot tribes of southern Alberta, the Stoneys and Sarcees along the foothills, and the Assiniboines of southwestern Saskatchewan.

Ethnohistorian John C. Ewers estimates that at least six thousand members of the Blackfoot, Blood, and Peigan tribes – or three-quarters of their population – perished in the epidemic,[37] as did 4,800 Plains Assiniboines.[38] The Gros Ventres suffered fewer casualties because they had gone through the 1801 epidemic and many had developed an immunity to the disease.

The smallpox continued unabated through the winter of 1837–38 and into the following year before it ended. The Blackfoot winter count for 1837–38 was recorded simply as "smallpox," and 1838–39 as "when it ended in winter."[39] The Carlton House journals note in July 1838 that "two Crees from Fort Pitt ... bring the news that the Small Pock was still among the Indians."[40]

One of the results of the epidemic was to completely decimate many bands and families, so that new bands had to be formed and new leaders chosen to replace those who had died. Also, time was needed to rebuild their depleted populations, but in the meantime, those less affected by the disease, notably the Crees, were able to invade enemy hunting grounds with ease. In Alberta, the Blackfoot tribe found it expedient to withdraw from the Battle River and centre its attention on the Bow River and Blackfoot Crossing. The devastated Assiniboines tended to migrate southward into Montana and left much of the southwestern Saskatchewan plains to the Crees. According to historian Arthur Ray, "As a consequence of the different experiences of the various tribes to the epidemic and the steady migration of Cree into the parkland-grass-land area from the woodlands, the Cree became one of the most popu-lous Indian groups living in the prairie provinces."[41]

Thirty years were to pass before the next – and final – smallpox epi-demic swept the Canadian plains. When it erupted in 1869, Edmonton House, Rocky Mountain House, Fort Pitt, and Carlton House were still the primary trading settlements along the North Saskatchewan River, with large Métis communities at St. Albert, Lac Ste. Anne, Victoria mission, and Whitefish Lake. In the south, a gold rush had brought a swarm of settlers into Montana, with the main trading post for the Blackfoot being at Fort Benton, a short distance from the present Great Falls.

The epidemic started in late August 1869, when a steamboat with a number of smallpox patients on board was allowed to proceed up the Missouri River to discharge its freight. According to a newspaper report, when the boat reached the mouth of the Milk River, an Assiniboine Indian crept on board and stole a blanket from one of the patients. "The dreaded disease broke out among the copper-colored devils," said the reporter, "and spreading like wild-fire from tepee to tepee and from camp to camp, has made a great havoc in their strength and numbers – sending them to perdition in quicker time than bullets and bad bread could do the work."[42]

Within weeks the disease spread to the Gros Ventres and Crows. The Peigans, who normally hunted in Montana, were the first Blackfoot tribe to contract the plague. It could not have come at a worse time for them. For almost a decade, relations between newly arrived American settlers and the Peigans had been marked by animosity and killings on both sides. Then, in the summer of 1869, a young Peigan murdered Malcolm Clark, a rancher and one of the most prominent men in Montana Territory. As a result, Mountain Chief and several other leaders were declared to be "hostiles" and were threatened with extermination. As the winter months set in, the smallpox and the threat of war swirled through the Blackfoot camps.

In January 1870, General James Hardie was convinced that the epidemic would make the Blackfoot even more hostile. "The smallpox prevailed to considerable extent among the Indians," he reported, "and is thought by some to have had the effect to intensify hostility of many of the Blackfeet against the whites, to whom they attribute the introduction among them of the disease."[43] In fact, the Blackfoot were cowed, rather than angered by the onslaught, but the supposed hostility provided a further excuse for the army to destroy their camps.

On January 23, a military expedition under Col. E. M. Baker attacked a smallpox-ridden camp that they believed belonged to the "hostile" Mountain Chief. Instead, it proved to be the village of a friendly Peigan leader, Heavy Runner. But it made no difference; by the time the attack was over, 173 Peigans had been killed, mostly women and children. Those who managed to escape travelled in bitterly cold weather across the border, seeking refuge in Canada. The American Indian agent, Alfred Sully, received a report later in the year from Alexander Culbertson, who had visited a Peigan camp on the Belly River, west of the present Lethbridge. "Mr. Culbertson," he said, "states that a very large number of squaws and children died on the way, from the severe cold weather, and from Small Pox which they had

One of the first chiefs to die in the 1869–70 smallpox epidemic was Seen
From Afar, head chief of the tribe. He is seen here in a Gusavus Sohon
sketch made in 1855 during a treaty with the American government.
Courtesy: Hugh Dempsey.

at the time. They also inform me that they should judge about (1400) fourteen hundred in all died last winter of this disease." [44]

According to the Blackfoot, they knew they were facing a disaster when they saw sun dogs in the sky. "People say the Sun is sorry for us," recalled Yellow Kidney. "After the sickness comes, it attacks all the camps." [45] They believed that the disease was carried through the air, that winds were beneficial in that they could blow the sickness away, and even birds could help because the flapping of their wings dispersed the evil.

There were several methods followed by the Blackfoot in trying to ward off the smallpox or to cure an afflicted patient. One was to have a mildly sick person chew dried meat and then give it to children to eat. It was believed that the children would then contract only a mild form of smallpox and survive. [46] A seriously ill patient might take a dose of boiled whiskey, then plunge headlong into a nearby stream, breaking a hole in the ice if necessary. According to Cecil Denny, "this nearly always resulted in death, although to my astonishment I have been told that in some few cases a cure was the result." [47]

One of the men struck down in the early stages of the epidemic was Father Of All, a Blackfoot chief. His wife was a Blood, and when they went to visit in the southern camp, smallpox broke out and the man came down with the disease. His wife fled in terror and, recalled a Blackfoot elder, "people were angry at her for leaving *Manistokos* sick like that." [48] When the Bloods moved camp, they took the ailing Blackfoot chief with them, but he died on the trail. "Everyone felt so sorry for *Manistokos*," continued the elder, "because alive he was beautiful and dressed up always, and had a good bed, but when he died, he was just laid on the ground and left – no grave at all." [49]

Another leader to perish in the early stages of the epidemic was Seen From Afar, considered to have been the greatest chief in the history of the Blood tribe. He was at Fort Benton trading with the Americans when the epidemic occurred. While camped near the fort, he had a dream on four successive nights telling him that he would be safe as long as he did not try to cross the Milk River Ridge that divided the American territory from the British. However, the chief was worried about his daughter, Mink Woman, who was camped on St. Mary's River near the present city of Lethbridge. In spite of his dream, he rode through the Blood camp, saying, "My people, my children, the Sun looks down upon me. I am going away. My dreams have told me not to cross the Milk River ridge. Four times I have been told. But I have no power to stay here. I must go to my daughter. My people, I may not see you again. Live good lives and do the best you can." [50]

Seen From Afar and his favourite wife went north and found Mink Woman alive and well and, reassured, they headed back south with her. However, when they reached the Milk River Ridge, Seen From Afar said, "I feel a pain in my back. I have the sickness." [51] He laid down in his lodge and died later in the day. His wife and daughter took his body back to the confluence of the Oldman and St. Mary rivers and placed it in his huge tipi beside a gnarled old cottonwood tree. With him were left his personal possessions, including six revolvers and two rifles, with twelve horses being slain at the tipi door so they could accompany him to the spirit world. [52]

A Sarcee named Many Wounds, who was ten years old at the time, recalled the terror of the epidemic. "We had encamped near the Blackfoot just north of the Red Deer River [when] smallpox broke out among us. It attacked the Indians in different ways. Some became red all over, but their skin did not break out into open sores; others were covered with red sores oozing pus. Some were attacked in the throat; their tongues swelled and they suffocated. Others felt pain in the spine and died in one night.... We broke up camp and moved south, abandoning the dead and the dying in their tents or dropping them beside the trail." [53] When it was over, Many Wounds had lost both his parents, two brothers, and a sister.

Chief Factor W. J. Christie at Edmonton House estimated that 1,080 Peigans, 630 Bloods, and 676 Blackfoot had died in the smallpox epidemic, as had two hundred Sarcees and a hundred Stoneys. [54] McDougall was told by a Stoney Indian that the whole area along the Bow River from Morley to the mountains was one vast graveyard. Others believed the death rate had been much higher than Christie's estimate. A traveller in northern Montana recalled seeing a large smallpox camp on the banks of the Marias River containing a thousand bodies, while estimates of Sarcee deaths were as high as five hundred. [55]

In the spring of 1870, the disease spread to the Plains Crees and the Métis along the North Saskatchewan River. It began when a war party of seventeen Crees from the Fort Pitt and Fort Carlton area raided a smallpox-ridden camp of Blackfoot. According to William F. Butler,

"Coming upon a deserted camp of their enemies in which a tent was still standing, they proceeded to ransack it. This tent contained the dead bodies of some Blackfeet; and altogether these bodies presented a very revolting spectacle, being in an advanced stage of decomposition; they were nevertheless subject to the usual process of mutilation, the scalps and clothing being also carried away. For this act the Crees paid a terrible penalty; scarcely had they reached their own country before the disease appeared among them in its most virulent and infectious form."[56] In June a camp of Métis buffalo hunters from St. Albert sent a delegation to treat with the Blackfoot, but instead of peace they brought back smallpox. Farther east, Cree scouts from the Methodist missions at Victoria and Saddle Lake discovered an enemy camp but were warned off by a Blackfoot who told them it was infected with smallpox. The chiefs kept their young men away, but it did not matter, for a short time later some visitors from Carlton House brought the disease into their camps.

As soon as the smallpox appeared, Edmonton House closed its doors, and as a result it had only one case, where a man contracted the disease and recovered. Downriver at Fort Pitt, there were about a hundred deaths in the region and three deaths inside the fort, while the Fort Carlton district had a hundred fatalities, including one European employee at the fort.

At Fort Pitt, the situation was desperate. According to Butler,

> In the immediate neighbourhood ... two camps of Crees established themselves, at first in the hope of obtaining medical assistance, and failing in that – for the officer in charge soon exhausted his slender store – they appear to have endeavoured to convey the infection into the fort, in the belief that by doing so they would cease to suffer from it themselves. The dead bodies were left unburied close to the stockades, and frequently Indians in the worst stage of the disease might be seen trying to force an entrance into the houses, or rubbing portions of the infectious matter from their persons against the door-handles and window-frames of the dwellings.[57]

Above: Fort Pitt, seen here in 1884, was at the centre of the 1869–70 smallpox epidemic. Angry Crees rubbed their infected sores on the door handles of the fort, hoping to spread the disease to the traders. Courtesy: Hugh Dempsey.

Below: Fort Edmonton is seen here in 1871, just two years after the tragic smallpox epidemic that wiped out large portions of the Indian and Métis populations. Courtesy: Public Archives of Canada C-4475.

The methods used by the Oblate priests and the Methodist missionaries to combat the disease were diametrically opposite. George McDougall cautioned his son, "If the small-pox reaches the Saskatchewan, isolate the people as much as you can." [58] As soon as the hunters brought word of the contagion, John McDougall closed the mission at Victoria and told his followers among the Cree and Métis to scatter to the winds and to avoid contact with other families. For some, this action saved their lives; for others already infected it was too late. As for the Oblates, according to George McDougall, "when the scourge first appeared they collected their people into large camps: the bodies of the dead, the infected, and the well, were all collected in the church." [59] As a result, they paid a heavy price. At St. Albert, most of the children at the orphanage were among the 320 who perished, and several years after the event the effects were still being felt. A reporter commented in 1881 that "Whole families were carried off, and in many cases the heads of families only, leaving the children to the charge of the mission." [60] There were about thirty children who survived, one having been blinded by the disease and others horribly disfigured. Meanwhile, Father Albert Lacombe permanently abandoned the mission of St. Paul des Cris, near the present Brosseau, but not before 150 Crees in the area had died.

Yet the missionaries from both congregations laboured long and hard on behalf of their parishioners, and some paid a heavy price. Fathers Leduc and Bourgine, and Brothers Doucet and Blanchet from the Oblates, and John McDougall from the Methodists came down with smallpox, but all recovered. Not so lucky were McDougall's sisters, Flora and Georgiana, and adopted daughter Anna, all dying at Victoria Mission. [61]

Although vaccine had been available at most trading posts during the 1837–38 epidemic, this was not the case in 1869–70. The only supply was at Winnipeg, and the people in the Manitoba area were vaccinated as soon as they learned about the disease. At Qu'Appelle, trader Isaac Cowie used the old variolation method, taking the lymph from the arm of a young Métis child. As a result, there were no deaths in that entire region. [62] At Fort Pitt, John Sinclair used vaccine matter from an Ojibwa. [63] When Hudson's Bay Company officers at Red River learned of the outbreak in the summer of 1869, they made arrangements to send vaccine into the afflicted areas, but the first shipments did not arrive until spring of the following year. By that time the epidemic was in full fury in south and central Alberta, and the vaccine's use seemed to have little effect. The vaccine that reached Edmonton House had been partially frozen on the trip and was worthless. And none reached the Blackfoot and other plains tribes who perhaps needed it most.

During the winter of 1871–72, trader Peter Erasmus could finally comment, "At last the epidemic was over. The terror and fear that had gripped the people was gone and no new cases developed. The people who had fled to the bush returned with the colder weather. Life went on as before except for the scattered graves and the missing places of those who were gone." [64]

One of the results of the epidemic was the formation of the Saskatchewan District Board of Health, which met at Edmonton House in April 1871. Its purpose was to prevent the export of furs from the area until the contagion had passed; to prevent anyone from leaving the district until they swore they had been free from smallpox for three months; and to warn residents to stay away from their settlements until the epidemic was completely over. It also directed that forts and missions be disinfected, and that a supply of vaccine be kept on hand. [65]

The smallpox epidemic of 1869–70 had a number of far-reaching consequences. Probably the most significant is that it occurred on the eve of settlement in the West, just four years before the arrival of the North West Mounted Police. The question arises as to whether the Blackfoot would have been as tractable to the police had their numbers been greater and if some of their great warrior leaders had survived. For example, when Blood chief Seen From Afar died, trader John Healy commented that "his death made the settlement of the north easier." [66] In Montana, General Hardie wondered – correctly – "whether the great calamities which have lately visited this nation will tend to subdue them and cause them to beg for peace." [67]

In addition, the epidemic was followed immediately by the invasion of scores of illicit American traders who flooded the southern Alberta prairies with whiskey. The smallpox had already caused a breakdown in tribal leadership with the deaths of so many of its leaders, and the whiskey trade further exacerbated the situation by creating dissension and chaos within the Blackfoot camps. By the time the Mounted Police arrived, the Blackfoot could not even cope with their own internal problems much less resist the first step in the invasion of their territory by white settlers.

Because of their weakened condition, the Blackfoot also saw further inroads of Cree and Métis hunting parties, until by 1875 enemy camps could be found in the centre of their domain at Blackfoot Crossing.

To a lesser degree, the Métis and their Catholic priests also suffered a setback because of the high mortality rate at St. Albert and other French-Cree communities. As an Edmonton reporter stated in 1881, "The Roman Catholic mission at Big Lake, at one time the largest and most flourishing settlement around here, has not yet recovered from the smallpox in 1870." [68] With the arrival of the Mounted Police in 1874 and the subsequent immigration of English-speaking settlers, St. Albert was ill-equipped to maintain the French language domination of the area. This was not due entirely to the smallpox epidemic, but the setback in population did not make the tasks of the Oblate priests any easier.

One of the side effects of the 1837 and 1869 epidemics was to create the legend of the smallpox blanket. According to this tale – which has had wide circulation in the native community – white people deliberately set out smallpox-ridden blankets in order to destroy the Indian population. This has been held as a prime example of the attempted genocide of the Indian race. Like so many other legends, it appears to have elements of truth. There is, for example, at least one documented instance in the East in which smallpox blankets were used to spread the disease. In 1763, at the beginning of Pontiac's uprising, Sir Jeffrey Amherst, commander-in-chief of the British forces in America, suggested to Col. Henry Bouquet that smallpox be introduced to the dissident Indians. Bourke replied, "I will try to inoculate ... some blankets that may fall into their hands, and take care not to get the disease myself." [69] Amherst countered with the statement, "You will do well to try to inoculate the Indians by means of blankets as well as to try every other method that can serve to extirpate this exorable race." [70] Later in the year, another British officer noted, "Out of regard for them (i.e., two Indian chiefs) we gave them two blankets and a handkerchief out of the smallpox hospital. I hope it will have the desired effect." [71] It did, and within a short time the epidemic was raging out of control among the tribes of the Ohio Valley. This incident was recorded by historian Francis Parkman and others and received wide circulation. This appears to have been the origin of the western legend of the smallpox blanket.

It received further credence in 1831 when smallpox was introduced among the Pawnee Indians camped along the Platte River. According to artist George Catlin, a year earlier, "some of the Fur Traders visited a threat upon these people, that if they did not comply with some condition, 'he would let the small-pox out of a bottle and destroy the whole of them.' The pestilence has since been introduced accidentally amongst them by the Traders; and the standing tradition of the tribe now is, that 'the Traders opened a bottle and let it out to destroy them.'" [72]

The earliest known fictionalizing of the smallpox blanket tale occurred when a story, "The Death Blanket," appeared in a Scottish journal in 1844.[73] The author, Percy B. St. John, obviously used the writings of Catlin as his reference as he told the story of a beautiful Blackfoot girl named Many Buffalo Calves. She was promised to an evil Blackfoot-Crow warrior, Buffalo Child, but she was in love with a fur trader, Henry Williams. While the two men were competing for her hand, the steamboat *Yellowstone* arrived and Buffalo Child obtained a blanket or poncho owned by a smallpox patient. "Some said the blanket was given him by a trader who hated the Blackfeet," said the author.[74] In council, Williams told the chiefs that Buffalo Child would die, and so would anyone who had contact with him. When the epidemic struck, the evil warrior was the first to perish. "Of the 2,500 families existing at the time the pestilence commenced," said St. John, "one or more of 8,000 only survived its ravages; and even to this hour do the bones of 7,000 or 8,000 Blackfeet lie unburied among the decaying lodges of their deserted village...." [75] Williams persuaded the girl to flee with him to St. Louis, where he later became a federal senator.

A second fictional story – this one about the 1869–70 smallpox epidemic – was written by Frank Wilkeson and published as "The Haunted Tribe" in a Montana newspaper in 1880.[76] The first part of the tale deals with a party of Crees and Métis who were killed by Peigans near the Cypress Hills, after which their ghosts began to haunt the enemy camps. In 1869, a whiskey trader named John "Liver-Eating" Johnson supposedly tried to build a fort on the Belly River but was driven off by the Bloods. In Wilkeson's story, "Johnson swore to have revenge on the whole Blackfeet tribe. Going to Fort Benton, on the Missouri River, that fall, he found that a steamer just arrived from the lower river had smallpox on board. Johnson eagerly bought the infected blankets. Packing them on two ponies he started at once for the upper Milk River." [77]

The two pack horses with the deadly loads were abandoned where they could be found by Peigan scouts. A short time later, the ghosts returned to the Peigan camps and on the following day the epidemic erupted in the tribe. "Of the ravages of this disease, introduced by Johnson, enough is known to justify the statement that one-third of the nation was swept away by it." [78]

In 1943, schoolteacher Gerald Berry picked up a variation of the latter story and published it as an historical fact. He said that, "The smallpox plague of 1869 which so ravaged the Blackfoot Confederacy was caused by the malevolence of a single white man. An American trader named Evans and his partner had trouble with the Blackfoot in 1868, the partner being slain and all their horses stolen. Evans made his way back to St. Louis, where he swore revenge. Purchasing several bales of blankets infected with smallpox, he set them out on the bank of the Missouri in Indian country, and the plague swept through the tribes like wildfire. The Blackfoot alone lost nearly 1,400 men, women and children in five months – truly, a life for a life, with a vengeance." [79]

Historian Paul Sharp drew from Berry's account in 1955 to write that "Blackfoot stories blamed the plague of 1869 upon the evil genius of an American trader who swore revenge for the loss of his horses to a raiding party. He allegedly purchased several bales of infected blankets in St. Louis and placed them on the banks of the Missouri River where innocent Indians filched them." [80]

The stories are pure fiction, but combined with the factual events in the Ohio Valley in the 1700s, they became the basis for the smallpox blanket legend that has gained a place in western folklore. It is now firmly believed by many to have really happened, but as yet no evidence has come to light that would give it any credence. Yet like many other legends, it has gained a life of its own and will continue to be told and retold as historical fact.

NOTES

1 Hugh A. Dempsey, *A Blackfoot Winter Count* (Calgary: Glenbow Museum, 1965), 14–15; interview with Many Guns, Julian and Jane Hanks Papers, Glenbow Archives, folder 35, box 300; C. C. Uhlenbeck and R. H. Van Gulik, *An English-Blackfoot Vocabulary* (Amsterdam Uitgave van de Koninklijke Akademie, 1930), 73, 135.

2 Dempsey, *Blackfoot Winter Count*, 7, 14.

3 David G. Mandelbaum, *The Plains Cree* (New York: American Museum of Natural History, 1940), 186.

4 Richard Glover, ed., *David Thompson's Narrative, 1784–1812* (Toronto: Champlain Society, 1962), 245.

5 Ibid.

6 Ibid., 246.

7 Claude E. Schaeffer, "Plains Kutenai: An Ethnological Evaluation" *Alberta History* 30, no. 4 (Autumn 1982): 8.

8 Glover, *David Thompson's Narrative*, 236.

9 Arthur J. Ray, *Indians in the Fur Trade: Their role as trappers, hunters, and middlemen in the lands southwest of Hudson Bay, 1660–1870* (Toronto: University of Toronto Press, 1974), 105.

10 Ibid.

11 Ibid.

12 Cumberland House journal, entry for December 11, 1781, Hudson's Bay Company records, B.49/a/11, Provincial Archives of Manitoba.

13 Jody F. Decker, "Tracing Historical Diffusion Patterns: The Case of the 1780–82 Smallpox Epidemic Among the Indians of Western Canada," *Native Studies Review* 4, nos. 1 and 2 (1988): 15–17.

14 Edward Umphreville, *The Present State of Hudson's Bay, Containing a Full Description of that Settlement, and the Adjacent Country; and likewise of the Fur Trade* (Toronto: Ryerson Press, 1954), 47–49.

15 Ibid.

16 John C. Ewers, *The Blackfeet: Raiders on the Northwestern Plains* (Norman: University of Oklahoma Press, 1958), 114.

17 Charles M. Gates, ed., *Five Fur Traders of the Northwest* (St. Paul: Minnesota Historical Society, 1965), 155.

18 Alice M. Johnson, ed., *Saskatchewan Journals and Correspondence* (London: Hudson's Bay Record Society, 1967), 317.

19 E. Wagner Stearn and Allen E. Stearn, *The Effect of Smallpox on the Destiny of the Amerindian* (Boston: Bruce Humphries, 1945), 53.

20 Ibid., 57.

21 Alexander Culbertson claimed that the steamboat had been the *Trapper*, not the *St. Peters*.

22 Hiram M. Chittenden, *The American Fur Trade of the Far West* (Stanford: Academic Reprints, 1954) 2: 621–22.

23 Clyde D. Dollar, "The High Plains Smallpox Epidemic of 1837–38," *Western Historical Quarterly* 8, no. 1 (January 1977): 22.

24 Charles Larpenteur, *Forty Years a Fur Trader on the Upper Missouri* (Chicago: Lakeside Press, 1933), 110.

25 Chittenden, *The American Fur Trade*, 625.

26 Ewers, *The Blackfeet*, 71.

27 Jack Holterman, *King of the High Missouri: The Saga of the Culbertsons* (Helena: Falcon Press, 1987), 50.

28 Ibid.

29 James H. Bradley, "Characteristics, Habits and Customs of the Blackfeet Indians," *Contributions to the Historical Society of Montana* 9 (1923): 278.

30 James H. Bradley, "Affairs at Fort Benton," *Contributions to the Historical Society of Montana* 3 (1900): 221.

31 Dempsey, *Blackfoot Winter Count*, 15.

32 Letter, Rowand to George Simpson, December 28, 1837, Hudson's Bay Company records, D.55/4, 360, Provincial Archives of Manitoba.

33 Hugh A. Dempsey, ed., "Simpson's Essay on the Blackfoot, 1841," *Alberta History* 38, no. 1 (Winter 1990): 4.

34 Fort Pelly journal, entry for September 20, 1837, Hudson's Bay Company records, B.159/a/17, 2, Provincial Archives of Manitoba.

35 Arthur J. Ray, "Smallpox: The Epidemic of 1837–38," *The Beaver* 306, no. 2 (Autumn 1975): 11.

36 Ray, *Indians in the Fur Trade*, 190.

37 Ewers, *The Blackfeet*, 66.

38 Ewers, *The Blackfeet*, 72. This is based upon the estimate of eight persons per tipi.

39 Dempsey, *Blackfoot Winter Count*, 9.

40 Carlton House Journal, entry for July 12, 1838, Hudson's Bay Company records, B.27/a/23, Provincial Archives of Manitoba.

41 Ray, *Indians in the Fur Trade*, 191.

42 *Helena Herald*, October 26, 1869.

43 Report of Inspector General James A. Hardie, January 7–15, 1870, cited in Ben Bennett, *Death, Too, For The-Heavy-Runner* (Missoula: Mountain Press, 1981), 90.

44 Letter, Alfred Sully to the Commissioner of Indian Affairs, Washington, July 10, 1870, "Letters Received by the Office of Indian Affairs, 1824–81," Montana Superintendency, 1864–1880, roll 490, National Archives, Washington, D.C.

45 Interview with Yellow Kidney by Claude Schaeffer, October 28, 1949, Schaeffer Papers, Glenbow Archives.

46 Ibid.

47 Cecil Denny, *The Riders of the Plains* (Calgary: Herald Co., 1905), 10–11.

48 Interview with Mrs. Takes the Gun Himself, by Julian and Jane Hanks, July 30, 1941, Hanks Papers, Glenbow Archives.

49 Ibid.

50 Interview with John Cotton by the author, December 26, 1953.

51 Ibid.

52 William F. Butler, *The Great Lone Land* (Toronto: Macmillan, 1910), 314.

53 Ibid., 7–8.

54 William J. Christie, "Smallpox Report," *The Manitoban*, Winnipeg, September 16, 1871.

55 Diamond Jenness, *The Sarcee Indians of Alberta* (Ottawa: National Museum of Canada, 1938), 7.

56 William F. Butler, *The Great Lone Land*, 367.

57 Ibid., 368.

58 John McDougall, *George Millward McDougall, The Pioneer, Patriot and Missionary* (Toronto: William Briggs, 1902), 154.

59 Ibid., 159.

60 *Edmonton Bulletin*, December 2, 1881.

61 William J. Christie, "Smallpox Report," *The Manitoban*, Winnipeg, September 16, 1871.

62 Ray, *Indians in the Fur Trade*, 192.

63 *The Manitoban*, Winnipeg, April 15, 1871.

64 Peter Erasmus, *Buffalo Days and Nights* (Calgary: Glenbow Museum, 1976), 212.

65 *The Manitoban*, Winnipeg, September 16, 1871.

66 "John J. Healy and the Bloods," Manuscript in Tappen Adney Papers, Montana Historical Society Archives.

67 Report of Inspector General James A. Hardie, January 7–15, 1870, cited in Bennett, *Death, Too*, 90.

68 *Edmonton Bulletin*, December 2, 1881.

69 Stearn and Stearn, *Effect of Smallpox*, 44.

70 Ibid., 44–45.

71 Ibid., 45.

72 George Catlin, *North American Indians, Being Letters and Notes on their Manners, Customs, and Conditions, Written During Eight Years' Travel Amongst the Wildest Tribes of Indians in North America, 1832–1839* (Philadelphia: Leary, Stuart & Co., 1913) 2: 29.

73 Percy B. St. John, "The Death Blanket," *Chamber's Edinburgh Journal* 1, no. 24 (June 15, 1844): 373–76. The author sets the date at 1828, but this a likely a typographical error for 1838, as the steamboat *Yellowstone* that figures prominently in his story had not yet been built by that earlier date.

74 Ibid., 376.

75 Ibid.

76 Frank Wilkerson, "The Haunted Tribe," *Benton Weekly Record*, September 24, 1880.

77 Ibid.

78 Ibid.

79 Gerald L. Berry, *The Whoop-Up Trail* (Edmonton: Applied Art Products Ltd., 1943), 15.

80 Paul F. Sharp, *Whoop-Up Country: The Canadian-American West, 1865–1885* (Minneapolis: University of Minnesota Press, 1955), 27.

PALE HORSE/PALE HISTORY? REVISITING CALGARY'S EXPERIENCE OF THE SPANISH INFLUENZA, 1918–19[1]

Janice Dickin

What makes an event something of historical importance or, for that matter, even simple historical interest? Our history books are filled with stories that have affected only very few and have had what might be called only near-reaching significance. In some instances, notably in political history, events are cited even though the main point is that they have had no effect at all on the course of human affairs. For good reason or ill, however, the daily commerce of what we call "politics" has been invested with historical importance, making it a touchstone for how we see ourselves, how we explain ourselves. Were it not for its characterization as "political," would the collapse of the World Trade Center and its aftermath still be in the news more than a year later? Would there indeed have *been* an aftermath? Certainly more Americans will have died in the meantime of tobacco and car crashes (and, probably, gunshots) than died in the admitted tragedy of September 11. And in terms of worldwide rates of death from disease and famine, all these tragedies constitute only a blip on the scale.

The fact is that we decide which incidents to remember as historic and which not. That choice need have nothing whatsoever to do with active historical agency. A good example of an incident of absolutely no historic importance whatsoever that nonetheless has a grip on at least recent North American consciousness is the sinking of *The Titanic*, at most instructive as a case of bad engineering, elevated to a lesson on punishment of hubris. Other, more damaging, events meanwhile slip by historians and the society they serve like ghost ships, leaving in their wake only pale history. One prime example of this is the worldwide pandemic of influenza that killed in excess of twenty million people in the fall and winter of 1918–19. In Canada alone, the death toll was in the nature of 50,000 in a few weeks, only a few thousand less than the nation lost in the four years of hostilities that ended just as the epidemic struck.

I first wrote about the effects of this epidemic in 1976,[2] in an article which forms the major part of my contribution here, and again in 1977 in an article expanding my examination to Canada as a whole.[3] At the same time, another graduate student wrote and published on the similar experience of another western city,[4] and a senior historian from the east chided me (at the major conference at which I presented the broader study) for beating him to press. The topic also attracted international interest, resulting in a book on the American social experience of the flu[5] and another with a more medical bent, looking at influenza in terms of its general threat to humans.[6] Predating all of these by a couple of years was another seemingly prescient study specifically on the 1918–19 flu as a pandemic.[7] This flurry of activity in the mid-1970s was spurred by a distinct historical panic of its own: a fear that something called "swine flu" was about to wreak worldwide havoc similar to the 1918–19 visitation. For a variety of reasons, one of which was that the panic had little basis in reality, this did not occur.

The scholarship produced by the scare was nonetheless sound and offered a new perspective ripe for factoring into historical discussion the changes the world underwent at the end of the Great War. In fact, the revelations of this scholarship have had no impact on historiography whatsoever, and we remain as ignorant as before when it comes to understanding the effect of this pandemic on human history. In preparation for this re-examination, I set a researcher the task of cutting a wide swath through (mostly general) works on Canadian history written after 1976 to ascertain how they handled the new material on the Spanish flu. For key words, she used "Spanish flu," "influenza," "epidemic," "grippe espagnole," "espagnole," and "maladie." In over a hundred general histories of Canada as a whole or of its provinces or specific municipalities, she found that only eight made any reference to the epidemic and that only four professional historians made any attempt to synthesize this new knowledge into a general understanding of Canadian history. Two of the works[8] are more or less chronological narratives, and the treatment of the epidemic as more or less just another anecdote is not immediately noticeable. In the two general histories that did, to their credit, make mention of the influenza epidemic, the event was subsumed in one, as an end to the Great War, and as the beginnings of a "small Department of Health."[9] In the other view, it is justly recognized as "one of the most devastating epidemics of modern time," but became in the larger narrative a segue linking the end of the war to the politics of the Red Scare of 1919.[10]

My return to the topic of influenza in the 1980s while in law school presented me with a slightly different problem. I attempted to find historical meaning in one of the greatest cases in English common law.[11] *Carlill v. Carbolic Smoke Ball Company* ([1892] 20 Q.B. 484; affirmed [1893] 1Q.B. 256) is followed to this day as a precedent in unilateral contracts by lawyers and courts with absolutely no inkling of its origins in an influenza pandemic (1889–90) rivalling the 1918 onslaught in killing ability. Frustrated in general by the lack of intellectual depth in my new discipline and by its eagerness to cloak itself as a science (i.e., jurisprudence) as a way of fending off accusations that it (albeit usually unwittingly) both engendered and prolonged endemic injustice, I sought solace in demonstrating that the judges who ruled in *Carlill*, really for the first time, against a quack medicine company could not have helped but notice the illness and death surrounding them. Medical historians were happy with my work and I had no problem publishing it. The legal historian with whom I had done the work as a "directed reading" was far less happy: he insisted that I could not say the judges were influenced by the epidemic unless I could produce a written statement by one or all of them making that precise assertion. Since I considered it highly possible that they knew not their own motives, I did not argue the point. In terms of the point I was trying to make, it simply didn't matter whether they had internalized this or not.

The structural truisms of professions die hard. Despite three decades now of social historians like myself producing complex scholarship on non-political topics, politics as the quintessential organizing principle in the history of Canada – and of all other countries, for that matter – remains unperturbed. Ironically, for that reason, it is possible for me to republish an article more than a quarter of a century old without making any fundamental changes to interpretation. The only work on the 1918 epidemic that has succeeded the scholarly flurry of the mid-1970s has been starkly anecdotal in nature. This is not to downplay the importance of getting a richer set of data on the record. Eileen Pettigrew's monograph is an excellent read.[12] Stephani Keer's chapter[13] in Ted Byfield's several edited volumes on Alberta history adds details beyond my original scope. And the Belyks' *Beaver* article of 1988,[14] largely confined to the experience in Vancouver, is interesting. My point is merely that, barring profound shifts in historiography in general, the 1918 flu epidemic is destined to remain only a disaster, not a defining moment in our history, but pale history.

Canadians are not alone in this affliction. The name I have given this rewrite comes from the Book of Revelations (6: 7–8), in which the Prophet John envisions, well, the end of history. One of the agents of destruction, one of the so-called Four Horsemen of the Apocalypse, is Death, astride a pale horse. This numinous image illuminates an unforgettable line in an Afro-American lament featuring a young woman whose life has been changed by the death of another: "Pale horse, pale rider, done taken my lover away." Katherine Anne Porter chose the title "Pale Horse, Pale Rider" for a story considered a masterpiece of twentieth century American short fiction.[15] Porter, a young reporter in Denver, was so ill from the flu that her newspaper set the type for her obituary. Her hair turned white and then fell out. In her first attempt to get up after a month in bed, she broke her arm and damaged her leg. She was told she would never walk again. Within six months, however, she was well on the way to full recovery. It would be years, though, before she could write the story of her lover's death – and of the death of the way of American life she had been raised in but which was rapidly giving way to one that is more recognizable to us.

The influenza epidemic came not only at the end of what we have come to call the First World War (such a term requiring the occurrence, undreamed of in 1918, of at least a Second), it came also at the beginning of women's suffrage, affordable automobiles, accessible roads, middle class affluence, and – soon and possibly most significant of all – radio. Porter used the device of the flu to snap a shot of American society at just that moment of change. Alfred W. Crosby, the major American historian of the flu, claims that this single story provides the most accurate depiction of the period, synthesizing material otherwise available only through endless newspaper consultation. Despite this, he says, "the story has attracted the attention of historians not at all, or only as a characteristic product of an important figure in American's postwar literary revival."[16] I refer to Porter's story here, not because the Canadian and American experiences were identical (which, given the differences in the geographical and racial realities of the two countries, let alone the political, simply could not be!), but to demonstrate that sometimes it is profitable to step outside traditional historical constructs when seeking historical truth. What follows is the best stab I could make a quarter century ago at understanding the impact the epidemic had on my own city a mere thirty years before my birth. I leave it intact as an artifact of its own time.

—

During the years 1918 and 1919, a pandemic of influenza swept all inhabited sections of the world except the tiny island of Tristan de Cunha in the South Atlantic.[17] It has been estimated that over half the world's population, more than one billion people, were attacked by the disease, and of these between twenty-one and twenty-two million failed to recover.[18] For Canada, the number of sufferers was set at about two million[19] and for Alberta 38,000,[20] of whom over 4,000 died.[21] The available statistics indicate that Calgarians got off extremely lightly, with only 341 deaths from epidemic influenza in 1918 and forty-three in 1919.[22] Non-statistical data indicates that the city's actual toll was considerably higher.[23]

The so-called "Spanish flu" made its official entrance into Calgary at 3 a.m. on October 2, 1918, with the arrival of a trainload of soldiers which had become infected en route from Quebec City to Vancouver. Calgary's Medical Health Officer, Dr. Cecil Stanley Mahood, had been forewarned by telegram from the last stop, Regina. He met the train at the station and took charge of fifteen sick men, making sure that no one but himself came into contact with the passengers. The soldiers were immediately put into isolation at the base hospital at Sarcee military camp and Mahood expressed hopes that due to the precautions taken, the flu would spread no further. This was not to be. Not only were two nurses from the hospital and a Calgary-based soldier contaminated within the next five days, but the disease entered the city through at least three other channels. One was via a family recently arrived from New Brunswick, the father dying in the city and the mother becoming sick. The others consisted of two soldiers transferred from Petawawa, Ontario, and the wife and daughter of a Calgary lawyer who had died of the flu in New York City and whose body they had gone to retrieve. These cases were immediately quarantined at the army base hospital, but there can be no doubt that the disease made other entrances into the city, and once introduced, it was too virulent to contain. By mid-

October, although doctors denied coming across any "true cases" of Spanish flu and would admit only to "a great many cases of grippe and ordinary influenza," [24] Calgary had an epidemic on its hands.

The man of the hour for the next four months was Cecil S. Mahood. Educated at the University of Toronto and with public health experience obtained in Denver, Colorado, the young doctor (born in 1882 in Huron County, Ontario) had come to Calgary in 1911 and was appointed medical health officer shortly thereafter.[25] In this capacity, he automatically became the leader in the fight against the flu. Throughout the duration, his tasks included the provision of care for the sick, imposition of quarantine, liaison with the provincial Minister of Health, A. G. Mackay, and such non-medical chores as quelling panic, demanding fair pay for those under his charge, and soothing the ruffled feathers of city officials and businessmen. Mahood excelled in these capacities, and it is undoubtedly partly due to his no-nonsense approach to the emergency that Calgary's toll was as light as it was. Tragically, his own wife, Ina Hodgins, died of pneumonia following influenza during a later wave of the same disease in August 1922.

The disease with which Mahood was dealing had already been described to the people of Calgary in the *Herald* of September 28. Its symptoms were described in layman's terms: chills, then fever with temperatures of 101 to 103 degrees, headache, backache, reddening and running of the eyes, pains and aches all over the body and "general prostration." This sounded not unlike the "grippe and ordinary influenza" Calgary doctors hoped they were faced with.

However, the 1918–19 flu had some special added features. One was its extreme contagiosity. Present in the mucous membrane of the sufferer or carrier, the influenza virus was broadcast by breathing, sneezing, coughing, and expectoration. It could also be picked up through contact with materials such as handkerchiefs, sheets, etc., that had recently been in contact with a sick person. Once infected, people suffered a sudden onset of symptoms, characterized by a great physical weakness causing some literally to drop at work, at home, or on the street. There were even some recorded cases of victims actually dropping dead.

A severe case of flu could mean a dangerously high fever, cyanosis – a condition causing a bluish discoloration of the skin and mucous membranes due to an excessive concentration of reduced hemoglobin in the blood – and possibly death. A mild case meant a few days in bed, but here too there was danger; a long, slow convalescence was needed to assure full recovery. If too little care were taken at this crucial period the flu could lead to the onset of pneumonia, a very serious matter before the discovery of antibiotics.

Not only were there no antibiotics, there was (and is) no drug that could cure influenza. The only effective measures that could be taken were bed rest, increased intake of fluids, and some sort of analgesic to relieve the pain. The only effective preventive was to avoid coming into contact with the flu. These seemed to be simple enough instructions, but in a city the size of Calgary and with the high percentage of people infected or convalescing at any one time, Mahood had his hands full. The city lacked sufficient hospital beds, equipment, and personnel; and the position of medical health officer lacked the authority necessary to provide for efficient prosecution of the job at hand. As long as Calgarians were frightened, Mahood faced little opposition to his sometimes extrajudicial tactics, but as soon as they declared a premature victory over the flu, his authority was challenged and his lack of power exposed.

Imposing quarantine was the first and most obvious step to be taken, and in doing so Mahood broke the law. The Alberta Health Act did not provide for the quarantine of influenza cases. Mahood admitted this in public, but said he intended to go through with it anyway. There was no public outcry and local physicians declared their full support. Six days later, on October 16, Sections 22 and 23 of the relevant Act were amended to include Spanish influenza among those diseases requiring modified quarantine.

However, flu had escaped quarantine before for some basic reasons. Difficult to diagnose, its symptoms were often so mild it appeared to be nothing more than a common cold. In such a case, the household might miss being placarded and the other members of the family were free to go anywhere they pleased, possibly carrying the flu with them. Some people, recognizing their condition for what it was, did not seek medical attention for fear of quarantine, which would prevent the rest of the household, most importantly the breadwinner, from carrying out necessary tasks.

And in mild cases where medical attention was sought, the doctors themselves must share some blame for the failure of quarantine. Some of the cases they saw were not reported – sometimes because of an honest failure to make a proper diagnosis, but also because they felt they were too busy to bother dealing with the necessary bureaucracy to have the residence placarded. Some failed to act because they were convinced that other doctors were not obeying regulations, or that such measures did no good. There was also a genuine sympathy for a family that could be cut off from the outside world and from its source of income for a set of symptoms that in ordinary times would interest practically no one. At any rate, quarantine was never more than partially successful against the spread of the flu. It has been estimated that despite the best efforts of the health department of Edmonton, the number of cases reported and quarantined in that city did not exceed 60 per cent of the actual cases in the community. [26]

If one believed the patent medicine advertisements in the *Herald*, Mahood could have used other means than quarantine to prevent further spread of the flu: Fruit-a-tives, Gravino Co.'s Hot Toddy, Carbolium Sweeping Compound, Wonder Health Restorer, Caro-Noleum, Peps, Laxative Bromo Quinine, Gin Pills, Horlick's Malted Milk and Morson's Scotch. The local Hudson's Bay store ran a special on a number of articles, guaranteeing every one as an aid in the pre-vention of Spanish flu, including gum camphor, Boral Throat Gargle, Listerine, Paraformic Throat Ease Tablets, Harry Lauder Vocalets, Cascara Bromide Quinine, Evans Famous Pastilles, Syrup of White Pine and Tar, Norway Pine Syrup, a concoction of white pine, eucalyptol and honey, and another of syrup of linseed and turpentine. McIvor's Drug Store listed some twenty-five remedies for flu, at the same time warning customers not to follow fads. People used such products throughout the epidemic. By October 21, Vancouver announced that it was running out of camphor, cinnamon, and "other anti-influenza drugs." [27]

In addition to patent medicines, large supplies of prescription drugs were consumed. The medical profession throughout the continent was as eager as the public to find a preventative or a cure. One Pittsburgh doctor announced no ill effects and full recovery following the injection of a solution containing iodine, creosote, and guaiacol. More conserva-tive practitioners recommended such standbys as acetylsalicylic acid (aspirin) and acetophenetidin, although later these were thought to have perhaps done great harm.[28] Narcotics were also popular. During the month of October, Chicago pharmacies filled 741,825 prescriptions, 441,641 of which were for flu or pneumonia, and of these 104,010 contained either opium, opium derivatives, cocaine, or chloral.[29] Demands for drugs were so strenuous that a Calgary druggist suggested that more women should take up pharmacy so that they would be available in such emergencies. A reversal of general over-prescription of drugs came from the doctors of osteopathy. One in Calgary claimed that sensualists suffered worst from disease and the best cure for the flu demanded not only strict avoidance of drugs but also no food for a week, enemas, and plenty of water. Still, he was probably closer to the truth than the Pittsburgh doctor.

People also suggested various homegrown concoctions: thyroid pills; a rub made from lard, camphor, and chloroform; a mixture of cream of tartar and rhubarb. But the main ingredient of most non-professional remedies was liquor. Goat's milk and rum was a sure cure; so was whiskey and quinine. In a province undergoing the rigours of prohibition, the only legal way to get liquor was by prescription, and as some wit in Lethbridge wryly observed, doctors prescribing whiskey got more patients than those prescribing castor oil.[30] There was repeated pressure on the local and provincial authorities to relax the liquor laws as was done in Toronto and Vancouver, but instead, on November 1, F. G. Forster, chief inspector of the Alberta Liquor Control Board, released some sad news. The liquor stock would not last ten more days at its current rate of consumption and he asked doctors to cut back on their prescriptions. There was no hope of replenishing stock. No brandy or Scotch was available in Canada and neither could any be obtained from Britain, where all potable alcohol had been commandeered for use by the army. Forster's proclamation did little to quell the demands for liquor. It was the most popular topic of letters to the *Herald* until November 7, when the paper announced its policy to publish no more on that subject.

Liquor had always been used as a folk medicine, its major appeal probably being that it felt as though it was doing something. The same psychology lay behind the popularity of compounds containing such aromatic substances as camphor, menthol, and eucalyptol, for even the mildest cases of flu manifested what has been called an "indescribable foeter" or stench.[31] Masking the odour must have seemed like a positive act even if any other advantages were questionable. Even though Mahood declared early in the epidemic that "Menthol, camphor, throat pastilles and other things of a similar nature will not prevent the disease,"[32] he made no effort to discourage the sale of such items and even recommended the use of camphor as a chest rub at one point. He concentrated on implementing two other methods of prevention: vaccine and masks.

Vaccination involves inoculation with a milder variety of the germ, but for the vaccine to be successful the disease in question must be subject to certain conditions. For one thing, it helps if one attack provides immunity from further attacks. For another, the doctors must be certain as to what disease is being dealt with. Influenza does not fulfill the first of these conditions, although infection sometimes does result in a tendency not to contract the same variety of the disease for a limited period. The 1918 variety also did not fulfill the second condition. Nobody really knew what it was, partly because there was such a short period between the onset of the disease and the major epidemic in the autumn. The other reason for the flu's mystery was the fact that a microscope powerful enough to allow for its proper identification had not yet been invented.[33] Nevertheless, several types of vaccine were manufactured and tried on various groups of people, but there was distinct disagreement among the medical profession regarding their worth.[34] The most rational approach to the subject was that it was time to get started on vaccine for the next epidemic.[35] Massachusetts health officials distributed several types of vaccine and came to the reluctant conclusion that inoculations should only be performed for scientific research. In Calgary, although vaccine was sent from the east by the CPR for its seriously depleted staff and Edmonton sent down enough to inoculate 15,000 people, there was never enough for the whole city, and even what was available could be distributed only on a volunteer basis. Not many people were interested, and vaccine played too small a part in the epidemic in Calgary to measure its effectiveness.

The use of masks was a different matter, and the enforcement of their use vied with the lack of liquor as the greatest flu-related controversy in the city. At first they were recommended only for use by those coming into constant contact with the sick, then were made compulsory for all railway and street car employees and passengers. The province eventually passed a law on October 25 ordering all persons to wear masks while outside their own homes or residences, except while eating. Although the order continued in effect until November 23, one should not assume that it was generally complied with. True, the *Herald* ran a front page picture showing the staff of a local Bank of Commerce looking for all the world like a large gang of well-disciplined bank robbers, but it also ran daily reports on the number of people appearing in court for appearing unmasked in public places. Many were fined, many more were warned. One defendant complained that the presiding judge wore no mask, and even the hospital board held meetings at which not one official's face was properly covered.

Complaints against the masks continued for the duration of the order. They were described as being grotesque, distracting, depressing, and most importantly, dangerous. Proper care and use presented no danger and, although some doubt was cast on their value in preventing the wearer from catching the disease, they certainly acted as a means of preventing the wearer from disseminating it – if only because of the deterrent effect upon what became known as "the careless spitter." However, masks were in many cases neither cared for nor used properly. The main problem was that one needed not one but several masks, each to be worn no more than two hours at a time, then thoroughly boiled before re-use. Moist masks incubated germs, and those complaining that their use was dangerous were right. Constant attempts were made to educate the public in this matter, but it is unlikely that much headway was made. Most people avoided the danger of unsanitary masks by simply not using them. On a visit to Calgary, the provincial Minister of Health complained that not 20 per cent of Calgarians were complying with the order. In certain situations, however, use was compelled, such as when boarding a street car or when being approached by a police officer. To prepare for such emergencies most offenders kept a mask tied around the neck which could be slipped into place. A picture taken of the victory celebrations on November 11 clearly shows several masks pushed down out of the way. Mahood did what he could to encourage the use of masks but, faced with a wall of civil disobedience, he could do little.

So, of the four major preventatives available – drugs, vaccination, masks, and quarantine – the first three were of doubtful efficacy and the fourth unrealistic. Since the flu would inevitably spread, the major efforts of Mahood, his small health department, and the many volun-

Canadian Bank of Commerce Staff during Spanish flu epidemic, 1918.
Courtesy: Glenbow Archives NA 964-22.

teers were aimed at simple relief of the symptoms, keeping the sufferer comfortable until recovery or death, and slowing down the spread of the flu as much as possible.

One of Mahood's first decisions was that flu sufferers would not be admitted to regular hospitals. If permitted, this could have resulted in the rapid spread of the disease within the institution, as was the case in eastern hospitals where it was allowed. The alternative was to set up and equip a new hospital. To this end, the hospital board met on October 17 and decided to take over the old hospital on 12th Avenue East that had been evacuated in preparation for its use by the army. [36] City council granted funds to fit the building for occupancy, and by October 19 it had twenty-three patients. When its capacity of sixty patients was reached by October 24, Colonel Walker School was occupied and provided with another forty-five beds. This was soon increased to ninety-five, and the capacity of the 12th Avenue East building, generally referred to as the Emergency Hospital, was increased by erecting two large tents to which pneumonia sufferers were moved at the first symptom. Tents were also raised at Colonel Walker, and on November 1, Victoria School was taken over and equipped with thirty beds for use as a convalescent hospital, thereby releasing space at Emergency and Colonel Walker for the more seriously ill.

Most of those patients actually admitted to hospital were from out of town or were members of entire families, all of whom were too sick to look after themselves. In cases where all adults in a family were sick but the children were well, the latter were moved to Stanley Jones School, which was fitted up on October 28 as a dormitory for fifty children. However, the greatest number of sick managed at home. For those families with at least one adult still functioning, endless columns of nursing advice were published in the *Herald*. But in other families, although one person might be capable of doing some chores while convalescing or under the influence of only a mild case of influenza, outside help was needed. Finding trained personnel to run the regular hospitals and emergency hospitals, visit the sick at home, and supply their bodily wants was a much bigger problem than simply opening new hospitals.

Many doctors had gone overseas with the troops. So had many nurses. Added to this shortage was the fact that, due to their constant contact with the sick, health personnel yielded to the infection in great number. As many as sixteen city doctors were sick at one time, the first death among them occurring on October 30. Nurses also suffered a high rate of sickness and death.

Mahood was then left with the double problem of filling more positions with fewer people, so his only alternative was to turn to the public. Salaries were offered to attract volunteers: first to any unmarried trained nurses not currently employed, then to unmarried V.A.D.'s (members of the Voluntary Aid Detachment), then to married nurses or V.A.D.'s with no dependent children, then to those with children who could make other arrangements for their care, then to just anyone who might not know anything about nursing but who could at least warm soup, get a drink of water, or empty a bedpan. Desperate notices asking for more volunteers appeared every day in the newspapers, and by the end of the year, even part-time help was sought. Even students served, one adolescent girl becoming infected while caring for sick children, and dying on November 17.

To carry volunteers on their rounds, women motorists with their own cars were called for. Women were also expected to join in the effort to provide the quarantined and bedridden with sufficient food. Soup kitchens were set up by October 26 in the domestic science departments of Ramsay, Victoria, Connaught, Riverside, and Hillhurst schools. Two days later another was opened at the Good Eats Cafe on 8th Avenue East to provision the many sick in downtown rooming houses, and on October 30 a kosher kitchen was opened in the Strathcona Block to supply Jews and anyone else who might apply. The kitchens at first concentrated on soup and later added junket and custard to the menu as the number of convalescents needing more solid food gradually increased.

Men seem to have largely escaped being persuaded, impressed, or shamed into volunteerism. There are several reasons for this, the obvious being that many men were overseas with the army and the regular employment of the rest was enforced by the "Loafer's Act." But another reason existed: the epidemic was seen as a chance for women to do their bit for the war and for civilization. Nursing was considered a maternal act, and maternalism was, after all, what women were thought to be all about. Some men, of course, helped in the epidemic. But these were given jobs in what was considered man's work – organization and provision of supplies.[37]

Provisioning was a problem. Just as many health personnel were involved in the war effort, so was a good deal of Canada's economic production. Any extra beds, blankets, or bedpans that the country owned were in military hands. Fortunately, the war was winding down by the time the epidemic hit Calgary, and the army could supply many of the items needed. The city of Montreal also helped. Mrs. Sheawood of the Alberta branch of the Red Cross, considered the best hospital buyer in Canada, was in Montreal when the flu hit, and in appreciation for her services, that city sent Alberta any sheets, blankets, pillowcases, towels, nurses' gowns, and dressing gowns left over from its own flu fight.

However, most provisions were scrounged from within city facilities. The Palliser, Alexandra, King George, Empress, and Yale hotels donated worn bed linen. The Red Cross made available its emergency equipment and supplied masks and pneumonia jackets by the score. The P. Burns Co. provided meat for the soup kitchens, and Associated Charities distributed milk, eggs, jellies, fruits, etc., it had received from various organizations and wholesale food stores from as far away as Okotoks. Private citizens also donated what they could.

In addition to looking after their own, Calgarians also helped smaller surrounding communities. From the first arrival of the flu in the area, Mahood served as medical health officer for virtually the whole southern third of the province. He sent pages of advice to small town doctors and officials, answered their phone calls regularly, and arranged for nurses, volunteers, and supplies to be sent out. Calgarians served in Drumheller, which suffered two thousand cases by November 1, perhaps the worst epidemic of the province. They helped at the Sarcee Reserve, where practically all teachers and pupils were taken sick, and after city inhabitants decided that flu was no longer a problem, many of Calgary's health personnel went to towns north of Edmonton where there were later but severe epidemics.

Calgary's premature declaration of victory over the flu came on November 11, 1918. Bill Hohenzollern, as the Kaiser was now patronizingly called, had been defeated and in fact would soon catch influenza himself. Thousands of people spilled onto the streets – police, firemen, city officials, and ordinary citizens – and as the *Herald* noted: "Influenza masks were forgotten and those who enjoyed the day least were those who remembered to bring their masks." [38] From the beginning, the epidemic had been tied psychologically to the war, although there is no evidence that Calgarians believed the rumours circulating elsewhere that the flu had really been caused by the Germans poisoning Allied water supplies.

However, though the two disasters, war and flu, were linked, it was simple-minded to think that defeating the Huns would also put an end to the "flooies." Yet all major North American centres lowered their restrictions soon after the day of victory and all suffered relapses. On November 15, the city of Hamilton, Ontario, which had not only suffered seriously from the epidemic but also had celebrated victory more vigorously than most, announced that it was undergoing a second wave of flu and found a connection between this setback and the peace celebrations. Calgarians' eagerness to forget about all the old problems at once was not an act of childish petulance. Since mid-October, the flu had changed their lives decidedly for the worse. Although the *Herald* occasionally published amusing flu poems and cartoons, Calgarians were not light-hearted about their situation. The health department phone rang constantly; many people kept their children at home as a preventive measure; others shunned the street car for fear of infection; some stopped reading the newspapers, and others asked that reporting on the epidemic be stopped and replaced by religious columns. And Mahood stressed: Don't worry. Don't get excited. Don't be afraid.[39]

Even those who wanted to live normal lives could not do so. One could avoid the mask restrictions with a little ingenuity, but other rules were unavoidable. On October 19, police and store managements were given orders to enforce a new "no loitering" rule. In addition, the following types of concerns were closed or forbidden: dance halls, pool rooms, dancing academies, cabarets, joy parlours, theatres, picture shows, roller skating rinks, second-hand clothing and furniture stores, rummage sales, private furniture sales, meetings of women's clubs and organizations, and all public meetings and parades. Schools closed the next week, partly to make the buildings available for use as flu hospitals or provisioning headquarters, and partly to release teachers for volunteer work. Eventually, all auctions, wedding parties, and public funerals were also banned. Even churches and Sunday schools were closed. Railroad and street car services were cut; garbage could not be burned because it bothered flu patients, and quiet was decreed, especially on downtown streets, for the same reason. Even Halloween celebrations were cancelled. Everywhere Calgarians went they were hounded by the reality of the epidemic. Ironically, the churches were the first to lead a

Wearing flu masks during Victory Parade, November 13, 1918. Courtesy:
Glenbow Archives NC 20-2.

rebellion against these restrictions; they wanted to hold a thanksgiving service to celebrate the end of the war, but it took pressure from the business community to get rid of the restraints.

At the end of October and again in the second week of November, Dunn's Review of New York announced that Canadian business was suffering general temporary slowdown due to the flu. In Calgary, advertising managers worked overtime to think up ways to lure customers into their stores. The Hudson's Bay Co. announced that it was "taking unusual precautions for the safety of its patrons," and ordered its sales personnel to wear masks three days before the order became general. It also prided itself on being the "best ventilated store in the west."[40] For those still not convinced, it offered a stepped-up telephone order service, as did Jenkins Grocery. Glanville's Department Store announced numerous sales, meanwhile admonishing its clientele to "Keep Moving," and Kolb's Restaurant repeated almost daily that it used "only thoroughly sterilized dishes and equipment." The losses of these businesses, however, could not be compared with the hardships undergone by those which actually closed down. Calgary sports promoters lost big money; theatres and moving picture houses were closed for over five weeks; and more than one acting troupe was stranded in the city, unable to give performances there or anywhere else in the West.

On November 14, the Calgary city council, dominated by businessmen, announced that it would petition the provincial government for the right to lift all bans. Mahood objected and the council retaliated by asserting that throughout the epidemic, the board of health had consistently overstepped its authority. It notified the government that it wanted any further decisions to be arrived at jointly by the board and the city council before being sent to the provincial board for approval. Health Minister Mackay fired back a reply the next day: the board was the sole power when it came to regulation of the flu epidemic and needed no confirmation from the council. But in the same telegram a response was made to the theatre cast of "Have a Heart," which had been stranded in Calgary since the flu began. Mackay strongly recommended in favour of them giving one show before they left and Mahood complied. Other theatres demanded and quickly received the same right, followed by businesses, labour organizations, and finally the churches, who considered it a sorry state of affairs when people were allowed to do everything but pray.

After Mahood had grudgingly approved the lifting of restrictions, the hospitals had closed down one by one, except for the Emergency, which took care of any convalescents, and the lack of volunteers became less noticeable as people recovered. By November 23 there were no new cases and the epidemic was declared over. Business returned to almost normal and doctors and morticians finally had a chance to determine just what the toll had been.

But the respite also allowed problems that had seemed unimportant while danger threatened to take on a new significance. The city council wanted to know who would pay for the expenses incurred by the flu hospitals.[41] There was also an uproar over the "outrageous" wages paid to nurses and volunteers. During the epidemic, people had been willing to pay as much as $40 a week for untrained nurses, the supply being so short and the need so urgent. This was now labelled as profiteering. Six school nurses were also under fire for receiving their regular salaries plus that paid for epidemic work by the health department, and the employees of that department also created an issue when they submitted a joint bill for overtime.

Mahood supported those who had stood by him in the time of crisis. He said that the nurses had earned every cent they got and fought for the health department overtime, asking for none himself. His victories were limited, for the actual pay finally received by all flu workers was less than he had personally supported. Probably his major accomplishment was to have the opening of schools delayed for a week so that teachers, most of whom had worked long and hard as volunteers, could relax and overcome their exhaustion.

Mahood also warned that a second wave would no doubt occur and that if the city refused to support those who had worked hard and to engender a wariness of the disease in the public mind, there would be a cutback in the number of volunteers next time.

In November, the American Public Health Association scheduled a special meeting in Chicago on the topic of the influenza epidemic and, as medical health officer, Cecil Mahood was granted both time and expenses to attend. The meeting started on December 9 and Mahood left several days earlier to allow for travelling.

The second wave actually started gearing up before Mahood left for Chicago, and before it was finished most of his predictions had come true. Most volunteers and public health workers who were serious in their vocation had left to help in the north as soon as Calgary's restrictions were lifted. Unconvinced that a real public emergency existed, others from the city failed to take their places in the fight. Perhaps others were disillusioned by the acrimonious pay dispute, convinced that helpers were not appreciated. By December 11, all beds at the Emergency were filled, pleas for nurses had reached the point of desperation, and Mahood was cabled for advice. He urged the taking of all necessary precautions, and when he arrived back from Chicago a week later he announced that the conference had supported his conviction that inoculations and masks were the most effective means, with added results coming from public education.

Schools were closed early for the Christmas holidays, mostly to release Stanley Jones and any other schools that might be needed later as hospitals. Otherwise the only restrictions were to keep children under sixteen out of public places and to provide for some shorter hours, anti-crowding regulations, extra fumigation, and masks for those serving the public. Schools were not to be reopened until the flu had totally disappeared, and vaccine was available to anyone who would consent to inoculation. In an attempt to lure volunteers, Mahood provided for shorter hours and assured married women that arrangements would be made to allow them to be at home on Christmas Day.

The second wave was over by January 27, 1919. It took those who had been spared by the first, mostly children and the well-to-do in Elbow Park and Mount Royal. Mahood stated that the first wave reported 1,800 cases, but he really felt 3,500 cases was closer to the truth. The second recorded 934, which he considered fairly accurate. However, more of those who caught the disease died.[42] Still, with fewer people sick there was not the crisis to supply beds and food. The Emergency was filled, Stanley Jones was converted to a two-hundred-bed hospital, and Central Methodist Church set up a soup kitchen, but that was all that was needed. Most people could successfully ignore the flu, and accounts of it were buried in the back of the papers.

For some, the flu would have long-lasting effects. Some families had lost their main wage earner; others faced crushing debts that had piled up while the person was off work with the flu, convalescing or laid off because of closure or business cutback. Associated Charities announced that never before had it ever had so many calls at Christmas by destitute households. Sadder yet, the Children's Shelter was filled to capacity with children available for adoption. On November 29 alone, sixteen children were brought in, nine of these available for adoption. They included six under thirteen months and another three who were aged two, four, and six, all from the same family whose father had died in September and the mother in November. By January 8 there were twenty children, all orphaned by influenza, available for adoption from the shelter. Added to this were an unknown number of children, similarly bereaved, who were simply taken by relatives or friends.

In addition, the epidemic brought more broadly based changes. Public health was seen as an urgently needed service, and in 1919 the federal government established a separate Department of Health. Many other countries did the same. Preparations also were made to allow for a better system of vital statistics. Public attention was drawn to shortcomings in sanitation systems, and many returned soldiers took courses and found jobs in areas relating to that field. The United Farm Women of Alberta pushed for health reform, and one alderman in Calgary ran on a ticket for rationalization of health services. Drumheller ratepayers voted for the establishment of a hospital to be built and run at their own expense.

Mahood lost a certain amount of popularity among officials because of his handling of the epidemic. He was criticized for overreacting to the flu and causing great expense to the business community; it was even suggested that the post of medical health officer be switched from an appointive to an elective position. The suggestion was not taken seriously and Mahood stayed on for many years. In 1924 he was considered prominent enough to be included in John Blue's biographical work *Alberta Past and Present*, wherein it was declared that "his work as a public official is deserving of strong commendation."[43]

The flu remained in the area for most of the first half of the 1920s, but it was largely ignored. After the epidemic of 1918–19, most wanted to forget.

Staff at Pinkham Hospital (later Grace Hospital) during flu epidemic, 1919.
Courtesy: Glenbow Archives NA 2267-7.

In Happier Times. Dr Cecil S. Mahood and Nurses, c. 1936. Courtesy:
Glenbow Archives NA 2361-8.

NOTES

1   Unless otherwise stated, all material for this paper came from day-by-day accounts in the *Calgary Herald* for the months of September, October, November, and December 1918 and January 1919. Direct quotes from the *Herald* are noted individually.

2   Janice Dickin McGinnis, "A City Faces an Epidemic," *Alberta History* 24 (Autumn 1976): 1–11. Reprinted with permission of *Alberta History*.

3   Janice Dickin McGinnis, The Impact of Epidemic Influenza: Canada, 1918–1919," *Canadian Historical Association Historical Papers* (1977), 121–40, reprinted in S.E.D. Shortt, ed., *Medicine in Canadian Society. Historical Perspectives* (Montreal and Kingston: McGill-Queen's University Press, 1981), 447–52.

4   Margaret W. Andrews, "Epidemic and Public Health: Influenza in Vancouver, 1918–19" *B.C. Studies* 34 (Summer 1977): 21–44.

5   Alfred W. Crosby, Jr., *Epidemic and Peace, 1918* (Westport, CT: Greenwood Press, 1976).

6   W.I.B. Beveridge, *Influenza: The Last Great Plague. An Unfinished Story of Discovery* (New York: Prodist, 1977).

7   Richard Collier, *The Plague of the Spanish Lady. The Influenza Pandemic of 1918–1919* (London: Macmillan, 1974).

8   John H. Archer, *Saskatchewan: A History* (Saskatoon: Western Producer Prairie Books, 1980), 183–84; and Howard Palmer and Tamara Palmer, *Alberta, A New History* (Edmonton: Hurtig, 1990), pp. 187–88.

9   Desmond Morton, *A Short History of Canada*, 3rd ed. (Toronto: McClelland & Stewart, 1997).

10 J. M. Bumsted, *A History of the Canadian Peoples* (Toronto: Oxford University Press, 1998).

11 "Carlill v. Carbolic Smoke Ball Company: Influenza, Quackery and the Unilateral Contract," *Canadian Bulletin of Medical History* 5, no. 2 (Winter 1986): 121–41.

12 Eileen Pettigrew, *The Silent Enemy. Canada and the Deadly Flu of 1918* (Saskatoon: Western Producer Prairie Books, 1983).

13 Stephani Keer, "In six hideous months the 'flu kills almost as many as the war," in Ted Byfield, ed., *Alberta in the 20th Century*, vol. 4, *The Great War and its Consequences, 1914–20* (Edmonton: United Western Communications, 1994), 326–44.

14 Robert and Diane Belyk, "Spanish Influenza 1918–1919: No Armistice with Death," *Beaver* 68 (October/November 1988): 43–49.

15 *The Collected Stories of Katherine Anne Porter* (New York: Harcourt, Brace, 1957), 269–317.

16 Crosby, *Epidemic and Peace*, 319.

17 Adolph A. Hoehling, *The Great Epidemic* (Boston: Little, Brown, 1961), 8.

18 Collier, *Plague of the Spanish Lady*, 305.

19   Charles Graves, *Invasion by virus: can it happen again?* (London: Icon Books, 1969), 180.

20   Of which 31,051 occurred in 1918 and 7,185 in 1919: Alberta, *Annual Report of the Department of Public Health of the Province of Alberta*, 1919 (Edmonton: King's Printer, 1920), 8.

21   Ibid., 65; and Alberta, *Annual Report of the Department of Public Health of the Province of Alberta*, 1918 (Edmonton: King's Printer, 1919), 35. There were 3,259 deaths from epidemic flu in 1918 and 1,049 in 1919.

22   Alberta, *Annual Report*, 1918, 77; and 1919, 109.

23   All contemporary statistics for the 1918–19 pandemic are very incomplete and always on the low side, for several reasons: difficulty of diagnosis, concomitance of similar diseases, a desire to avoid public panic, the confusion general to keeping statistics in wartime, a desire to hide the true situation from the enemy, the failure of overworked personnel to report accurately, and so on.

24   *Calgary Herald*, October 15, 1918.

25   John Blue, *Alberta, Past and Present*, vol. 2 (Chicago: Pioneer Historical Publishing Co., 1924), 347–48.

26   T. H. Whitelaw, "The Practical aspects of quarantine for influenza," *Canadian Medical Association Journal* 9 (December 1919): 1,070–74. Whitelaw was Edmonton's medical health officer.

27   *Calgary Herald*, October 21, 1918.

28   Graves, *Invasion by virus*, 201.

29   Ibid., 200.

30   Ibid., 185.

31   Lieutenant-Colonel C. E. Cooper Cole, "Preliminary report on influenza epidemic at Bramshott in September-October 1918," *Canadian Medical Association Journal* 9 (January 1919): 42.

32   *Calgary Herald*, November 2, 1918.

33   Graves, *Invasion by virus*, 47.

34   For this range of opinion, see Major F. T. Cadham, "The Use of a vaccine in the recent epidemic of influenza," *Canadian Medical Association Journal* 9 (June 1919): 519–27; John W. S. McCullough, "The Control of influenza in Ontario," *Canadian Medical Association Journal* 8 (December 1918): 1,084–86; and Graves, *Invasion by virus*, 30.

35   See J. J. Heagerty, "Influenza and Vaccination," *Canadian Medical Association Journal* 9 (March 1919): 22–28; and F. H. Wetmore, "Treatment of Influenza," *Canadian Medical Association Journal* 9 (December 1919): 1,075–80.

36   Minutes of Calgary Hospitals Board and Committees, 1915–1919, entry for October 17, 1918, Calgary Hospitals Board Papers, 1905–1970, Glenbow-Alberta Institute.

37   The only woman with a high organizational position was Dr. Gertrude Oakley, head of the school nursing program. During the epidemic, she was in charge of all nursing and volunteer work. Her role was also seen as strictly feminine – women were urged to volunteer and help their "sister" Gertrude fight the good fight. She was second-in-command only to Mahood throughout the worst part

of the flu, and when the second wave became serious during his absence from the city, she immediately took charge, as Mahood had provided for. However, within two days, she had had Dr. A. Fisher, superintendent of the General Hospital and unfamiliar with health department proceedings during the flu, quietly placed in command over her.

38   *Calgary Herald*, November 12, 1918.

39   *Calgary Herald*, October 18, 1918.

40   *Calgary Herald*, October 19 and October 30, 1918.

41   Minutes of Finance, Special and Auditing Committees of Calgary Hospital Board, 1914–1919, entry for December 14, 1918, Calgary Hospitals Board Papers, 1905–1970, Glenbow-Alberta Institute.

42   As noted, statistics are sketchy. This state is based on experience of the second wave recorded for other centers in North America.

43   Blue, *Alberta, Past and Present* 2: 348.

THE GREAT ROCK SLIDE AT FRANK

Lorry W. Felske

At 4:10 a.m. on Thursday, April 29, 1903, the top of Turtle Mountain cracked loose and hurtled toward the coal mine town of Frank nearly three thousand feet below. Eighty million tons of limestone smashed and ground its way across the valley floor, pulsed tremors through the ground and pushed forward gusts of wind and dust with a noise like "a thousand express trains ... tearing at full speed over the house-tops."[1] In ninety seconds it was over. Thirty million cubic feet of rock had carved a wide and destructive path and covered nine hundred acres.[2] Buried by the jumbled limestone boulders were seventy unfortunate victims, sections of the Crow's Nest River and its tributary, Gold Creek, seven thousand feet of the CPR's main line and mine spur lines, the Frank mine entrances, its surface structures, six miners' cottages, and tents and buildings from a neighbouring construction camp and ranches. Hit and killed instantly as they worked just outside the mine opening were a haulage driver and a trapper boy, a young assistant who opened and closed ventilation doors in the mine.[3] Sealed inside the workings were another seventeen miners, alive and uninjured, but with no route for escape. Trapped with them were several haulage horses. The miners would survive their ordeal; the horses would not. They would eventually succumb to starvation before feed could be got to them in the weeks following the Slide.[4]

The Turtle Mountain Slide is a notorious event in the history of the Crow's Nest Pass and southern Alberta. Yet, despite its tragic reputation, it only ranks third in terms of lives lost. In comparison, the Coal Creek mine explosion of 1902 took 120 lives and the Hillcrest mine disaster of 1914, the largest mine disaster in Canada, killed 189 men and boys who were underground at the time. Smaller mine disasters and numerous deaths from individual mining accidents would take more lives than those killed in the Great Rock Slide at Frank.[5] Despite these larger numeric losses of life in other Crow's Nest tragedies, the Turtle Mountain Slide has claimed the more distinct historical profile. The Slide is frequently recounted in family histories, not only in the Pass, but throughout Alberta; it has inspired novels, poems, paintings, plays, songs, and several debates about its cause and the details of this fateful ninety seconds in Pass history. There are a number of different reasons for the enduring fascination it sustains in the public imagination.

Certainly the incredible scale and visibility of the Slide partly explains the lasting attention it receives; nature's power, and the corresponding vulnerability of humanity, is a lesson quickly gained from visualizing the rocks and the nearly vertical mountainside from which they slid. The spectacular event was also well recorded visually by the cameras of professionals and amateurs in its aftermath.[6] Several poignant photographs of the Slide made their way into newspapers and contemporary journals, graphically capturing the dramatic twists and turns of the events that unfolded in the newly opened eastern district of the Crow's Nest Pass.[7] Photographs of Slide debris and Turtle Mountain adorned numerous postcards and spread its reputation far and wide. Long after the disaster, the photographic power of the Slide remained. Many personal and public archival collections have pictures of people standing beside, on top, or in front of large limestone boulders.[8] Travellers through the Pass still stop on the roadside to capture pictures of themselves with massive rocks in the background. The Slide's popularity resurfaced when it came time to name the area's historical interpretative centre: rather than the Crow's Nest Pass Interpretative Centre, the building, perched on the flanks of the Slide, and looking toward Turtle Mountain, was named the Frank Slide Interpretative Centre, although the building explains far more than this one event.

Undoubtedly the visual reality of the Slide partly explains its large historical shadow, but its notoriety also comes from the context of western Canadian development at the time. By 1903, western Canada was a region in full-scale development. With poor progress in the late nineteenth century giving way to the greater prosperity and interest in the West by the late 1890s, western Canada was a region bursting with promise by 1903. Faith in this progress had produced talk of more transcontinental rail lines through the area. Immigration into the West was in full swing and the numbers looked promising. Farming activity was expanding while new cities and their industries sprouted across the western plains. The campaign by the CPR and others for new settlers was escalating rapidly by 1903.[9]

Above: Frank townsite shown below Turtle Mountain before 1903. Frank's main street, untouched by the Slide, is on the far right. The large building behind main street, also missed by the Slide, is the Frank School. Courtesy: Photo in possession of author, photographer unknown.

Below: Turtle Mountain many years after the Slide. Site of town on the middle right has been abandoned. Road and train tracks pass through middle of Slide debris. Circa 1950. Courtesy: Photo in possession of author, photographer unknown.

In this context, the Frank mine and the Crow's Nest Pass district had both a very specific role and a much broader regional significance. In specific terms, the Frank mine was the first commercial mine on the eastern side of this new coal district. It was hoped that the Frank mine would rival developments on the western, British Columbia, side of the Pass, where a flurry of activity was already underway. On the western side, the ambitious and well-connected principals of the Crow's Nest Pass Coal Company (C.N.P.C. Co.) had negotiated the Crow's Nest Pass Railway into existence by bringing the CPR and the federal government into partnership in 1897.[10] With their transportation problem solved, the C.N.P.C. Co. began a coal mine, with some housing, at Coal Creek, and a larger town nearby at Fernie where coke ovens were also built. By 1901, when the Canadian American Coal and Coke Co. at Frank started production, the C.N.P.C. Co. also had additional mines and towns underway at Morrissey and Michel.[11]

Operations at Frank, then, represented the expectations for industrial development on the Territorial side of the Pass. The Frank mine would provide the tremendous quantities of affordable bituminous coal needed to heat prairie homes, to fire industrial enterprises, but most importantly, to fuel the railways spreading quickly through the West. Most intrigued with these developments was the powerful Canadian Pacific Railway, which needed cheap and abundant coal supplies to run its trains through the Pass, but also out on the Prairies. Dependent on expensive Pennsylvania coal for most of its needs, with additional production coming from the Lethbridge and Banff area mines, the CPR saw the Crow's Nest district as an important strategic development. Deposits of high quality steam coal of superior quality would guarantee efficient western transportation. From its opening in 1901 and for several years following, the CPR bought Frank's entire production, nearly a thousand tons daily, up to the time of the Slide in 1903.[12] Many felt the development of the Frank mine, and others to follow on both sides of the Pass, would pace the speed and extent of western Canadian settlement. R. Barnwell, who was the Fuel and Tie Agent for the CPR, made this point clearly in 1906 at a meeting of CPR officials. Barnwell claimed that any serious problem in these first years at the Frank mine "would have been disastrous" for the railway, which was eager expand its sources of locomotive coal.[13] Immediately upon hearing of the Slide, the CPR dispatched its officials to the scene and the decision was made to rebuild the line. With 1,100 men and two boxcars crammed with blasting powder, the task began. One newspaper reported that the CPR had told its contractors, Breckrenridge and Lund, that "time not money" was the important consideration. In twenty-three days the line reopened.[14] The company that tamed the Roger's Pass and battled its tremendous snowfalls proved ready for the challenge of reopening the Crow's Nest line through the largest known rock slide in the world to that point.[15]

A disaster at Frank clearly threatened a new coal district and its necessary supplies of railway coal for western expansion. A Crow's Nest Pass blocked for any length of time also imperilled other economic developments. If the Slide that spread across the valley floor permanently cut or seriously hindered travel, an important link would also be lost with the other side of the Pass. Here were newly developing industries in southern British Columbia and the Pacific Northwest area of the United States.[16] In these regions a series of hard-rock mining and smelting districts had developed from the mid-1880s. Dependent on large quantities of coal and coke, these industries also needed continued access to growing Pass mining operations. Substantial freight revenue for the CPR was also at stake, both for carrying coal and coke to the smelters and moving their production to market.

In the days following the Slide, an answer to this question of the area's future was nervously awaited by a variety of interests to the east and west of the Pass. Dispelling any sense that the Slide had long-term consequences was extremely important to the larger economic interests involved in the area. The serious nature of the event was signalled by the visit, shortly after the Slide, by Sir Thomas Shaughnessy, the President of the CPR from 1898 to 1918. Travelling with his handpicked geologist, Shaughnessy was there to confirm that the Slide was a rare event that would neither reoccur nor threaten the closure of the Crow's Nest Pass railway and its coal, and future coke, operations. Shaughnessy's visit sent a clear message that the CPR had decided that all Pass-related investments and development plans could proceed.[17] And, In the early period of western Canadian development, astute business people listened carefully to CPR pronouncements.

The Turtle Mountain disaster was a multiple economic threat, and it menaced other facets of western development. It jeopardized, for example, the campaign for thousands of additional settlers and investors in the western region. A horrendous disaster in this new western territory could undo all the positive mythology about western settlement that was flowing from so many quarters. And this mythology was important in these industrial contexts as much as it was in agricultural settlement circles. Industrial development needed its own myths and odes to progress to sustain faith in the glorious future awaiting the West and the individuals who invested in its natural resources. Too often we think of the West as a ranching frontier, a farming frontier, or even an urban frontier. But western development was also an industrial frontier, replete with its industrial pioneers whose strong and expansive visions rivalled other sectors of western society. These beliefs were particularly trenchant in the Crow's Nest Pass, in the hard-rock mining and smelting areas adjacent to it in southeastern British Columbia, and in the similar American areas just across the border.[18]

What was clear in these areas was the incredibly powerful vision held by these pioneers of the relative importance of their particular contributions to western progress. They were the key actors from their perspective. For these individuals and communities it was the industrial pioneer who was the backbone of western development, and any progress in these endeavours would fuel the advance of civilization. Mine owners, mine workers and the townspeople who flocked to the business opportunities in these communities all saw themselves as pioneers with the same intensity as someone on a Prairie homestead. So strong were these beliefs that some reinterpreted this disaster in positive terms. One example can be seen in the promotional literature produced by the Hillcrest community that immediately neighboured Frank to the east. In their pamphlet, Hillcrest boosters advocated buying Hillcrest lots because the Slide had given their town an advantage. The Slide made more difficult the wagon and horse connections between Frank and the farming and ranching communities bordering the eastern side of the Pass. Consequently, Hillcrest would be the new Pass centre, and the wise investor should respond accordingly. Another example of such heady confidence was the twist given to the effect of the disaster on Frank's mine operations. A coal company official, awkwardly trying to remain positive, claimed the event was a blessing in disguise, as the coal seams would be accessed with two additional openings.[19] The point being made was that more openings in the seam meant more production and less chance that future "problems," presumably rock slides or mine explosions, would interrupt operations. In other words, the disaster had positive consequences – a more efficient coal mine had been created.

In these early years, then, the Frank mine was a special mine, and the reaction to the disaster on April 29 was intensified accordingly. A sense of this importance was clearly on display in Frank's 1901 opening celebrations. Attending the fall event and giving speeches were the Territorial Premier, F. W. Haultain, and Liberal Minister of the Interior, Clifford Sifton. A day of varied festivities had been organized to attract miners and their families, those wanting town lots for business development, and those with heavy pockets who might buy company shares. To ensure a robust crowd, the CPR had put on extra trains carrying guests from Lethbridge and Cranbrook. There were mine tours in canvas-covered coal cars and inspections of the new miners' cottages, which featured running water, electric lights, and spacious yards for gardens; athletic events with medals for the winners; a band; a ton of fresh fruit and ice cream brought from Spokane for the free dinner served out in the open to nine hundred hungry people, all combined into one gala event. As a local booster observed in the Frank newspaper, "… what was one year ago the haunt of the deer, where the howl of the coyote was heard nightly, is now a hive of industry, furnishing homes and employment for hundreds of families."[20]

Organized by its two prominent American owners, Samuel W. Gebo from Wyoming and Henry L. Frank from Montana, the opening celebrations underlined the hopes and expectations attached to Frank and the new coal district emerging on the territorial side of the Pass. By the time of the Slide two years later in 1903, significant steps had been taken in accomplishing these plans. The main entry had been driven over a mile into the mountain's side. Production was reaching significant levels at the mine: 1901 output was 15,000 tons, and in 1902 it jumped to 160,000 tons, an unusually dramatic increase for a coal mine starting production.[21] By 1903, Frank's operations were complemented by many more prospectors and developers scouring the Pass and promising new mine developments. Already there was significant investment at Lille to the north; the company here, West Canadian Collieries, a group of investors from France, had completed their branch railway connecting their operations to the CPR's mainline at Frank. A mile and a half of this rail line would be buried by the Slide. Closer to Frank, at Bellevue and Hillcrest, prospecting and initial development were proceeding.

A few miles further west from Frank at Coleman, more developments were in motion. Soon Passburg, Burmis, and Lundbreck would join them to the east, and some miles to the south, another CPR spur line would open Beaver Mines. Blairmore, just west of Frank, would see coalmine development begin in 1908 and accelerate in 1912 with the start of work on the Greenhill Mine.

Into this heady mix of plans and partial beginnings came the disaster at Frank on the morning of April 29, 1903. In a mere ninety seconds, this tragedy placed a region, a coal district and the specific plans of individual entrepreneurs at serious risk. Immediately imperilled by the event were the dreams and schemes of Samuel W. Gebo and Henry L. Frank. Classic western North American entrepreneurs who had worked their way up from humble origins as they moved across the American West, Gebo and Frank planned a comprehensive development at this mine and its associated townsite. Henry L. Frank, the one with more financial clout and already a celebrity in Montana, attached his name to the operations. Away from the town at the time of the disaster, both men arrived on the scene shortly after the catastrophe. Most personally affected was Henry Frank who exhausted himself rebuilding the mine and the town's reputation. According to one newspaper account of Frank, at his death at age fifty-seven in 1908, he was "sympathetic to a degree [and] sustained a shock at the time of the disaster...in which many of his employees [*sic*] lost their lives from which he never fully recovered."[22] Gebo, on the other hand, eleven years younger than Frank, proved somewhat more resilient. He remained connected to Frank operation for many years, before finally selling his investment and concentrating exclusively on American business ventures.[23] By the 1930s, however, life had changed for Gebo. Hit by illness and economic loss in the Depression, Gebo ended his own life in 1937 by way of a gas oven in the kitchen of his Seattle home.[24]

The Great Rock Slide at Frank was a traumatic event on a number of different levels. It was a human tragedy, taking the lives of men, women, and children without a moment's warning. It threatened the entrepreneurial plans of Gebo and Frank, and those of many others in the immediate area. It endangered the development of western Canada and the fortunes of the CPR and impinged on the development of the hard-rock mining and smelter industries adjacent to the area. Its notoriety stems from all these contexts and another one as well.

For western Canadians, people living in a developing frontier, the story of those killed and of those who escaped had a particularly strong appeal. Pioneering, of whatever kind, whether agricultural or industrial, was a risky business filled with stories of struggle, defeat, and success. The anxieties created by the dangers and uncertainties of western settlement were best soothed with a romantic belief in a positive outcome, or the belief that fate was indiscriminate, that good luck or misfortune was randomly assigned. This approach was prominent in the novelists of the era, such as Ralph Connor or Nellie McClung. A pure heart, most often a Christian one, and good intentions were usually rewarded, but fate had an equally important role. In the events at Frank, many western Canadians undoubtedly saw a microcosm of their own experience, confirming their nervousness about the dangers in this frontier while also allowing them a way to imagine how they might avoid those perils. Many individual memoirs told of good fortune with respect to the Slide, of plans to be in Frank that night that were changed at the last minute. Indeed, if everyone's plans had been reversed, Frank might have been a very large town on the morning of April 29.[25]

In the contemporary newspaper accounts of the event, in later writings, and, more recently, in a documentary dramatization of the Slide, the persistent storyline is one of fortunate escape alongside tragic demise. Presenting these two sides of the coin, these two possible outcomes, danger and unpredictable disaster beside tales of survival and heroism, made living in an uncertain western environment seem a more rational choice. In a region where nature could easily take lives by blizzard, flood, fire, disease, and any number of accidental causes, a positive counterweight was always needed on the other side of the scale. Some of the Frank stories were useful in righting that balance.

Other underground mining disasters, before and after the Slide, were less useful in this way. Although the mine explosions at Coal Creek or Hillcrest were equally tragic, they were different than the disaster at Frank. At Coal Creek and Hillcrest, no one survived. There was no hope, no encouragement to continue the struggle, no reason to accept more risk, no sense that some might die but some might live. In those disasters there could be no spark of optimism, only grief for all those who had succumbed. Recounting these events was simply morbid fascination; they offered no way of salvaging even a small glimmer of hope. The Slide, however, provided both outcomes, both possibilities:

a sense of loss but also a way to imagine yourself among the lucky ones. And there was even room for heroes in the Slide story, the idea that human effort, in some limited way, could also overcome such destructive events. Efforts by individuals did make a difference, a lesson that was important in a region where life could be taken so easily. And for this reason as well, the Slide is a more remembered event than other disasters in the Crow's Nest Pass that were equal or greater in their level of human tragedy.[26]

Examples for both sides of the balance, tragedy on one side and survival or heroics on the other, are numerous in accounts of the Slide. One story with both elements was the discovery of the Alexander Leitch family. In the ruins of their house were found the bodies of Alex, his wife, and their four boys. Still alive and pulled from the room were two of their daughters. A short distance away, crying, was their baby daughter. Many stories of this child's good fortune circulated after the Slide. For years, in fact, Marion, the "Frank Slide baby," was hounded by frequent inquiries about that day although only an infant at the time.[27] For another family, that day was even more tragic. William Warrington, one of the miners who had been trapped underground, emerged from the mine only to learn that his wife and three children had been killed in the Slide.[28] Placed alongside this event was the incredible luck of the Innes family, whose house had been hit by the rocks and reportedly turned over three times – and yet the family of five escaped.[29]

Success in the struggle to survive was especially prominent in the story of the seventeen men trapped in the mine. While in the midst of their work in different parts of the mine, these men heard a loud "rumbling noise like the beating of drums" that was suddenly followed by a gust of air that snuffed their lamps. After the men collected together and relit their lamps, the search for exits began. A jog to the main entry found the passageway blocked some forty feet in from the opening. The next option was to try for an airshaft four thousand feet back in the mine and four hundred feet higher up in the workings. But this proved futile was as well. One eight-foot passageway was squeezed so tightly that no man could push through. With water filling the lower workings and continuing to rise, and every exit covered and clogged, the situation looked bleak. A final decision to tunnel up a different airshaft closer to the main entry opening was a last resort. For the next twelve hours their intense work continued, and after fifty feet of digging, tree roots appeared and a small hole was poked through to the surface. Within minutes the breach was expanded and the smallest man was shoved through to the surface. More furious work widening the gap let the remaining men scramble above ground with waves and shouts to the surprised rescue crew below, who were digging at the opening to the main entry in a vain attempt to rescue their fellow miners.[30]

Besides these survivor stories, either in the mine or from the houses crushed by the rocks, were the narratives of heroes, those who risked their lives and contributed to defeating this destructive power of nature in some small way. Most prominent in this category were those who immediately made their way to the rocks once dust had settled and daylight lit the scene. One group headed to the mine entrance, where they frantically shifted rocks and gravel in the vicinity of the mine mouth with the hope of finding main entries intact and the men inside alive. Despite a dangerous shower of rocks that continued falling from the mountain, these men stuck to their task throughout the day until they heard the shouts from above.[31]

Equally heroic was another group of people who rushed from their houses and hotel rooms to the town's edge where a row of miners' cottages had sat. Here the devastation was breathtaking. Huge boulders carpeted the valley floor. With some houses completely gone, and the parts and pieces of others scattered through the rocks, men shifted debris, called out names and scrambled back and forth listening and looking for survivors. Without knowing what further danger might arise from the mountainside, and with a threatening dam of water building from the blockage of the Crow's Nest River and its Gold Creek tributary, these men continued their efforts to find and free survivors.

As rescue work began, another crisis produced more heroic action. Two CPR men, Sid Choquette and fellow brakeman Lowes, remembered the train due shortly from the east. The CPR's luxurious passenger train, the Spokane Flyer, was heading directly at the Slide. An express passenger train that started in Minneapolis-St. Paul, the Spokane Flyer traveled north to join the CPR's western Canadian mainline, then south through the Crow's Nest Pass and into Spokane. A service aimed at competing with parallel American routes offered by the North Pacific and Great Northern, the Spokane Flyer, with its mahogany-panelled cars, 250-volume library, velvet curtains, green leather upholstery, and

Swiss servants, was due in Frank minutes after the Slide.[32] Knowing someone must stop this train, Choquette and Lowe set off across the rocks ignoring the possible dangers awaiting them: unsteady boulders that could shift and crush them instantly, rocks still tumbling down the mountain's side, or perhaps a hidden crevasse into which they could slip and never escape. With a rough bearing taken and railway lanterns tightly gripped, they headed through the field of slippery, jagged rocks. Although Lowe was winded and forced to pause, Choquette continued on and stopped the oncoming train.[33]

As Frank's residents and others in the area reacted to these first concerns, telegrams about the Slide reached the outside world and raised the call for help. Responding to the event were all the main players involved in western Canadian development. James A. Smart, the Deputy Minister of the Interior, ordered William Pearce, Chief of Surveys in the West, to gather a force of NWMP and proceed to Frank, where he would take charge until F. W. Haultain, Premier of the North-West Territorial government, arrived. The CPR immediately dispatched Taylor, the Divisional Superintendent, and shortly after Chief Engineer McNenry; the Acting Minister of the Interior, William Mulock, ordered the Acting Director of the Geological Survey of Canada to dispatch two geologists to the scene, R. G. McConnell and R. W. Brock.[34] The range of the responses signalled the seriousness with which the event was taken in the dominant western institutions of power.

Along with the telegraphed calls for help went the first versions of what had happened to Turtle Mountain and the inhabitants living in the mountain's shadow. These theories, and an ongoing debate about the causes of the Slide, also explain the large space the Slide occupies in the western imagination. An initial explanation for the Slide was the occurrence of volcanic activity. Several reasons explained this response. Dust from the event was considerable, and in the dim morning light, dust from a distance appeared like steam that might accompany volcanic activity. Wind that some reported as hotter than normal, generated by the fall of rocks, and the tremendous sound that was produced, also seemed to indicate a volcanic event.[35] Coupled with the shock waves through the ground, which were widely felt, the sudden eruption of a volcano seemed a plausible framework to suggest. But with no lava flow, no volcanic crater, and no continued volcanic activity, this theory soon collapsed.[36]

Above: Many such photos have been taken of the large rocks involved in the Slide of 1903. C1911. Courtesy: Provincial Archives of Alberta A.1771. Photo by Rev. W. J. Young.

Below: View of the Slide looking west, c. 1930. The town of Bellevue is to the left. The swath of rock on the flat (middle foreground) is over two miles long. Courtesy: Photo in possession of author, photographer unknown.

Another explanation that gained even more support was the possibility of an earthquake in the area. The ground tremors were important in this regard, as people far from the Slide had experienced vibrations at roughly the same moment in time. With the knowledge of previous seismic activity in the region, some observers considered an earthquake as a sensible possibility. However, as no windows were broken in the main part of Frank or in the buildings in neighbouring towns, and no aftershocks occurred, this too was a theory that quickly lost its punch.[37]

In the more creative explanation category were a number of entertaining possibilities. One of these was the meteorite theory.[38] With dust clouds drifting through the air, and the incredible size and large distances that huge boulders had been thrown, a collision between mountain and meteor was just as reasonable. The force of such contact explained the sound, the event's sudden nature, and the great force that had obviously been at work in the Slide. As no confirmations arose about streaking meteorite tails in the moments before the Slide, these and other ideas lived briefly, and then faded, as the "invention[s] of the fertile brain of a penny-a-liner."[39]

Another possible cause of the Slide was the explosion theory, the idea that deep inside the mountain, a combination of materials had suddenly blown the rock apart. First suggested was that a mixture of coal, lime, and water had produced a pocket of acetylene gas that was inexplicably ignited.[40] More reasonable in this regard was the argument that a large cavity inside the mountain had filled with methane gas, and was then ignited accidentally by the men underground at the time. Proposed in a pamphlet by Gordon H. Crayford, and attributed to his father who was in Frank at the time, this theory had certain attractions. It explained the Slide's ground tremors and noise reported in Frank and at several places distant from the Slide. The explosion theory also helped with comprehending the peculiar distribution of rocks. It is hard, for example, to understand how several large boulders travelled such a great distance from the mountain.[41] As well, at the time of the Slide, there were reports of light or fire that also supported the evidence of explosion.

In considering the explosion theory, however, a number of problems exist. Evidence of combustion on the rocks or debris has never been reported. In addition, none of the accounts of the men underground mentioned that they were engaged in blasting. The night shift was a repair crew, fixing timber supports, repairing brattice (the special cloth used to direct air flow in coal mines) and moving coal cars in the mine. No account included blasting as part of their activity. An explanation of how blasting in the mine workings could reach a gas-filled chamber high in the mountain was also difficult to rationalize.

As geologists climbed and reclimbed Turtle Mountain, observing and measuring in the days and weeks and years that followed, more reasonable understandings emerged. Two interrelated factors were considered crucial to explaining the event's occurrence: the unique structure of Turtle Mountain and the cumulative affect of water freezing and thawing within fissures at the mountain's top. What was peculiar about Turtle Mountain's shape, and was unknown to those in Frank at the time, was the nature of rock at its peak, positioned, if sufficient force was applied, to release on a slope aimed directly at the mine and town. Into this situation came the power of freezing and melting water, by way of rain and snow, which worked its way into the cracks and crevices, constantly pushing apart rock layers and eventually prying them free from the mountain's side. With high precipitation levels the previous year, and during that spring of 1903, coinciding with unusually distinct periods of warm and freezing weather, sufficient force finally knocked the rock from its perch.

Another factor that has centrally figured in the explanation of the Slide, having an early popularity, then a period of rejection, and more recently a renewed sense of relevance, was the action of coal mining at Turtle Mountain's base.[42] Soon after the Slide, many suggested the culpability of coal mining as an important factor in understanding what had occurred.[43] Probably this factor would have received more credence, but two factors muted its status. In the first instance, those who felt coal mining responsible did not believe that the officials of the Canadian and American Coal and Coke Co. were at fault. In the context of the time, no one would have expected the company to study Turtle Mountain in such detail before beginning operations. In addition, it is uncertain if Turtle Mountain's dangers could have been determined, even if studied, before the Slide occurred. For this reason, those who suspected coal mining were tame about announcing its responsibility. Potential lawsuits, against the company or the government, would have been unfair in the context of this situation. William Pearce, the Chief of

Surveys for the Dept. of the Interior, explained these problems clearly in a letter to his boss, James A. Smart, the Deputy Minister. Pearce wrote that:

> The Mining Management, of course, would dispute that [coal mining's involvement], and you will understand that, owing to suits which will probably arise out of this, that it is not advisable that I should give this opinion officially, at least not at the present juncture. It is probable that the Territorial Government would come in for censure for permitting operations to be carried on.[44]

Another reason for muffled statements about coal mining's involvement related to the importance of this particular mine. If a vague message about coal mining's responsibility circulated too widely, an improper image would have been created about the work at Frank and the work about to begin at other spots in the Pass. Explaining the fine points of coal mining's contribution to an already risky geological situation might simply become a message that coal mining was an excessively dangerous and unstable economic proposition. With so much dependent on coal mining, and this particular district, few were willing to aggressively pursue the point – although, ironically, the danger of Pass mining did later prove to be the normal, rather than the exceptional reality.

When looking at the responsibility of coal mining in producing the Slide, several reasons emerge with special relevance. First of all, the coal seams under development by the Frank company lay in a particularly unique position.[45] Sitting nearly perpendicular to the surface, these seams formed a wall or ribbon across the bottom section of Turtle Mountain, like a layer cake lifted ninety degrees, sitting on its side. Pushed from a horizontal to a vertical position by upthrust of limestone that formed the mass of Turtle Mountain, these seams were also relatively thick: measurements put the "Great" seam at fourteen to thirty feet in width.[46] Extracting coal at Frank required a different approach, and in this method and its application, questions arose concerning the responsibility of coal mining in triggering the Slide.

To extract the coal from these seams, the company drove a main entry (tunnel) into the seam with a slight slope toward the outside.[47]

Above this main entry, a second entry, or counter entry, was dug parallel to the main entry below. Between these two entries was a block or pillar of coal, thirty-five feet thick, forming the roof of the main entry and the floor of the counter entry. At various points along the main entry, other tunnels were dug into its roof, vertically into the coal seam hanging above. These tunnels sectioned out the coal seam into very wide rooms. William Blakemore, a man with wide extensive experience, claimed some rooms were three to four hundred feet in width with only twenty-foot pillars of coal between each room.[48] A more reliable assessment provided by the Mine Inspector indicated rooms at a hundred feet wide with a forty-foot pillar between, and a manway run up the centre of these pillars.[49] Chutes at the bottom of each room, opening into the main entry, allowed coal to be drained into mine cars and taken outside to the tipple.

For the miners this method of extraction was rewarding but dangerous work. Paid by the ton of coal extracted, the Frank miners were offered large rewards but riskier work than at other Pass mines. Rather than hewing coal from a vertical coalface or wall, the miners were essentially taking coal from the roof overhead, or hanging wall, following the nearly vertical seam to its outcrop on the surface. The coal fell to their feet or the bottom of the room where coal chutes could be opened to fill coal cars stationed in the entry below. Timbering, which was a tedious task in more normally positioned seams, was less frequently required in these rooms. Once all the coal had been loosened in the room, the chute could be opened and the coal drained.[50] In some rooms, however, coal came freely from the roof and miners never entered their places for weeks. Coal would be loaded from the chutes and credited to the miners without them entering the mine.[51]

What was more dangerous about these methods in the Frank mine were the possibilities of unexpected coal falls from the roof. Picking and drilling into coal overhead was a perilous proposition. In the limited light conditions of a mining room, it was not always possible to see the size of coal that might come down. The company's position, however, was that with the miners "on top of the coal...as long as the ... [rooms] are kept full there is very little danger to practical miners from falling coal as they are so close to their work."[52] Nevertheless, a coal fall killed Robert Belshaw, an experienced miner aged forty-seven, in December 1902. As Mine Inspector F. B. Smith noted:

The working of coal in this mine will always be dangerous owing to the peculiar conditions, of a perpendicular seam and the disturbance to which the seam has been subjected, forming in many cases wedge shaped masses which may sound good when tapped by the pick but often easily loosened at some particular key point of the wedge.[53]

Equally dangerous in this system of mining was the vertical climb, up manways adjacent to the mining room. Men travelled up these vertical shafts, then crossed horizontally over to the level at which work was occurring in their rooms. One letter to a local newspaper illustrated concerns that arose about this journey where "men coming off shift are obliged to swing out upon this rope [into the manway] to descend [200 feet] and if the rope should break [from falling coal] they might be maimed for life or killed outright."[54] In response to this complaint, the Mines Inspector F. B. Smith noted "there is nothing in the mine that could be considered absolutely unsafe, but as I have already pointed out...there are conditions and always will be in this mine that makes it more dangerous to work than any other mine under the jurisdiction of the Department."[55]

There was no doubt that this mining method in a nearly vertical seam raised specific problems. These questions, however, were still within the realm of normal mining discussions. Continual negotiation about these types of safety issues among the owners, the inspectors, and the miners was the typical pattern in all Crow's Nest Pass mines.[56] What was safe one moment in one part of one mine might not be safe the next moment or in another part of the same mine. What was more important in relation to the disaster was the overall impact of the mining method used in Turtle Mountain. This question was raised soon after the Slide for one obvious reason – the width of the rock slide was very close to the width to the mining activity occurring at the mountain's base. Remembering that the coal seam sat as a perpendicular wall or slice next to the mountain's side, the hypothesis was that mining in this seam created instability that transferred up the mountain to the precariously poised rock overhanging at its peak. R. W. Brock, one the Ottawa's geologists sent to report on the Slide, and who later became the Director of the Geological Survey of Canada, was particularly adamant about the connection, and the fragility of the arrangement. According to Brock:

> These things are so nicely adjusted in nature that the slightest disturbance is apt to bring down a landslide. A readjustment of an eighth of an inch due to the removal of coal might do it. That the...slide was caused by the mining of coal there is no doubt in my mind. It is true the mine was only one of a number of causes, but if it or any other of the causes had been absent, I do not believe the slide would have occurred. It is of course possible that an earthquake shock might some day have brought Turtle Mountain down, but it is scarcely likely that it would have had the same dimensions.[57]

What made the suspicions even stronger about the connections between mining and the Slide was the fact that coal had been extracted quickly and in great quantity from this seam. Production figures for 1902 were very large: 160,000 tons compared with 15,000 tons in 1901. J. E. Woods, the mine's surveyor, who was also convinced mining caused the Slide, noted that coal was gone from a block 2,500 feet long by three to six hundred feet high. With that much coal taken out and a greater quantity loosened and ready for removal, only the pillars between the rooms held apart the mountain and valley walls bordering the seam.[58] Many, like two miners who were in the mine at the time of the Slide, felt these pillars were too small.[59] If these blocks of coal began compressing then movement in the walls might occur – movement that could transfer up the mountaintop and trigger the release of rock.[60]

No definitive proof of these connections could, then or now, be found to prove definitively such a claim. Geologists have generally doubted that activity at the base could have connections to the top of Turtle Mountain.[61] Re-examining the mine's interior might make firmer conclusions possible, but re-entering the mine would be a foolish and dangerous proposition without restoring ventilation and retimbering throughout. Even without new evidence from inside the mine, the connection between mining and the Slide should be given more weight, as existing historical sources do exist that suggest a close relationship.

In the observations immediately after the event, these connections can be seen. In discussing the effect of the Slide on the mine workings, the predominant description has stressed that everything inside was left intact, with the exception of debris filling the airshafts and main entry. However, in the description of one miner who was trapped underground, already cited, he does explain that a passageway, formerly eight feet in width, had been nearly compressed as a result of the Slide. Where that passage sat, how it came to be so squeezed, and whether there was other evidence of extreme pressure in that area, are important questions that were not asked. The answers to them might have indicated movement on the mountainside wall of the coal seam and a possible connection to the Slide.

Other links between the mine workings and the Slide come from the area of the main entry. Here significant pressures were recorded as a result of the Slide. The large entry timbers were either buckled or crushed and "considerable coal" had broken loose from the roof.[62] Rocks from the Slide moving over the seam outcrop on their way into the valley does not seem a reasonable explanation for this event. Connections between the Slide and the mine's interior were also found when the miners re-entered. A few months later, once back in the mine, a significant quantity of gas was encountered, preventing entry for a three-month period, a very significant occurrence. The implication here is that the Slide had changed pressures in the mountain in some manner that affected gas release in the mine.[63]

In shifting the focus back prior to the Slide, more connecting evidence is available. In the months before the Slide, there were numerous situations that suggested unusual stresses at work in the Frank mine. J. E. Woods, the mine's surveyor, remembered "tremendous pressure" in the entry which sent large pieces of shale popping off the mountain wall.[64] One specific incident involved a slab of rock, eighty feet long, fifteen feet tall, and five feet thick, coming free from the mountain wall bordering the coal seam. Other evidence of unusual pressure was also common. Timbers two feet in diameter were often crushed, and replaced, then replaced again the following day. Over time, timber replacement happens in all mines, but to have it replaced within twenty-four hours is exceptional. In addition, the company's initial disregard for timbering may also be of relevance. One of the first government inspectors to tour the mine worried openly about mining in a vertical seam. The coal could, he thought, release from the sides, plunge directly down and crush the main entry. No amount of timbering could prevent this occurrence of an entire seam shifting its position.[65] The Mine Inspector's concern was made more plausible with the knowledge that the company pushed the entry 627 feet into the mountain without placing any timber supports.[66] Whether waiting this long to start timbering allowed unusual stresses to build in the mine and the mountain is open to debate. However, this delay was not usual practice in opening a main entry tunnel.

As well, men in the mine before the Slide reported that there had been strange noises "coming from the mountain."[67] As noise in a mine is extremely important, these sounds should not be overlooked. In a mine there were always different noises, and miners' lives depended on knowing these noises and interpreting what they meant. Survival in limited light conditions depended on interpreting sounds. An experienced miner could tell, for example, from the sound of his pick, if gas was about to erupt from the face or if roof rock was about to fall.[68] Reports about unusual noises and "deep rumblings" before the Slide should not be ignored; a miner's analysis of sound is not of the same order as someone who has never been underground. What undoubtedly contributed to giving the testimony of Frank miners less consideration in unravelling the cause of the event was Gebo's decision, just three weeks prior to the Slide, to fire all the supervisory staff underground.[69] Information about occurrences preceding the Slide, from an informed group, was consequently lost. Most of these men had probably left the area by April 29. Nevertheless, accounts from those who remained provide significant evidence of the mine's involvement.

One final factor about practices in the mine before the Slide deserves additional consideration in terms of its impact on Turtle Mountain and the stability of rocks at its peak. Unlike most other mines, shot firing, that is, blasting in the coal, was done simultaneously in the mining rooms at Frank.[70] The effect must be considered of multiple shots in all the rooms igniting as one blast, along a possible length of four thousand feet, sending their percussions simultaneously in the base of Turtle Mountain. Over time, it is conceivable, added to other factors of mountain structure and the work of freeze-thaw cycles, that mining made a significant contribution to the Great Rock Slide at Frank.

Debates about the Slide, its cause, and the nature of the path and movement of the rocks as they hit the valley floor, have been a substantial reason for the continued popularity of the Frank disaster.

No such reoccurring debate has been generated by the Coal Creek explosion of 1902 or the Hillcrest mine explosion of 1914. What also has given memory of the Slide more persistence was the continuing possibility of more rock downfalls. In the immediate hours and days after the Slide, no one knew if an additional limestone avalanche was about to occur. On May 2, after an official party examined the mountain's top, Premier Haultain ordered the town's evacuation.[71] This was a rushed and anxiety-ridden experience, and many thought the town was doomed. As more information was gathered, and the threat of more rock falls dismissed, the townspeople returned and the task of recovery began. But nervousness remained and was rekindled in 1912 when a government reported forced the town's relocation to the north of its original position.[72] Over nearly a century that followed the Slide, rock falls from Turtle Mountain continued. The threat of a serious downfall from the southern peak remains a real possibility and was confirmed in a new study commissioned by the Alberta government in 2000. In the summer of 2001 a large rockslide reminded everyone of the mountain's remaining potential for disruption.

The Great Rock Slide at Frank in 1903 impinged upon many realities and many projected plans. The Slide brought tragedy for those unfortunate people in its path, and it threatened the destiny of those nearby and those in the wider western regions. The story of the victims, the survivors, and the heroes engaged western Canadians, an interest that still exists today. Although other disasters deserve as much or more concern, the Slide still makes headlines. What sustains this interest most, whether it derives from real threats of more falling rock, a scientific desire to prove its origins, or from some more broader cultural purpose such as mediating the past and present dangers and uncertainties of western settlement, is an interesting question. Regardless, the Slide remains a persistent part of western Canadian heritage whose dusts have not yet settled.

NOTES

1   *Engineering and Mining Journal*, July 4, 1903. This description was provided by Thos. J. Cooper, who was in Frank the morning of the Slide. Cooper had worked for the journal, *The Canadian Engineer*, and seems to have been employed by the Canadian American Coal and Coke Co. at Frank, probably as part of their office staff, at the time of the Slide.

2   S. Rodney, K. Read, Wayne Savigny, Franco Oboni, David M. Cruden, and C. Willem Langenberg, *Geotechnical hazard assessment of the south flank of Frank Slide, Hillcrest, Alberta*, Abstract, Alberta, 2000. The estimate of area covered comes from Frank B. Smith, "The Frank Disaster," *Canadian Mining Review* 22, no. 5 (May 30, 1903): 102–3. Smith was Inspector of Mines at the time.

3   Work at a coal mine involved a great many more occupations than just men working at the coal face. Although these were the more skilled workers, there were a host of other occupations associated with a coal mining operation. The union contract in 1911 listed over a hundred different jobs below and above ground. Frank B. Smith, in "The Frank Disaster," 102–3, claimed there might be "a few more Slavoians [*sic*] or Russian Poles not accounted for." The exact number will never be known. See Frank W. Anderson, *The Frank Slide Story* (Calgary: Frontier Publishing, 1968), 36 or J. William Kerr, *Frank Slide* (Priddis, Alberta: Barker Publishing, 1990).

4   One horse was alive thirty-one days later when entry was regained to the mine. Another forty horses were killed when the rocks hit a large stable that C.A.C.C.Co. had erected: see Thos. J. Cooper, "Frank, Alta, April 30, 1903," *The Canadian Engineer* (May 1903): 154, 164–66; see also Walton E. Dowlen, "The Turtle Mountain Rock Slide," *Engineering and Mining Journal* (July 4, 1903): 10–12.

5   In its 17 years of operation from 1901 to 1917, the Frank Mine claimed an additional 27 lives in individual accidents. See the Mine Inspectors' Reports (hereafter cited as MIR), Provincial Archives of Alberta (hereafter cited as PAA), Accession 77.237, Mine No. 48. At the Morrissey and Michel mines, thirty-nine deaths occurred from July 1903 to December 1905: see Lorry W. Felske, "Studies in the Crow's Nest Pass Coal Industry From Its Origins to the End of World War I," Ph.D. dissertation, University of Toronto, 1991, 190–91. Another thirty men were killed at the Bellevue Mine in 1910. See David J. Bercuson, "Tragedy at Bellevue: Anatomy of a Mine Disaster," *Labour: Journal of Canadian Labour Studies* 3 (1978): 221–31.

6   Thomas Gushul Photograph Collection, Glenbow Alberta Institute Archives (hereafter cited as GAI); Jim Kerr Collection, Crow's Nest Museum, Coleman, Alberta. See Ira Flatow, *They All Laughed: From Light Bulbs to Lasers* (New York: Harper Collins, 1992), 50–51. Kokak introduced the Brownie in 1900. See also Ulrich Keller, "Early Photojournalism," in David Crowley and Paul Heyer, eds., *Communication in History* (Don Mills: Addison Wesley Longman, 1999), 178–87.

7   William Pearce, "The Great Rockslide at Frank, Alberta," *Engineering News* 49, no. 23 (June 4, 1903). Pearce's article is a good example of this trend.

8   The Slide probably rivals Lake Louise as one of the most photographed sites in western Canada.

9   See Gerald Friesen, *The Canadian Prairies: A History* (Toronto: University of Toronto Press, 1984).

10 Lorry W. Felske, "Crow's Nest Pass Coal Industry," Chapter 1.

11 Ibid., Chapter 7.

12 RCMP Papers (hereafter cited as RCMPP), Public Archives of Canada (hereafter cited as PAC), RG18 A1, vol. 1515, file 2–1903, October 1903; Canadian Pacific Railway Papers (hereafter cited as CPRP), GAI, Box 201, file 1981, July 8, 1904; the *Blairmore Enterprise*, March 21, 1912, reported that Frank was producing a thousand tons daily.

13 R. Barnwell, "Western Coals," talk given to a Field, B.C., meeting of CPR officials, May 21, 1906, CPRP, GAI, Box 52, file 548.

14 A company that had pushed a rail line through the Rockies and battled the snows of the Roger's Pass was well prepared to face the obstacles thrown at its operations by such an event: see Dowlen, "The Turtle Mountain Rock Slide." Another source claims the CPR sent the first train through on May 24, 1903: see Cooper, "Frank, Alta, April 30, 1903," 164; and *Cranbrook Herald*, May 28, 1903.

15 So committed to developing coal deposits in the Crow's Nest Pass, the CPR would open its own mine at Hosmer in 1908. Despite investing millions in the mine, however, the CPR was defeated by the geological conditions found at this site. See Felske, "Crow's Nest Pass Coal Industry," Chapter 5.

16 Discovered after the Kicking Horse and Yellowhead Passes, the Crow's Nest Pass was the lowest of these passes and the only one discovered from the west, rather than the east. Located in the 1870s by gold prospectors traveling up the Elk River Valley, the Crow's Nest was opened because of its coal deposits, not its gold possibilities: see Felske, "Crow's Nest Pass Coal Industry," Chapter 1.

17 See *The Canadian Engineer* (May 30, 1903): 154; see also W. A. McKay and W. Stewart Wallace, *The Macmillan Dictionary of Canadian Biography*, 4th ed. (Toronto: Macmillan, 1978), 762.

18 Indeed, it was the American entrepreneurs in the Spokane region who would recognize and act on investment possibilities in the region before western Canadian capitalists, who were busy with other projects on the Prairies: see Felske, "Crow's Nest Pass Coal Industry," Chapter 2.

19 These comments were made by E. C. Spriggs, an ex-Governor of Montana and a director of the C.A.C.C. Co. New openings were placed at 3,780 and 5,780 feet from the original entrance: see Dowlen, "The Turtle Mountain Rock Slide," 10.

20 *Frank Sentinel*, October 25, 1901. See also Anderson, *The Frank Slide Story*, 4.

21 MIR, PAA, Accession 77.237, Mine No. 48, February 12, 1903. Production for 1903 was 101,591.96 tons.

22 *Butte Miner*, August 18, 1908.

23 Frank bought out Gebo's interest for $200,000 in 1905, but shortly after Frank's

death, Gebo renewed his involvement in the Frank operations, then exited the scene again around 1910: see *Canadian Mining Journal* 11 (June 1, 1908); RCMPP, PAC, RG18 A1, vol. 292, file 218-05; MIR, July 7, 1910.

24 Seattle *Tribune*, July 12, 1940; Seattle *Post-Intelligencer*, July 11, 1940, 13; Seattle *Times*, July 11, 1940, 10. Seattle *Tribune*, July 11, Dec. 23, 1940.

25 See for example, Paul M. Cyr, who, if he had not broken his leg and been moved to Pincher Creek hospital in the days before the slide, would have been at Frank. *Prairie Grass to Mountain Pass* (Pincher Creek Historical Society, 1974) and the numerous family histories in *Crowsnest and its People* (Crowsnest Pass Historical Society, 1979), such as the biography of Steve Magdall, Sr., 684.

26 Anderson's account, *The Frank Slide Story*, is the best example of this approach, but it appeared first in the numerous newspapers' reports and still appears in more current forms. See, for example, the new video produced by the Frank Slide Visitors' Centre.

27 Interviews by the author with Jessie Hamilton, who was a friend of the Leitch family, 1982, Calgary; see also the *Calgary Herald* (weekly edition), May 7, 1903.

28 Anderson, *The Frank Slide Story*, p. 42.

29 See *The Canadian Engineer* (May 1903): 164.

30 Raoul Green, "The Frank Disaster," *Canadian Mining Review* 22, no. 5 (May 30, 1903): 103–10; Pearce, "The Great Rockslide," and Dowlen, "The Turtle Mountain Rock Slide," also have descriptions of the escape.

31 Smith, "The Frank Disaster," 102.

32 Felske, "Crow's Nest Pass Coal Industry," 61.

33 Anderson, *The Frank Slide Story*, 24, 30.

34 Item in the *Engineering News* 49, no. 23 (June 4, 1903): 492; see Dowlen, "The Turtle Mountain Rock Slide." McConnell later became Deputy Minister of Mines for the federal government in 1914; Brock would later serve as the Director of the Geological Survey of Canada. See McKay and Wallace, *Macmillan Dictionary of Canadian Biography*, 487; and R. W. Brock Papers, Special Collections, University of British Columbia. See also William Pearce Papers, Archives, University of Alberta (hereafter cited as WPPAUA).

35 Almost all accounts tell of a tremendous noise that accompanied the event. Raoul Green's description claimed everyone in Lille, four miles up Bear Valley, was awakened by the Slide: see Green, "The Frank Disaster," 103.

36 The powder magazine of Poupore and McVeigh, contractors working on the branch railway to Lille, had exploded in the slide and contributed to the popularity of the volcano theory. Geological Survey of Canada Papers (hereafter cited as GSCP), file 2306, vol. 45, PAC.

37 William Blakemore, "The Frank Disaster," *Canadian Mining Review* 22, no. 5 (May 30, 1903): 122. Blakemore had been mine manager of the Crow's Nest Pass Coal Co. and had also held senior management positions in Nova Scotia.

38 This theory was recorded by the Northwest Mounted Police. See Royal Canadian Mounted Police Papers (hereafter cited as RCMPP), file 139, vol. 1527, RG18 B1, PAC.

39 Blakemore, "The Frank Disaster," 122.

40 The methane gas and lime explosion theory can be found in *The Canadian Engineer* (May 30, 1903): 154. See also Green, "The Frank Disaster," 103–10.

41 Gordon H. Crayford, *Recollections of the Frank Slide* (Lacombe, Alberta: G. H. Crayford, 1986). See also Cooper, "Frank, Alta, April 30, 1903."

42 Felske, "Crow's Nest Pass Coal Industry," Chapter 4.

43 Those who attributed the Slide, in whole or in part, to coal mining formed an impressive list. They included Frank B. Smith, then Inspector of Mines, R. W. Brock, who was a geologist with the Geological Survey of Canada, and William Pearce, Chief of Surveys in western Canada for the federal government. See Smith, "The Frank Disaster"; Pearce, "The Great Rockslide"; and MIR.

44 WPPAUA, letter, May 5, 1903.

45 Such comparisons are always difficult to make. Mining engineers usually stress that every deposit is always unique and presents important fundamental differences. There were, however, few companies mining vertical seams.

46 Pearce, "The Great Rockslide."

47 One source describes two small tunnels, one above, but also one below the main entry in 1901: Geological Survey of Canada Papers (hereafter cited as GSCP), PAC, RG45, vol. 218, file 1902, Leach 1769-71.

48 Blakemore, "The Frank Disaster," 122. See also GSCP, Leach 1769-71, which reports that eighty rooms had been opened in 1901.

49 MIR, February 4, 1902.

50 There may have been more than one chute per room, as William Pearce states that these chutes were every thirty to forty feet: see Pearce, "The Great Rockslide."

51 Interview by author with Jock Shearer, Calgary, 1981. Jock Shearer had been a pit boss in the Hillcrest Mine; see also Blairmore *Enterprise* and Frank *Vindicator*, 10 Apr. 1914.

52 Ibid., September 29, 1901.

53 Ibid., December 11, 1902.

54 *Lethbridge Herald*, January 31, 1906.

55 MIR, letter dated August 26, 1905.

56 Felske, "Crow's Nest Pass Coal Industry," Chapter 6.

57 Ibid., letter from R. W. Brock to John Stocks, Deputy Minister, Alberta Government, Department of Mines, March 26, 1910.

58 L. D. Burling, "The Landslide at Frank, Alberta," *Science*, N.S. 29, no. 754: 947–48. Burling reported that all the coal had been loosened or taken out by the time of the Slide.

59 Item 1052-10810, Box 77, Frank 1901–1906, Department of Municipal Affairs, PAA, Savey Steen and Walter Wrigley. The underground foreman, Ed Ash, also noticed the entry timber problem before the Slide: *Lethbridge Herald*, April 24, 1958.

60 Smith, in "The Frank Disaster," claimed the coal had been extracted for a length of three thousand feet. William Pearce, Chief Inspector of Surveys for the Territorial Government, reported that the main entry had been driven six

thousand feet by the time of the Slide: see Pearce, "The Great Rockslide," 490–492. At four hundred feet into the mine, the cover or height of the seam to the surface was four hundred feet; at four thousand feet from the entrance it was eight hundred feet. See also W. W. Leach, "The Blairmore-Frank Coalfields," *Geological Survey of Canada, Annual Report*, vol. 15, New Series, 1902–1903, Report A. Leach noted that by the summer of 1902 the main entry had reached 4,500 feet. A company director claimed that the entry had reached nine thousand feet by May 28, 1903 and that there were three million tons of coal loosened in the mine and ready for withdrawing: *Cranbrook Herald*, May 28, 1903.

61 Rodney, Read, Savigny, Oboni, Cruden, and Langenberg, *Geotechnical hazard assessment.*

62 It took thirty-one days before the debris blocking the entry could be cleared and access made by a party of ten into the mine. Coal was shipping again by July 4, 1903: see Pearce, "The Great Rockslide," and Dowlen, "The Turtle Mountain Rock Slide."

63 MIR, August 1903; December 9, 1903; February 11, 1904. This gas problem persisted into 1904 and undoubtedly contributed to the underground fires that soon plagued the Frank mine.

64 File 2306, vol. 45, RG45, PAC.

65 MIR, letter from D. Evans, Inspector of Mines, North-West Territories, to the Deputy Minister, Department of Public Works, April 16, 1901.

66 MIR, May 12, 1901.

67 W. Blakemore, "The Frank Disaster," 121–22.

68 Felske, "Crow's Nest Pass Coal Industry," 206.

69 MIR, April 4, 1903. During the course of its operation from 1901 to 1918, the Frank mine employed 21 different managers.

70 MIR, February 4, 1902.

71 Smith, "The Frank Disaster," 102–3; Green, "The Frank Disaster," 103. Those making the climb were Frank B. Smith, Inspector of Mines, J. C. MacArthy, the Canadian American Coal and Coke Co.'s manager, and F. L. Bryon, a long-time Pass resident and coal prospector.

72 R. A. Daly, W. G. Miller, and George S. Rice, *Report of the Commission appointed to investigate Turtle Mountain, Frank, Alberta, 1911* (Ottawa: Government of Canada, 1912).

HORROR STORIES TALES OF FROZEN PRAIRIE SETTLERS DURING THE BRUTAL WINTER OF 1906–7*

Joe Cherwinski

> I come from a land that is harsh and unforgiving
> Winter snows can kill you
> And the summer burn you dry
> When a change in the weather
> Makes a difference to your living
> You keep one eye on the banker
> And Another on the sky
>
> ....
>
> 'Cause that big old flatland
> She doesn't suffer fools lightly
> Watch your step if you're new around
> Brown broke down in a blizzard last winter
> Tried to walk and froze to death fifty feet from town
> Connie Kaldor, "Harsh and Unforgiving"[1]

Although the land was quite level, with only a few clumps of bush to force detours, Sergeant Hy Lett of the Estevan Detachment, Royal North West Mounted Police, had to fight his way through metre-high snow drifts as he headed southwest that February day in 1907. The snow, according to pioneers, was the worst in a number of years, and the strong winds which had been blowing incessantly since November had filled the hollows with fine frozen granules. While the drifts could support Sergeant Lett, they could not hold his team and cutter, which he often literally had to excavate.

Although he should not have been out in such conditions, his orders from headquarters in Regina, which in turn was responding to Ottawa, were of the highest priority. It had been reported that an English family named Ratcliffe had been found frozen, and a full investigation was

---

* An earlier version of this article appeared in *Canadian Ethnic Studies/Etudes Ethiques au Canada* 31, no. 3(1999): 20–43, and is hereby reprinted with permission.

imperative. By the time he got back, however, his name had appeared in most of the country's major papers, and within hours the story had reached the desks of several cabinet ministers in Ottawa, their senior bureaucrats, the president of the Canadian Pacific Railway and the Canadian High Commissioner in London. This macabre news received such attention because it threatened to scuttle years of work to sell Canada as a safe haven for newcomers, particularly those from the British Isles and the United States. Its potentially detrimental impact had to be minimized quickly and effectively. But, as one of the more prominent events of that traumatic winter, the incident helped to erode the belief of some confident imperialists that the environment could be easily tamed. It also showed that information, once released, was difficult to control, especially when unexpected conditions effectively strangled communications.

—

The winter of 1906–7 has become so legendary for its severity that countless prairie pioneers have used it as a benchmark for their personal pasts, as they would a marriage or a death.[2] Almost every local history contains numerous references to it.[3] Literary references are also common. For example, Jake Trumper, W. O. Mitchell's hero of the "Jake and the Kid" stories, extolled its severity during a later prairie blizzard:

> She'll never be as bad as the winter my lumbago predicted in Ought-Six an'-Seven. What we got! Winter! this ain't real winter! Just a long skinny sort of fall, that's all she is! Any snow? hardly any till last week. Blizzard? Not a twinge, uh, not a blow. No siree, Bob. There ain't gonna be one.[4]

A more tragic perspective was provided by Frederick Philip Grove's generic story "Snow."[5] Also on a serious note, Wallace Stegner devoted an entire chapter of his memoir *Wolf Willow* to the "winter of the blue snow" in the ranching country of southwestern Saskatchewan.[6] So too did long-time cowboy and illustrator R. D. Symons, who opened his nostalgic tribute to the cattle industry with his own experience of that year.[7] In a less positive vein, the journalist-homesteader Georgina

Binnie-Clark confessed to "getting up late and going to bed early to economize fuel."[8] Meanwhile, Dr. L. H. Neatby, a newly arrived medical practitioner from England, tried to cut wood for his family without proper tools, expertise or clothing.[9]

With urbanization came a great deal of independence from the weather; as a result, climatic anomalies have tended to lose significance. But since the winter of 1906–7 posed a major crisis, the documentary legacy is significant.[10] Nevertheless, few scholars have viewed it as a matter for serious study, perhaps because they have seen significance primarily in things urban. Following in the footsteps of the early ranching historian, L. V. Kelly, David Breen's important study of the ranching industry on the southern Prairies describes how it rang the death knell for the region's massive ranches – a message repeated by John H. Archer and Don C. McGowan.[11] Most recently, Paul Voisey devotes a few sentences of his seminal community study of Vulcan to this same message.[12] Strikingly, J.F.C. Wright's earlier provincial history of Saskatchewan provides a much fuller treatment.[13] The transport problems of that winter are described by Canadian Northern Railway authority Ted Regehr, who rationalizes the poor service by reference to the weather, while R. B. Fleming presents the crisis from the perspective of one of the Northern's principals, Sir William Mackenzie.[14] Passing references have been made by David Jones and by Don Kerr and Stan Hanson.[15] Only the glossy second volume of the planned eleven-volume "Alberta in the Twentieth Century" series gives the crisis its due, albeit in a popular vein.[16]

Despite neglect by the Canadian academic community, scholarly work elsewhere has increasingly concluded that weather is a significant contributor to social change.[17] A careful examination reveals that while conditions between the Red and the Rockies during the winter of 1906–7 may not by themselves have altered the direction of developments, they certainly made contemporaries consider the implications of similar occurrences. This is the subject of an extended study in progress on the multiple facets of prairie life affected by the winter of 1906–7. Its impact on Canada's immigration campaign, and the efforts made to minimize the damage created by exaggerated reports and persistent rumours, is the subject of this essay.

The summer of 1906 had been almost ideal in Manitoba, Saskatchewan, and Alberta, and the harvest showed signs of being close to a record. Most of the crop was threshed by the end of October, thanks to a warm, sunny fall. While some farmers were actively involved in fall field work or in cutting and hauling wood for the winter, bachelor homesteaders fresh from overseas or the north-central United States left the construction camps and their town jobs to spend the winter fulfilling the residence requirement for "proving up" their quarter sections.[18] Still others busied themselves with enclosures for their livestock, poultry, and families against the winter, grumbling that they were cash-strapped because the boxcars to ship out the harvest were not parked at the nearest siding, an annual complaint which had become chronic. The CPR, the dominant carrier, blamed cautious farmers unwilling to order boxcars until the crop was assured. Farmers, meanwhile, spoke of dark conspiracies to create a glut to drive down prices.

The only other cloud on an otherwise clear horizon that fall was the lengthy strike by the United Mine Workers in Lethbridge, where Galt coal, the staple in most prairie stoves, was mined. But pressure on Ottawa by the premiers of Saskatchewan and Alberta suggested that the dispute would be settled well before the onset of really cold weather.

Outside of these irritants, the National Policy seemed finally to be operating as it should. Prairie farm land, the collateral to underwrite national development within an imperial framework based on a tariff to protect domestic industry and a sophisticated railway network, had been Canada's since 1870. Despite land at giveaway prices to newcomers willing to fulfill minimal requirements, progress had been painfully slow. The completion of the CPR main line in 1885, as well as branch lines north from Regina and Calgary in 1890 and 1891, respectively, followed by a concerted advertising campaign focused on agriculturalists, offered hope to Canada's imperialists, but the magnet still seemed too weak; most settlers still preferred the United States.

Those responsible for promoting western Canada's charms had long known that her climate was part of the reason it was a hard sell. It was still considered "a dreary, desolate region, only suitable as a habitat for arctic animals"[19] well into the nineteenth century, and it had taken publicly sponsored expeditions in the 1850s by Palliser and Hind to confirm that the region was fit for agriculture. Although aridity was an obvious concern, the geologist George Dawson minimized this.[20] Yet neither he nor his predecessors devoted much time to describing winter conditions. Palliser's report, however, did warn that the southern Prairies lacked sufficient wood for fuel and construction.[21]

In 1880, the Department of the Interior dispatched a party under the enthusiastic botanist, John Macoun, for more information; his 687-page report, *Manitoba and the Great North-West* (1882), concluded that winters were comparatively mild even in the Peace River country. The chapter on "Fuel Supply," while supporting Palliser's conclusions about the lack of wood, pointed to the extensive coal reserves as a superior alternative for the future settler.[22]

While some critics branded Macoun as a charlatan, the Canadian government liked the rosy picture he painted.[23] There was considerable concern expressed about the potential damage when the imperialist icon, Rudyard Kipling, referred to Canada as "Our Lady of the Snows" in an 1897 poem,[24] and more bad press was created by the experiences of the ill-starred Barr colonists in 1903.[25] Nevertheless, the tide of opinion appeared to be turning. As proof that the weather in the Northwest was gradually improving in the public mind, it was variously described by itinerant writers as "tolerable" and "healthy."[26] "For certain pulmonary complaints" it was "said to be beneficial" and bracing.[27] Meanwhile, Macoun's prophesies were fulfilled when the railways began to link prairie dwellers with the coal mines to the west and the supply lines which had traditionally transported firewood from the north rapidly withered from disuse. If coal was costly it was also more efficient, required a lot less work, and could be acquired readily from the lumber dealer's stockpile in a nearby village. The settler could purchase provisions from one of the many general stores established to make life as comfortable as that enjoyed by anyone anywhere. As an indication of the sophistication of the transportation network, general merchants offered a surprisingly wide variety of consumer goods to farm families and townsfolk alike. For Christmas Dinner 1906, for example, the citizens of Fernie in the southeastern corner of British Columbia could choose such delights as lobster, prime rib of beef, young Turkey, and "Spring" Chicken from the menu at the Royal Hotel.[28]

With the West rapidly becoming "civilized,"[29] and with the development of faster maturing wheat, by the turn of the century the campaign to win the hearts, minds, and pocketbooks of Englishmen, Americans and others seemed to be working. From a sophisticated network of offices in every major city in Britain and the northern United States, agents armed with posters, literature, newspaper ad money, lantern slides, display cases, essay contests, and public lectures, all pitched the West as a natural extension of the American garden,[30] where restless agriculturists and entrepreneurs could find ample opportunities.[31]

The central thrust of the campaign directed at potential British migrants is revealed in a lengthy memorandum from the advertising manager of *The Times* of London to Lord Strathcona, Canada's High Commissioner to the U.K. He argued that since his paper was "read by the whole of the educated and superior class," whose principal concern was "the problem of the younger sons" cut loose from economic and social success at home due to England's inheritance laws, the North American dominion was an ideal refuge. With a small amount of capital, "these educated, athletic, clean, healthy young Englishmen, anxious to work for themselves ... will in many cases ... go into much harder work and rougher conditions in Canada than they would care to undertake in England." As for the deterrent effect of the Canadian winter, *The Times* suggested that its series of stories would point out that because it was "so dry and crisp, with plenty of sunshine," it was even "in the coldest parts not so disagreeable as an ordinary English winter." Besides, "the snow and frost are of enormous commercial value to the country as they break up the soil and save a great deal of labour to the farmer." All in all, Canada would benefit from these "younger sons of English gentlemen" who would "keep up the intellectual and social status."[32] This and other marketing campaigns were working; by the time Saskatchewan and Alberta became provinces in 1905, immigration officials could proudly proclaim that Canada had attracted almost as many European immigrants as had the United States.[33]

In due course the Laurier government granted charters for two more rail networks, the Grand Trunk Pacific and the Canadian Northern, to meet increasing demand. In part because of this added capacity, from July to September 1906 immigrant arrivals through seaports were up 49 per cent over 1905, while overland they were up 15 per cent from the Unites States.[34] So great was the demand for good homesteads that many chose land in districts where only a promise for a future branch line existed.[35] Recent mild winters convinced them that the little fuel needed could be hauled either from the northern woods or the lignite mines to the south.[36]

To everyone's surprise, however, on November 16, 1906 winter hit early and hard across the southern Prairies with a three-day blizzard pioneers described as the worst early storm in living memory. Before spring arrived the following May, high winds, record low temperatures, and unprecedented snowfall caused widespread discomfort, destruction, and numerous deaths from exposure or self-inflicted injuries throughout the region. Meanwhile, the mid-November blizzard brought a sense of urgency to ongoing problems. Even while the CPR was still trying to explain away the wheat glut, the yet unsettled coal strike forced the Saskatchewan government to canvass every community in the province on anticipated needs should a fuel famine occur.[37] Reports of the storm and survey soon reached Lord Strathcona at the British High Commission in London. Ever sensitive to the speed with which publicity campaigns could unravel, the venerable politician, business magnate, and imperialist wired the Minister of the Interior in Ottawa for clarification. Frank Oliver replied by cable on November 27 that fuel was indeed scarce but only in central Saskatchewan and that the strike would be settled that very day. Meanwhile, he assured London that "Weather now fine after short cold snap & no present danger."[38] The High Commissioner blanketed the British press with Oliver's assurances and wrote back that despite the "mischievous" stories that had received "undue prominence in the press," his comforting words had had a "reassuring effect."[39]

The damage control statement came too late, however, and could not compete with a front-page story on November 29 in the *London Morning Leader* with a headline that screamed: "FUEL FAMINE IN N. CANADA – FEARS THAT ENGLISH SETTLERS MAY DIE OF COLD." Its Montreal correspondent described how settlers, faced with "terribly cold weather since the middle of the month," were twisting hay, straw, and grain into fuel, "as well as burning their furniture." Even schools were closed for lack of fuel.[40] Despite Oliver's further assurance that the Saskatchewan government had arranged for the CPR to supply its own coal to settlers, reports of hardship continued to appear, including one originating from Reuters in Winnipeg on December 11 about the "alarming" situation in which "vast numbers of settlers unable to procure fuel" were forced to burn straw, grain, and lumber from buildings.[41] British readers worried that family and friends caught in Canada's glacial grip would soon succumb.[42] In obvious frustration, the London office appealed for "actual facts" to counter the damaging publicity.[43]

The speed, nature, and scope of the government's response indicates how seriously it viewed this unexpected public relations disaster. Over the next four months Ottawa mobilized every available resource to accomplish four objectives: to investigate the hardship climate and circumstance had inflicted on settlers; to report the "true" situation; to exhibit the greatest flexibility so that homesteader success would not be jeopardized; and to assist materially those in need in order to minimize both hardship and dissatisfaction.

To determine the degree of suffering and to devise practical solutions, Ottawa called on those unofficial ambassadors of the National Policy, the Royal North West Mounted Police constables, whose regular patrols put them in touch with every settler and whose authoritative voices had considerable credibility at home and abroad.[44] Told to focus on the Eagle Lake district south of Battleford, where many homesteaders were forty to fifty miles from the railway, Immigration received the first of many detailed reports by mid-December. Following an exhaustive homestead-by-homestead investigation, the Mounties concluded that while conditions differed from place to place, reports of destitution were exaggerated. But they also concluded that if the bad weather continued, by spring there would be suffering, "as so many of the new homesteaders taken this year are so far away from fuel of any sort."[45] In fact, the situation worsened because stands of wood were cut down by fuel-starved homesteaders. Moreover, drifting snow, distance to wood supplies (in some cases up to sixty miles), the reliance on oxen (which were useless in deep snow), and the disruption of traditional trails due to fencing of land made the situation worse. The Mounties recommended that for safety's sake settlers go north in convoys to cut and transport wood or to procure supplies from town. As for alternate sources of fuel, "C" Division's Inspector McGibbon searched fruitlessly for Macoun's reported coal deposit on the Sweetgrass Indian Reserve.[46]

As winter's grip tightened after Christmas, most issues of prairie papers included at least one story of hardship, many of which were repeated elsewhere in Canada and abroad.[47] Moreover, to add immediacy to the situation, hardly an issue was published without at least one report of death due to exposure.[48] When reports were punctuated by stories of desperate farmers commandeering carloads of coal to keep

The Battleford, Saskatchewan detachment of the Royal North-West Mounted Police on parade in 1907 under the command of Superintendent J. A. MacGibbon. This detachment was responsible for seeking out settlers experiencing hardship due to a lack of fuel and provisions in the area south of Battleford and west of Saskatoon, and offering assistance. Courtesy: Glenbow Archives NA 557-2.

---

from freezing,[49] it appeared that civilization in Canada's Northwest had disappeared entirely. As a consequence, early in the new year the Department of the Interior ordered an even broader inquiry. Its fifty-nine Dominion Lands agents and sub-agents in Manitoba, Saskatchewan, and Alberta were told to investigate climatic conditions, transportation, and the availability of fuel and provisions.[50] The Mounties were also asked to cooperate; while they were reluctant because of a lack of resources, they felt compelled to comply. As MacGibbon, the Officer Commanding the Battleford detachment, noted, "I do not wish particularly to send a patrol, but if the Minister of the Interior asked for information again, I could not give it, and if any Settler perish I do not want to be held responsible so I came to the conclusion it would be better to send a patrol." MacGibbon also concluded, however, that the Department had been architect of its own fate: "I think it is a mistake that the Immigration Department did not place an agent down there [in the area south of Battleford] in the fall, to instruct settlers, and to look after them."[51] Their reports said supplies of fuel and other essentials like sugar and coal oil ranged from adequate to non-existent with three places hit hardest: south of Battleford, along CN's newly acquired branch line from Regina to Prince Albert, and the southeastern corner of Saskatchewan around Estevan.[52] Since those south of Battleford had no close rail link and were thus most vulnerable, the police established an emergency relief camp at Tramping Lake to dispense fuel, food, and other provisions to those in obvious need.[53]

Elsewhere, where need was obvious the government provided direct aid for fuel and provisions, securing the debt with liens and mortgages wherever it could. When homesteaders were forced to reside off the farm to preserve fuel, they were given additional time to fulfill residency requirements. In addition, farmers were permitted to cut firewood anywhere they wished until the first of May. In short order, Ottawa was able to tell the world that while the weather was uniformly bad, the stories of hardship were exaggerated and the alarm was unwarranted because Canada had matters under control. As confirmation, one press dispatch confidently predicted that the 1907 "Influx Will Be Greater Than Ever – A Busy Year Expected."[54] As in the previous year, British immigrants would come in droves.

Recent arrivals Joseph Ratcliffe and his family were just the kind of people Canada wanted to attract. Not only English, and therefore able to contribute to strengthening the "right" stock, but also from an agricultural background, Joseph was born to John and Mary Swendells Ratcliffe in October 1870. As the third son, he had little chance at the family dairy farm near Dovedale at the end of the Pennines in Derbyshire. Forced to leave the farm, he quit school at the age of eleven to work as a gardener and stable hand at Ilam Halls. After becoming a proficient horseman he got employment at an estate in Bournemouth, where he met Margaret, two years his junior and an experienced cook. They married in 1902 and went to Scotland to work at Belmaghie Castle Douglas in Kircudbrightshire. With responsibility for three boys, twins Ernest and Dick followed by Jim, and with prospects of a future of menial jobs working for various landowners, the family succumbed to the siren call of free land and decided to migrate to western Canada.

Their odyssey to the new world was typical. After a twenty-one-day crossing they arrived in Montreal on May 2, 1906 and boarded a CPR colonist car for Moose Jaw. While Margaret remained with the boys, her husband took the train to Weyburn to file on a homestead in a recently opened area south of that community. He chose the northeast quarter of 18-2-15, which was the furthest from the railway in the neighbourhood, although a branch line was promised soon. He then purchased the basic necessities to begin farming: two oxen, a wagon, a walking plough, a cow, ten hens and a rooster, a bachelor's stove with a pipe oven, and some lumber to build a shelter. The shack which rose from the prairie within days of his arrival had one large room with adjoining storage shed, all lined with lumber. It took Joseph three weeks to make it liveable. He then wired Margaret and the boys to join him in Weyburn. When they arrived on June 15 they traveled for two days to reach their new home.[55]

During the summer and fall of 1906 the Ratcliffes busied themselves adapting to their greatly changed circumstances, together with the dozens of British, American, and Scandinavian settlers who had arrived in the previous eighteen months. One of the first chores was to protect their priceless livestock by building barns of sods and lumber similar in design to the house but much larger.[56] Otherwise they spent that summer and fall breaking five acres for the next spring's seeding and laying in a supply of fuel and provisions for winter.[57] Residents had it easier in terms of fuel than most of those residing on the southern Prairies because they had lignite coalmines around Estevan. While the trip was lengthy, the coal was cheap and plentiful.

As winter approached, many bachelors left to spend the winter someplace warmer, but the Ratcliffes were stuck because their oxen needed constant attention. The mid-November storm ended yard work and left them to settle into a dull routine of twice-daily chores during the rapidly diminishing daylight hours. Periodic visits to the nearest post office for papers and news from home broke the monotony, but even these trips were severely restricted after the beginning of December as they experienced the full fury of the winter with its high winds, heavy snowfall, and brutally cold temperatures. At such times even routine activities were difficult; if the Ratcliffe experience was typical, the only way to get from the house to the stable and back during a blizzard was to hang onto a rope stretched between the two structures. When the severe weather broke occasionally, they were unable to get to the nearest general store for supplies and mail because the snow was too deep for the oxen. Even if they had made it to town, transportation disruptions were so serious that commodities like coal oil, tea, and sugar were in short supply and the mail and newspapers were weeks late, if they arrived at all. With nowhere to go and no visitors, the days were uneventful at best.

—

 Cut off as they were, the Ratcliffes were unaware of the stories about frozen settlers that had been circulating throughout the southern Prairies. One of the first appeared on January 23, 1907 in a report attributed to the St. Boniface, Manitoba police about a party of Galician immigrants aboard a Canadian Northern train which became snowbound. Thinking they were no more than a mile from home they detrained. But they were wrong about their location, and five men and one woman froze, the latter still clutching a living child.[58] The ethnic overtones of the story took on a moral dimension in the last week of January when a German settler living six miles south of Stoughton allegedly went to Estevan for coal and "became the worse for liquor;" by the time he returned home three days later his wife and three children had frozen due to his folly. Meanwhile, one of his other children was found frozen near Minot, North Dakota. Subsequent reports placed this disaster in a different location and increased the number of child victims to five.[59] This was followed by an account from Saskatoon of three homesteaders found frozen in their shack a hundred miles from Dundurn.[60] A story which received even greater publicity involved six men reported frozen at Darwin, Ontario.[61] A variation involved eight men who froze to death on the Arcola line south of Regina, "four of the victims dropping off the sleigh as they gave up the ghost, and the remaining four being found sitting bolt upright while the horses trotted along the road."[62] Yet another account in the *Edmonton Journal* concerned Sergeant Gillespie of the Lethbridge detachment, who encountered a shack in the middle of a slough while on patrol during a mid-February chinook. Inside he found a family of six huddling in a garret with two feet of water on the floor. To make matters worse, the father had gone for coal during the previous cold spell and on his way back got lost and had his feet frozen.

His horses got away and when the thaw came the shack was surrounded by water, making escape impossible. With the Mountie's assistance, however, they were saved.[63]

The Department of the Interior ordered its agents, with or without the help of the Mounted Police, to investigate and disclaim each story, no matter how outlandish. Their task was urgent because the Department wanted to prevent more serious damage to Canada's reputation. Consequently, many personnel travelled numerous miles over difficult terrain to discover that reports were without substance. Not surprisingly, Sergeant Lett was skeptical when he first heard about the Ratcliffe family. But on returning from patrol, he visited the detachment at Weyburn on February 19 to find the story had spread.[64] Moreover, the next day a Jewish farmer, Dave Trapper, who was in town for supplies, said he had seen the bodies at the shack in the Dirt Hills. While Trapper had a reputation for fabrication, he swore that another homesteader named McAlpine had seen the bodies and also had found the husband and his team frozen on a nearby river, his wagon full of coal.[65] Then Lett received a crude note from the Postmaster at Hamar, Saskatchewan, attached to another note from homesteader G. A. Goslin dated the 16th: "Family frose [sic] to Death on sec. 18-2-15 have been there for Over 2 weeks. No one to look after them Please notify Athorities [sic]."[66] This was followed by a report from G. A. Bell, the Department of Interior's Homestead Inspector at Alameda who, while on the lookout for cases of destitution, found nothing until he encountered Trapper. Alarmed, he notified his superiors and the police and requested that someone deliver the bodies to Macoun, the closest community.[67] While in Macoun he heard that the bodies could not be moved without the coroner's permission, so he requested the police to perform this gruesome task. Meanwhile, news reports of the tragedy appeared in the Estevan and Weyburn papers,[68] so Heffernan ordered Lett to travel to Macoun and from there "proceed to the scene of the disaster."[69]

The Sergeant, weighing the Force's policy of having two-man patrols in such dangerous circumstances against the costs associated with hiring someone to accompany him, chose the latter option, hired a team and proceeded after collecting almost three months of the Ratcliffes' mail at the Macoun post office.[70] He was able to make good time until the trail ran out. Knowing only that he had to find the

31 FROZEN TO DEATH.

Farmers in Canada Burning Their Homes Owing to Fuel Famine.

Special to The New York Times.

ST. PAUL, Feb. 13.—Telegrams from Canadian territory just north of the North Dakota boundary show that a terrible situation exists there owing to the fuel famine and the blockade of railroads.

Three families of settlers merge their effects into one household, while the homes of the remaining two are torn down and burned to keep the families from freezing. This plan has been adopted by a score of families. Where grain was not shipped it is being burned as fuel.

Thirty-one bodies found frozen in homestead shacks or on the prairie have been brought into various towns of the Northwest, and it is expected that the list will be swelled to half a hundred by the time the snow disappears.

Cortelyou in Town.

WASHINGTON, D. C., Feb. 13.—Postmaster General Cortelyou left this afternoon for New York to attend to pressing business. It is likely he may be absent for three or four days.

Clipping: Exaggerated accounts of the situation on the Canadian Prairies during the winter of 1906–7, like this one which appeared in the February 14, 1907 issue of the *New York Times*, caused considerable concern for government and railway officials involved with prairie development. Some believed that rumours like this were intentionally printed to discourage American residents from seeking opportunities north of the border.

northeast quarter of Section 18 in Township 2, Range 15 west of the second meridian, Lett was about as well informed as anyone about the Ratcliffes because their very existence on this farthest homestead from the railway was largely a matter of conjecture to their neighbours. When he sought directions from the McAlpines at 26-2-14, he was informed that they did not know the Ratcliffes but thought they lived in the hills fifteen or sixteen miles away. Although they had heard about the tragedy from three transients, they had not investigated because of the deep snow. They had seen Trapper around, but dismissed him as crazy and therefore unlikely to have witnessed the circumstances with which he was associated.[71]

Lett plodded on and reached the G. A. Goslin homestead at 2 a.m. on the 22nd. The owner admitted to sending the note that triggered the investigation, but confessed that he had not been over to the Ratcliffes, again because the snow was too deep and because he did not want to face the prospect of seeing four frozen corpses. Nevertheless, he had it on good authority from Pete Fossner, an American on his way home to Rugby, North Dakota, who said he had seen Mrs. Ratcliffe and the three children frozen in their beds two or three weeks earlier, their shack devoid of both food and fuel.[72]

Fearing the worst, the Mountie took the reluctant Goslin as a witness and to help break trail because the remaining six or seven miles were "very rough." Once they reached the homestead they went first to the stable, where they found the yoke of oxen, which meant that all was well, a fact confirmed when they knocked on the Ratcliffe door to be greeted by the entire family, very much alive and "a picture of health." Not only did they have two and a half tons of coal but also plenty of provisions to last the winter. The only thing they lacked was a sleigh with which to break free from the winter isolation.[73]

When the Mountie showed Joseph Ratcliffe the clippings about the family's death from the Estevan and Weyburn papers, he was at a loss as to the origin of the rumour. The only explanation he could think of was that another nearby English homesteader named Cozens had got lost in a blizzard and was still missing.[74]

His investigation complete, Lett hurried back to his detachment headquarters to file his report before the rumour spread further. But he was too late because the story had already been flashed far afield the day he left on his mission; over the next few weeks it was regurgitated in a wide variety of places with varying degrees of accuracy. Later attempts at correction were either half-hearted or non-existent.

The spread of the story appears to have been accomplished in three phases by three separate, but interrelated, methods. North American dailies were the first to pick it up, apparently as a result of Dave Trapper's "eyewitness" report. Before Lett had even reached 18-2-15 on February 21, a version of the story appeared in *The Gazette* (Montreal), *The Daily Herald* (Calgary), and *The Manitoba Free Press* (Winnipeg), indicating that the deaths were the result of isolation and a lack of fuel. The next day, people in Halifax, Moncton, Toronto, and New York read the news, but it was the story in *The Globe* which caused the greatest concern in official circles in Ottawa.[75] The headline – "ENTIRE FAMILY FROZEN. APPALLING TRAGEDY FROM RIGORS OF WESTERN WINTER" – gave Lett as the source.

One of the first people with a vested interest to hear about the tragedy was the president of the CPR, T. G. Shaughnessy, who received word on the morning of the 22nd. His version was that while there were three sacks of coal in the "shanty," Mrs. Ratcliffe had died from illness and "the children were too small to keep the fires going and froze to death." While he was bothered by this, he was more concerned that this was the first death reported on a CPR line and, more important, that despite the story's origin in a company telegraph office, he heard about it only after it had been reported in the *New York Herald*. He instructed his chief official in Winnipeg, William Whyte, to investigate this communication *faux pas*.[76]

Immigration Branch headquarters in Ottawa also received early word of the deaths, but they had been receiving reports of deaths from regional agents for some weeks, so the Ratcliffe tragedy was not so shocking. Nevertheless, the widespread publicity was a grave concern since much time and effort had been expended earlier to minimize the damage further north. The fact that the Ratcliffes were recently arrived English settlers made it even worse. Immigration therefore requested Branch headquarters in London and the Canadian High Commissioner to implement damage control measures similar to those used in the fall.

Lett's correct version of the Ratcliffe story arrived in Ottawa almost immediately, which allowed Frank Oliver, the Minister of the Interior, to assure Lord Strathcona that the story was "absolutely without foundation." The High Commissioner responded that he was "contradicting the report in advance of the possibility of the first untrue statement receiving wide publicity in the press in this country."[77] A press release was issued which urged that "sensational reports of this kind should be treated with much circumspection."[78] Meanwhile, in Canada it took three days for *The Globe* to publish a correction. When it did appear in the top, left-hand corner of page 4 on February 25, the headline – "NEWS TO THE RATCLIFFS" [sic] – the tone was considerably less sensational than the original story. It briefly described how Lett had "had to use the shovel to excavate the horses in order to make the Ratcliff's[sic] house," only to find Ratcliffe, his "wife and three fat, red, roundfaced nor'-westers ... all comfortable and [with] lots of provisions and fuel to last until navigation opens."[79] The *Montreal Gazette* and the *Calgary Daily Herald* also published corrections, while the *Halifax Herald* and the *Moncton Transcript* did not. Significantly, the *Regina Leader*, the daily newspaper closest to the tragedy, felt no need to retract a story it had not printed in the first place.

When London finally received copies of the story and the retraction early the following month via Immigration's Assistant Superintendent, the office drafted another press release reaffirming that the "sensational reports of settlers being frozen to death in the North West of Canada during the winter now closing ... have proved to be an ... absolute fabrication."[80] In due course more balanced accounts in the British press, based at least in part on such high level statements, were clipped and sent to Ottawa by Strathcona's staff.[81] But the damage had been done and negative reports on the Canadian Prairies continued to appear. The *Sheffield Weekly Telegraph*, for example, early in March published a lengthy article "IN WESTERN CANADA: A SEVERE WINTER" which described the winter as the worst since 1881, in part because adequate services were not in place to cope with "the howling blizzards, sweeping at hurricane speed across the prairies, carr[ying] great swirls of snow that cut like a knife." Yet, perhaps because of British pluck, "[w]estern settlers have refused to share the depression of the thermometer.... It has warmed their hearts, when their bodies were cold, to recall the fact that there has never been a hard winter, with plenty of snow, that has not been followed by a bumper harvest."[82]

While the Ratcliffes reaped that harvest and many others,[83] the report of their deaths took on a life of its own in the dozens of weekly regional newspapers long after the dailies had put the story to rest. Of the dozens of weeklies from Manitoba, Saskatchewan, and Alberta consulted, a significant number carried a version of the alleged tragedy.[84] Moreover, like the reports in their big-city cousins, the spelling of the names of the chief "victims" varied widely. Few, however, printed corrections once the rumour turned out to be a hoax. One exception, the *Carman* (Manitoba) *Standard*, placed the blame on "imaginative correspondents" seeking "heart-rendering occurrences" to telegraph to papers outside the region.[85] Another, *The West* (Regina), in a lengthy editorial entitled "No Truth to Wild Rumors," concluded that their American origins were part of a sinister plot to discredit the Canadian West, which was attracting American settlers in frightening numbers.[86] This suspicion is not surprising in light of a belief widely held throughout the region that American newspapers were intentionally distorting the Canadian situation to dissuade their citizens from emigrating. For example, a story in the *New York Times* from St. Paul, Minnesota, claimed that thirty-one "bodies found frozen in homestead shacks or on the prairie have been brought into various towns in the Northwest," and that this number was expected to rise "to half a hundred by the time the snow disappears."[87] Similarly, the *Calgary Daily Herald* some weeks earlier took issue with what it termed "Fairy Stories" originating in Bellingham, Washington, which predicted a veritable stampede of expatriot Americans "who are not used to extreme cold experienced on the windswept regions of the Alberta country."[88]

Prairie editors were also quick to direct salvos at the "Eastern" press for trying to portray the western Canadian experience in the worst possible light. For example, the *Western Canadian* from Manitou, Manitoba, pointed to the story of J. J. Browne, homesteading near Saskatoon, who read his own obituary claiming that he had frozen to death on the prairie. The Manitoba weekly blamed it on the "Ontario papers," which

> in order to stop the rush of young men to the west, will grasp at every possible straw if the west can be given a black eye, and seize upon every opportunity to enlarge upon the severity of the winter just past [*sic*], even though it is necessary to kill and bury the man in one issue, and many are the tales told by these papers about loss of life in this

country. In this case, however, things did not turn out as pictured and the supposed corpse is still able to sit up and take a little nourishment.[89]

In light of the fallout from the Ratcliffe story the Commissioner of the RNWMP, A. Bowen Perry, wanted a more tangible culprit and contacted the Deputy Attorney-General for Saskatchewan to have the most visible perpetrators, Dave Trapper and Pete Fossner, charged under section 126 of the Criminal Code because "this false news was ... detrimental to the public interest."[90] Whether Perry's eagerness to apportion blame was to save face is difficult to know, since he had been the first to lend credibility to the story by ignoring advice from the field to be cautious and wiring Headquarters in Ottawa that tales of the frozen "Ratchcliffe" family were indeed true. The message had been immediately relayed to the Immigration Branch.[91]

While Perry sought scapegoats, other sources attributed the spread of the accounts to the well-known and highly respected temperance advocate, Rev. J. G. Shearer, who while traveling the region referred to the German imbiber version of the story to punctuate his message, and likely repeated it for local newspaper publishers in the communities in which he spoke.[92] In fact, almost everyone in the region had an interest in the story for their own personal reasons. For the Police Commissioner, the Ratcliffe "tragedy" was tailor-made to enhance the size and influence of the Force. Ever since the first attempts to determine the number of needy cases in the area south of Battleford, the various detachments were badly strapped for personnel and had to "borrow" officers from elsewhere to do Ottawa's bidding. When the Mounties were ordered to patrol "every settled section" of Saskatchewan and Alberta early in February and to furnish relief in extreme cases, Perry was, by his own admission "at wits end now to supply all the requirements. Divisions are short handed, and should be filled up before spring." In a subsequent memo to Headquarters in Ottawa, he reiterated that "[u]nless we can get more men, I anticipate a great deal of trouble during the coming summer."[93] The fact that the Force's strength, particularly in the badly over-extended Battleford Detachment, increased during the next two years indicates that Perry's strategy worked.[94]

The many agents and almost five dozen sub-agents of the Dominion Lands Branch of the Department of the Interior scattered throughout the Prairies were just as motivated as the Commissioner to find and report victims. Officials managing the headquarters of the Immigration Branch were aware that their failure to prepare the hundreds of greenhorn homesteaders who had entered in the summer and fall of 1906 had contributed to the problem. This was the reason the Mounties had been asked to step in, especially in the treeless area west of Saskatoon and south of Battleford.[95] When the Department ordered the fact-finding inquiry in February, the staff searched high and low for cases of want and reported back with care and in detail, almost as if they feared some information might slip by them. Agent Bell from Alameda sought police assistance immediately when he heard about the Ratcliffes from Dave Trapper, even though rumours of multiple deaths had been prevalent for some time.[96]

Only the mounted police in the field on routine patrols emerged from the incident relatively unscathed. With their grassroots experience they were careful not to cause unnecessary anxiety before they investigated. An excellent example was provided by Corporal G. Greenlay of the Carnduff Detachment when ordered to track down a rumour similar to that involving the Ratcliffes. He wrote that "[i]t is hardly likley [sic] that they would freeze as with all of the reports it is stated that the settler had went to Town for coal if he did he must have had a team and consequently would have a stable, and it is hardly likley [sic] that anyone would freeze where there is a stable."[97] He correctly concluded that the body heat of the animals would prevent freezing. Meanwhile, Sergeant Lett's common sense made him reluctant to pursue the Ratcliffe story knowing the risk involved in travelling to the sparsely settled area near the U.S. border; he only went after Bell had intervened with his superiors.

Once the story of the "tragedy" had been put to bed, some Mounties could not resist spreading the story both for its instructional value and to enhance the force's reputation. A case in point was relayed by Lillian Turner, a young woman helping her brothers establish a homestead near Saskatoon, who was told by a patrolling constable of the difficulties he once had reaching a woman and children reported frozen with the husband gone, albeit this time for wood. "But having reached them he found them alive and happy [with] enough to eat of everything but meat." As they were soon joined by more police from the Medicine Hat detachment far to the south, Lillian was able to assure her family in

Above: CPR train near Regina snowed in for two days. Though this photograph is from the 1890s, similar situations existed during the winter of 1906–7. Courtesy: Glenbow Archives NA 155-20

Below: Casualties of a bitter Western Canadian winter. Courtesy: Glenbow Archives NA 2084-24.

Ontario with the tale that they were "all cared for in the best possible [way]."[98]

The question to be addressed is why stories which were so quickly proved false travelled so far even after their credibility had been questioned. The answer lies at least in part with the nature of prairie newspapers and the towns and villages they served. For most fledgling communities in the region, the press followed soon after their founding. Development came extremely quickly: a place designated by the railway for a townsite grew in a matter of weeks. In a gold-rush-like frenzy, the general store was soon joined by a hotel (with bar), lumber yard, barbershop/pool room and an implement dealership, as well as a newspaper office. The editor-publisher, usually from Ontario, was motivated not by a desire to contribute to the literary tone of the community but primarily by an opportunity to make money and, if he was lucky, to sell out at a profit. Commercial printing of auction notices, billboard signs, wedding invitations, and whatever else was needed in the way of local information was the mainstay of the operation.

The weekly newspaper complemented the printing business in many ways. Its main income came from advertising the wares and charms of local businesses, while the dollar-a-year subscription paid for paper and postage to reach a trading area of perhaps four hundred local farmers within a radius of ten to twenty-five miles. Consequently, there was every incentive for the weekly to be an unabashed community booster, since the publisher's own prospects were inextricably bound with those of his town. Therefore, the newspaper's mandate was to chronicle every minute improvement in the community's condition as proof that it was on its way to reaching metropolitan status.[99] As the *Ponoka Herald* proudly proclaimed from its masthead, "Ponoka District, First, Last and All the Time." When the village was not given its due recognition, the editor was quick to correct the oversight. For example, when the *1906 Census for the Prairie Provinces* was released in December, the *Vegreville* (Alberta) *Observer* noted that "Vegreville is credited with only 344. Of course this dates back to the pioneer days of June, but we were sure we had over 400 then. There is one satisfaction in it though and that is that one Vegreville man is equivalent to three or more in other towns."[100]

On the subject of the severe winter of 1906–7 the newspapers reflected a certain ambivalence depending on how the editor felt such conditions would be considered by outsiders. For example, the *Hartney* (Manitoba) *Star*'s owner-operator, Walpole Murdock, commented extensively with wit and a sense of irony on the weather and its impact, as well as on almost everything else. Meanwhile, the *Elkhorn* (Manitoba) *Advocate*'s editor, W. J. Thompson, seldom mentioned the weather, assuming that adverse news was bad for business, a view shared by the *Abernethy* (Saskatchewan) *Abernethan*.

There was a downside, exacerbated by conditions that winter, for those who subscribed to the booster school of prairie journalism. The following doggerel which *The News* in Belmont, Manitoba, borrowed wholesale from the *Swan Lake News* illustrates the problem confronting the prairie editor when weather brought most activities to a standstill:

> When It's Forty Under Zero
> Buried in the midst of winter
>> In a Manitoba town,
> With snow full sixty inches deep,
>> And the mercury way down;
> When blizzards greet us twice a week
>> And the weather's always rough,
> When it's forty under zero
>> I tell you boys, it's tough.
> With the snow piled on the railroad
>> And the snow plow's in the ditch
> And the traffic all congested
>> Alike for poor and rich;
> When the grist mill ceases grinding
>> Cause she cannot get the stuff,
> And it's forty under zero
>> I tell you boys, it's tough.
> With the town clean out of coal oil
>> And provisions running low,
> When you scarce can find your wood pile
>> Underneath the piles of snow;
> When you have to grind your axes
>> And seek fuel in some bluff,
> And it's forty under zero
>> I tell you boys, it's tough.

When all the world is silent
(For we get no outside news),
When all the town's in darkness
And the storm king is let loose,
When the wood pile's getting slender
(Though we've still got food enough)
And it's forty under zero,
Don't you think now boys, that's tough?

EPILOGUE

Long, long years since such effusions
Were regularly all the go;
And we smile to think of legions,
O' just such chaff marked zero.
Not such a dearth of news in ages,
Else such mellifluous stuff,
Never would have dimmed our pages
For "I'll tell you, boys, it's tough."[101]

The structure of prairie weekly papers made no news bad news. Except for their local coverage most were identical. While they may have contained between six and sixteen pages in any given issue, all but two to four pages were the same from paper to paper because the remainder came in by rail as "ready prints" on a weekly basis from elsewhere in North America. To these the local publisher added the local content as a cover and perhaps as an insert. The problem was that it was difficult to generate sufficient local news on a weekly basis in small towns with so few people. If the publisher was lucky he might court and win a column from a contributor in a nearby community that lacked a paper, thereby increasing the number of potential subscribers and also the trading area to be tapped by his advertisers. Most often, however, even after reporting on the comings and goings of everyone who passed through the train station, after describing every wedding and funeral in detail, and after commenting on every block of wooden sidewalk laid, there was still not enough news to fill the allotted pages. Blank spaces, as sometimes appeared, would not sit well with advertisers, so the only option was to "borrow" and reprint stories selected for their interest to locals from papers received by the editor from nearby communities or elsewhere in the region, modified to suit the space available. The poem above is a case in point. So also were the many tales of suffering and hardship like the Ratcliffe case. That they may have been inaccurate or downright lies really did not matter because the incidents they described were curiosities which might be discussed by folks killing time while waiting at the local elevator or post office and then forgotten. Besides, they confirmed how tough prairie life was and how strong, intelligent, and virtuous they were to have survived.

It was likely not a coincidence that the "victims" in southeastern Saskatchewan that winter bore the profiles they did. The tippler of German descent conformed to the generally held image of the "foreigner," whose weakness for Demon Rum was the seed of the tragedy which befell his family that brutal winter. As a result, the story did not get the attention it deserved from authorities; the same was true for the Galicians in Manitoba. Evidence suggests that homesteaders from continental Europe were considered quite hardy and able to adapt to severe conditions, provided they maintained their senses, something assumed to be in short supply.[102] The fate of the Ratcliffe family was an entirely different matter. Here was an English family who conformed to the view held of this special group of immigrant homesteaders. While they had certain desirable qualities for the Canadian Prairies, they were also more civilized and therefore delicate, thus requiring special nurturing in this rugged environment. When they fell victim to the worst the Prairies had to offer, it was due to their nature and inexperience. The tale of the family who built its shack in a hollow was proof of such shortcomings. To locals they represented newcomers too effete and too "green" to be prepared for harsh conditions.

When the story of the Ratcliffe "tragedy" began to circulate at the worst point in that dreadful winter, other homesteaders interpreted it as an example of the most vulnerable succumbing to the environment. For officials the story meant the fulfillment of a worst-possible scenario. From the early onset of the winter in November 1906, it was apparent that there could be suffering among recent immigrants. In fact, the records indicate a growing sense of foreboding as the danger signals increased.[103] Hence the thorough investigation undertaken by Immigration in December and again in January to find all cases of want and to offer aid. An occasional single homesteader reported frozen after wandering off the trail in a blizzard, while unfortunate, was considered routine. When the victims included an entire English immigrant family freezing from a lack of fuel, it became a crisis. Consequently the need *to report and then investigate* was immediate.

It appears obvious that the fabricated stories which made the rounds during the winter of 1906–7 on the Canadian Prairies reflected the deepest fears of those who created them, heard them, and passed them on. This was not only the case with individuals responsible for immigration matters but also for the population at large. The very perceptive Corporal Greenlay from the Carnduff Detachment summed up the root cause when he said that "the reports ... are likley [*sic*] started by people who have been short of fuel."[104] The concern about coal and wood supplies experienced by only a few unfortunates in November was described widely as a "fuel famine" by December. The combination of inadequate stockpiles locally, the railways' unwillingness to supply boxcars early in the season, the reduced availability due to strikes, the inordinate transportation delays caused by faulty equipment and drifting snow, and the prolonged spells of severe cold created fear and panic which led to long lineups on rumours of coal shipments, the imposition of quotas, and a rapid increase in prices for both coal and wood. This in turn resulted in desperate acts such as theft and the hijacking of coal cars as occurred at Windthorst, Saskatchewan and other places. A scramble for fuel became a struggle for survival, as most of the necessities of life became in short supply.

Similarly, the disruption in routine activities was common for most settlers. Isolation brought on by extreme cold and blizzards exacerbated the loneliness associated with homesteading. News from elsewhere through mail and newspapers, essential comforts in this strange and hostile environment, was drastically delayed, and even infrequent social intercourse, such as church services, sporting and other social events, was disrupted. When settlers did assemble, likely in a line of wagons waiting for too little coal to be unloaded at a local siding, they recounted their own experiences and compared them with those less fortunate, like the Ratcliffes, mother, father, and three to five youngsters, who had died in the Dirt Hills west of Estevan of cold and starvation.

NOTES

1   From Connie Kaldor, "Wood River: Home is Where the Heart is ... ," Coyote Entertainment Group, Inc., 1992.

2   Between 1919 and 1923, the Regina Branch of the Women's Canadian Club requested pioneers to recount their experiences. These accounts were eventually collected by A. S. Morton and are now housed in the University of Saskatchewan Archives in the A. S. Morton Collection (MSS C555). A considerable number refer to conditions during the winter of 1906–7. See, for example, MSS 555/1/ 1.19 and 1.21.

3   See, for example, Local History Committee of Rural Municipality No. 7, *The Saga of the Souris Valley.*

4   W. O. Mitchell, "The Man Who Came to Rummy," in *According to Jake and the Kid: A Collection of New Stories* (Toronto: McClelland and Stewart, 1989), 125–26.

5   Frederick Philip Grove, "Snow," *Queen's Quarterly* 39 (February 1932): 99– 110.

6   Wallace Stegner, "The Whitemud River Range," in *Wolf Willow: A History, A Story and a Memory of the Last Plains Frontier* (New York: Penguin, 2000), Section 3.

7   R. D. Symons, *Where the Wagon Led: One Man's Memories of the Cowboy's Life in the Old West,* 2nd ed. (Calgary: Fifth House, 1997), xvii–xxxi.

8   Georgina Binnie-Clark, *Wheat and Woman* (Toronto: Bell and Cockburn, 1914), devotes almost two chapters to problems with the cold temperatures and deep snow after a disagreement with her hired hand forced her to fire him.

9   L. H. Neatby, *Chronicle of a Pioneer Prairie Family* (Saskatoon: Western Producer Prairie Books, 1979), 7. This medical pioneer began the Neatby line which became so prominent, particularly in academic circles.

10 See, for example, Castell Hopkins, ed., *The Canadian Annual Review, 1907* (Toronto, 1908), 90–97.

11 L. V. Kelly, *The Range Men: The Story of the Ranchers and Indians of Alberta* (Toronto: W. Briggs, 1913), 376–83; David H. Breen, *The Canadian Prairie West and the Ranching Frontier 1874–1924* (Toronto: University of Toronto Press, 1983), 136–62; John H. Archer, *Saskatchewan: A History* (Saskatoon: Western Producer Prairie Books, 1980), 141–42; Don C. McGowan, *Grassland Settlers: The Swift Current Region During the Era of the Ranching Frontier* (Victoria: Cactus Publications, 1983), 104–6.

12 Paul Voisey, *Vulcan: The Making of a Prairie Community* (Toronto: University of Toronto Press, 1988), 88.

13 J.F.C. Wright, *Saskatchewan: The History of Province* (Toronto: McClelland and Stewart, 1955), 129–30.

14 T. D. Regehr, *The Canadian Northern Railway: Pioneer Road of the Northern Prairies, 1895–1918* (Toronto: Macmillan, 1976), 184–85.

15 David C. Jones, ed., *"We'll all be buried down here": The Prairie Dryland*

Disaster 1917–1926 (Calgary: Historical Society of Alberta, 1986), 46–47. Don Kerr and Stan Hanson, *Saskatoon: The First Half-Century* (Edmonton: NeWest Press, 1982), 87–88.

16   "The Killing Winter of Aught-six Aught-seven," in *Alberta in the 20th Century: A Journalistic History of the Province in Eleven Volumes. Volume Two: The Birth of the Province* (Edmonton, 1992), 230–33.

17   William James Burroughs, *Does The Weather Really Matter? The Social Implications of Climate Change* (Cambridge: Cambridge University Press, 1997).

18   *Saskatoon Phoenix*, December 5, 1906.

19   Charles Elliott, *A Trip to Canada and the Far North West* (London: W. Kent, 1887), 87.

20   Doug Owram, *Promise of Eden: The Canadian Expansionist Movement and the Idea of the West 1856–1900* (Toronto: University of Toronto Press, 1980), 149–51.

21   Irene Spry, ed., *The Papers of the Palliser Expedition 1857–1860* (Toronto: Champlain Society, 1968), 176, 241, 345.

22   Chapters 9, 10, 18, and 29. See pp. 294–310 for the discussion of coal reserves.

23   R. G. Moyles and Doug Owram, *Imperial Dreams and Colonial Realities: British Views of Canada, 1880–1914* (Toronto: University of Toronto Press, 1988), 126–27.

24   "Our Lady of the Snows," in Margaret J. O'Donnell, ed., *An Anthology of Commonwealth Verse* (London, 1963), 26–27; "Suggestions for Headings and Subheadings of 10 Literary Advertisements on the Dominion of Canada," no. 3, 1-2, National Archives of Canada (hereafter cited as NAC), RG25 A2, vol. 197, file "Interior and Immigration, 14-8 to 15-96."

25   H. R. Whates, *Canada The New Nation: A Book for the Settler, the Immigrant and the Politician* (London: Dent, 1906), 116-17; Mary Hiemstra, *Gully Farm* (Calgary: Fifth House, 1997), provides a personal memoir of the first winter in the Lloydminister area experienced by a Barr colonist family.

26   Elliott, *A Trip to Canada*, 87, 89.

27   Peter Mitchell, *Notes of a Holiday Trip: The West and Northwest, Reliable Information for Immigrants* (Montreal, 1880), 45.

28   *Fernie Ledger Nightcap*, December 22, 1906.

29   A. A. den Otter, *Civilizing the West: The Galts and the Development of Western Canada* (Edmonton: University of Alberta Press, 1982).

30   Owram, *Promise of Eden*, discusses early efforts to portray the Canadian prairies as a North American Eden. Henry Nash Smith, *Virgin Land: The American West in Symbol and Myth* (Cambridge, MA, Harvard University Press, 1970), is a classic treatment of role of the prairies in the American mind. See also Ellen Scheinberg and Melissa K. Rombout, "Projecting Images of the Nation: The Immigration Program and its Use of Lantern slides," *The Archivist* 111 (1996): 13–24.

31   Canada, *Sessional Papers*, 41, no. 10, 1906–7, Sessional Paper 25, pt. 2, *Immigration*, 3–72; Carla J. Wheaton, "'Advertise Judiciously': Canadian

Immigration, William J. White and the Lord & Thomas Advertising Agency, 1896–1904," unpublished Honours Essay, Memorial University of Newfoundland, May 1994.

32 Rupsell to Strathcona, November 9, 1905, NAC, RG25, A2, vol. 177, file "Interior and Immigration 14-8 to 15-96."

33 Ibid., 61.

34 *Saskatoon Phoenix*, December 5, 1906. In all 211,653 entered Canada that year: see M. C. Urquhart and K.A.H. Buckley, eds., *Historical Statistics of Canada* (Toronto, 1965), Series A254, 23.

35 W. A. Mackintosh, *Prairie Settlement: The Geographical Setting* (Toronto: Macmillan, 1934), 53. A total of 1,451 cars of settlers' effects passed through Regina between January and June 1906 bound for the area west of Saskatoon and north of Battleford where no branch lines existed.

36 Canada, *Sessional Papers*, 41, 1906–7, 88.

37 W. R. Motherwell to City Council, November 10, 1906, City of Regina Archives, file CR5-339.

38 Telegram, Oliver to Dominion, London, November 27, 1906, NAC, RG76, vol. 416, file 602204, pt. 1.

39 Ibid., Strathcona to Oliver, December 1, 1906.

40 Ibid., Clipping, *London Morning Leader*, November 29, 1906, attached to J. Bruce Walker, Assistant Superintendent of Emigration, London, to W. D. Scott, Supt. of Immigration, Ottawa, December 4, 1906.

41 Ibid., Telegram, Government, London to Interior, Ottawa, December 11, 1906.

42 Ibid., Receipt of cable, Oliver to Strathcona, December 1, 1906, acknowledged in Strathcona to Oliver, December 5, 1906. Clippings from fifteen English, Irish, Scottish, and Welsh newspapers which printed Strathcona's November 29 press release attached.

43 Ibid., Telegram, Government, London, to Interior, Ottawa, December 11, 1906.

44 R. C. Macleod, *The North-West Mounted Police and Law Enforcement 1873–1905* (Toronto, 1976).

45 MacGibbon (Battleford) to Commissioner, Regina, November 19, 1906, NAC, RG18, vol. 2767, file unnamed.

46 Ibid., J. A. McGibbon to Commissioner, RNWMP, December 16, 1906; Report, Perry to Comptroller, Ottawa, December 17, 18, and 31, 1906; J. A. McGibbon to RNWMP, Regina, December 19, 1906; Report, Constable H. R. Handcock, December 25, 1906.

47 *Moncton Daily Times*, January 1, 12, 21, 26, 31, and February 2, 1907; *The Times* (London), February 11, 1907; *New York Times*, January 12, 13, 16, 29, and February 3 and 14, 1907 contain stories of extreme cold and hardship in the entire region, including Minnesota, North Dakota, and Montana.

48 The many newspaper stories of the deaths of homesteaders due to exposure are confirmed by the crime reports prepared by RNWMP detachment personnel sent to investigate. See particularly NAC, RG18, vol. 1594, file 49, pts. 1 and 2.

49 *Regina Leader*, January 21 and 30, 1907.

50 List of Sub-Agents of Dominion Lands, March 3, 1907, NAC, RG76, vol. 416,

file 602204, pt. 2; *Saskatoon Phoenix*, February 4, 1907.

51 MacGibbon to Commissioner, Regina, November 19, 1906, NAC, RG18, vol. 2767, file unnamed.

52 NAC, RG76, vol. 416, file 602204, pt. 2. See reports from agents and sub-agents, January 10–February 8, 1907.

53 Telegrams, Constable McIllree to Commissioner, Regina, February 13 and 14, 1907, NAC, RG18, vol. 2767, file unnamed.

54 Ibid., "Hardship Rumours Are Not Correct. Western Stories of Death by Freezing Have No Foundation in Fact," n.d.

55 The description of the Ratcliffe family background, the transatlantic crossing, and their first few months in Canada is drawn from *Settlers of the Hills* (Lake Alma, Saskatchewan: Lake Alma over 50 Club, c1975), 253–55, and *Saga of the Souris Valley* (Oungre, Saskatchewan: Souris Valley No. 7 History Club, 1978), 730–32.

56 Sworn Statement of Joseph Ratcliffe, July 8, 1909, Saskatchewan Archives Board (SAB), Homestead Records, file 1898698.

57 Ibid.

58 *Moose Jaw Times*, January 25, 1907.

59 G. Greenlay Report to O. C. Regina, February 14, 1907, NAC, RG18, vol. 1594, file 49, pt. 2; *Ponoka Herald* (Alberta), March 15, 1907; Kisby to Deputy Minister, Department of the Interior, February 15, 1907, NAC, RG76, vol. 416, file 602204, pt. 1; *The West* (Regina), March 6, 1907.

60 *The West* (Regina), February 8, 1907.

61 Ibid., February 15, 1907.

62 Ibid., March 6, 1907.

63 *Edmonton Journal*, February 18, 1907. The RCMP records contain no reference to this story.

64 Memo, Commissioner to O. C. Regina, February 13, 1907; Sergeant Lett to O. C., Regina, February 17, 1907, NAC, RG18, vol. 2767, file unnamed.

65 Ibid., Lett Report "Re: J. Ratcliffe and Family Freezing to Death in Dirt Hills," February 24, 1907.

66 John Gulbranson, Hamar, to RNWMP," Estevan, February 18, 1907, NAC, RG18, vol. 1594, file 49, pt. 2.

67 A. Bell to R. C. Kisby, February 25, 1907, NAC, RG26 (Department of the Interior Immigration Branch Records), vol. 416, file 602204, pt. 1.

68 Lett Report "Re: J. Ratcliffe and Family Freezing to Death in Dirt Hills," February 24, 1907, NAC, RG18, vol. 1594, file 49, pt. 2; undated clippings from *Estevan Observer*, *Estevan Mercury* and *Weyburn Herald* indicating Trapper as their source.

69 Ibid.

70 Telegram, Inspector J. Heffernan to all subdistricts, February 9, 1907, NAC, RG18, vol. 2767, file unnamed.

71 Lett Report, February 24, 1907, NAC, RG18, vol. 1594, file 49, pt. 2.

72 Ibid.

73 Ibid., *The West*, March 6, 1907.

74 Ibid.

75 *Halifax Herald, Moncton Transcript, Toronto Globe*, February 22, 1907.

76 Shaughnessy to W. D. Matthews, February 22, 1907; Shaughnessy to Whyte, February 23, 1907, NAC, MG28, 3, 20, Canadian Pacific Railway Papers, Shaughnessy Letterbooks, Letter Book 89 (May 1906–December 1907), Reel M-3052.

77 J. Walker to Strathcona, March 12, 1907, NAC, RG25 A2, vol. 199, file "Interior and Immigration."

78 Ibid., draft press release, n.d.

79 *Toronto Globe*, February 25, 1907.

80 J. Walker to Strathcona, March 12, 1907; draft of press release, n.d, NAC, RG25 A2, vol. 199, file "Interior and Immigration."

81 Clipping, "Hardship Rumors Are Not Correct: Western Stories of Death by Freezing Have No Foundation in Fact," no name, no date, NAC, RG76, vol. 416, file 602204, pt. 2.

82 Ibid., Clipping, "In Western Canada: a Severe Winter," *Sheffield Weekly Telegraph*, March 9, 1907.

83 The two local histories from southeastern Saskatchewan which contain references to the Ratcliffe family describe how, in 1908, the family dwelling became the local post office for nearby homesteads, which in 1926, with the advent of a CPR branch line, became the focus for the new hamlet of Ratcliffe which exists to this day. The successors to the original Ratcliffes are still well represented in the area. See *Settlers of the Hills* and *Saga of the Souris Valley*, for various references to the Ratcliffes and their successors.

84 For example, the *Wolseley News*, February 28, 1907, *Battleford Press*, February 28, 1907, *Moose Jaw Times*, February 21, 1907, and *Saskatchewan Herald* (Battleford), February 27, 1907, all carried the Ratcliffe story.

85 *Carman Standard*, March 7, 1907.

86 *The West*, March 6, 1907;NAC, RG 76, vol. 416, file 602204, pt. 2, contains a clipping from a "leading Ill. Paper" which claimed that there were 50,000 "dead carcasses" against the barbed-wire fences in Calgary and that "thousands" feared perished on their homesteads. Meanwhile, the *Calgary Daily Herald* carried a report in mid-January from a Bellingham, Washington, paper which described minus 57 degree temperatures near Calgary, where "farmers for miles around have gathered in one building and all are huddled about a stove in which pieces of fences, barns, outhouses, and ... living houses are being burned." Consequently, the report predicted a massive exodus of Americans out of "the windswept region of the Alberta country" (January 19, 1907). Meanwhile, Canadian agents operating in the United States complained about "various state organizations ... brought into existence for the purpose of retaining their people; [and] newspapers ... subsidized to publish articles detrimental to Canada." Canada, *Sessional Papers*, 41, no. 10, 1906–7, Sessional Paper no. 25, 1906–7, 79.

87 *New York Times*, February 14, 1907.

88 *Daily Herald*, January 19, 1907.

89   *Western Canadian*, April 11, 1907.

90   Perry to Sask. Attorney-General, March 2, 1907, NAC, RG18, vol. 1594, file 49, pt. 2. Frank Ford informed Perry that there was no legal basis for such charges because the Criminal Code section involved was limited to "seditious offenses": Ford to Perry, March 12, 1907.

91   Ibid., Telegram, Perry to RNWMP Comptroller, Ottawa, February 21, 1907. A copy of this telegram also appears in RG76, vol. 416, file 602204, pt. 1.

92   *The West*, March 6, 1907; *Carman Standard* (Manitoba), March 7, 1907.

93   "Recruits, Recruiting," Perry to Lt. Col. Fred White, February 1 and March 6, 1907, NAC, RG18, vol. 1608, file 157.

94   Canada, *Sessional Papers*, 1907 and 1908.

95   MacGibbon, Battleford Detachment, to Commissioner Perry, Regina, January 24, 1907, NAC, RG18, vol. 2767. MacGibbon had no qualms in stating the root of the problem from his perspective: "I think it a mistake that the Immigration Department did not place an agent down there in the fall, to instruct settlers, and look after them." His report also appears in Immigration Branch Records, RG76, vol. 416, file 602204.

96   Telegram "Wire present condition fuel, provisions and railway service" sent to 22 Dominion Lands Agents in Saskatchewan, February 14, 1907, NAC, RG76, vol. 416, file 602204, pt. 2.

97   G. Greenlay Report to O. C. Regina, February 14, 1907, NAC, RG18, vol. 1594, file 49, pt. 2.

98   Lillian Turner to Mother and all, March 3, 1907, Glenbow Archives, Lillian Turner Fonds, M8244, file "1907."

99   See Paul Voisey, ed., *A Preacher's Frontier: The Castor, Alberta Letters of Rev. Martin W. Holdom, 1909–1912* (Calgary: Historical Society of Alberta, 1996), for a classic example of the pretensions held by Castor, Alberta in its early years.

100 December 17, 1906.

101 January 31, 1907.

102 For example, in early February 1907 the Canadian government received an appeal for enough money for bread and seed from a group of destitute Mennonites who had settled in the Star City, Saskatchewan area the previous summer but because of the condition of the roads arrived too late to put in a crop. Immigration authorities translated the request but there is no evidence that any action was taken: Rev. G. P. Neufeld to "our honourable Government, Ottawa," February 3, 1907, NAC, RG76, vol. 416, file 602204, pt. 2.

103 Just after the November 16, 1906 storm which officially began the winter the Mounties received a complaint from new homesteader Malcolm Cole that if he could not get any fuel he and his family would perish. The Officer Commanding, C Division, Battleford, J. A. MacGibbon, wrote Immigration "I am afraid that before spring we will have numerous cases of this kind, as so many of the new homesteaders taken this year are so far away from fuel of any kind." MacGibbon to Commissioner, Regina, November 19, 1906, NAC, RG18, vol. 2767.

104 Greenlay to O. C. Regina, February 14, 1907, NAC, RG18, vol. 1594, file 49, pt. 2.

IT'S AN ILL WIND THAT BLOWS NOBODY GOOD
REGINA'S 1912 "CYCLONE"

Patrick H. Brennan

Alternating periods of prosperity and depression, the rewards and dis-appointments of opening up a new country, and the anguish of war all characterized the first four decades of Regina's history. But only on one occasion, when a tornado[1] struck the city on June 30, 1912, were the city and its residents required to cope with a major natural disaster. This paper will focus on the manner in which public and private resources were channelled to meet the immediate crisis as well as the longer-term problems which the disaster posed, with an emphasis on both the challenges which confronted the city's dominant business and professional elite and their responses to those challenges.

There are numerous historical accounts of the dramatic events of that sultry late summer afternoon.[2] Suffice to say that a cyclone, a rarity on the northern plains, swept across the city from south to north, and in a matter of minutes left some five hundred destroyed or severely damaged public, commercial, and residential structures spread over a thirty-six block area. Twenty-five hundred out of a population of slightly more than thirty thousand were rendered homeless, and property damage reached approximately $1.2 million. Miraculously, the storm claimed only twenty-eight lives, although a further two hundred persons were injured, many of them quite seriously.

The immediate relief needs were obvious: tending to the injured, searching the wreckage for survivors, providing food and temporary shelter for the homeless, re-establishing essential services like electricity, and protecting private property left vulnerable by the storm. Fear of looting was a universal concern though it largely proved groundless, not the least because hundreds of militia, RNWMP officers, and city police, augmented by 150 "special constables," most of whom were business-men, guarded the devastated area. Newspapers attributed most of the "pilfering" to illiterate foreign labourers who were also prone, the news reports smugly concluded, to discard valuable belongings when helping to clear debris. "Law and order, those characteristics of British administration," the *Province* proudly declared, "were maintained with commendable strictness."[3]

The city's administration acted quickly to confront the emergency. A proclamation issued by Mayor Peter McAra on Dominion Day set up three committees, two to organize relief activities on the north and south sides of the city, and a third, the General Executive Committee for Relief (or Relief Executive as it quickly came to be called), to coordinate overall relief matters. The latter group comprised the mayor, the five aldermen of the city council's Finance Committee, the city commissioner, and three private citizens: W. P. Wells, J. A. Allen, and John A. Reid.[4] Among the first tasks undertaken by these committees was a complete canvass of the city to determine the precise nature and dimensions of public and private needs so that they could direct assistance where the requirement was greatest.[5]

Volunteerism played a dominant role in the initial relief effort. Most of the injured were cared for in small temporary hospitals staffed by volunteer medical personnel. While the city provided temporary shelter and food in tent cities and undamaged schools, most of the homeless were taken care of by friends and relatives. Realtor D. S. McCannel, a member of the south side committee, freely acknowledged four days after the disaster that "not over one-twentieth of the temporary relief work has been done by the city," and that public expenditures on temporary relief, mostly food, had come to less than $400.[6] Indeed, so restrained was the demand for municipal relief that the mayor finally appealed publicly for those in need to come forward with the promise that "everything is absolutely private and confidential.... The clothing, food, or anything else you need is yours by right."[7]

With the injured and dead accounted for, clearing rubble and repairing damaged residences and business premises became the priority. For a variety of reasons, most of this work was done by private arrangement, although the civic authorities did organize several large gangs of labourers and carpenters to speed the process along. By pure chance, the storm had completely devastated the city's most prestigious residential district, home to many of Regina's business and professional elite. Newspaper reporting of their trials greatly outnumbered accounts of conditions in the working class districts on the city's north side, where the destruction was equally severe. It is also clear that there were noticeable differences in the rate at which repair work was undertaken and debris cleared in the two areas. Money rather than need determined the allocation of the materials and labour required for reconstruction, as the rapid pace of repair of the businesses – especially warehouses – and the homes of the well-to-do attested.

Nevertheless, one of the dominant themes promoted in contemporary newspaper accounts maintained that all citizens were enduring the same trials, and that by pulling together they would also share a common victory over their shared adversity. While such wishful thinking could not belie the realities of the city's class, religious, and ethnic divisions, it was not for the lack of printer's ink expended to prove otherwise, the following editorial being typical of the effort:

> The problems which the city will be compelled to solve ... can be solved only through the united endeavours of a united people who will allow no petty things to hamper them in the task of building up a Greater Regina. The task is worthy of men who are men. It will not be a task for weaklings or for men of small minds who cannot give to questions which arise their proper places in the scale of relative importance.... Such differences of class as may have existed have been cast aside as unworthy.... Trivial things are thrust away. The people go forward with the watchword 'Regina First'.[8]

Conditions among the urban labouring classes in western Canada during these years were far from pretty, and Regina was certainly no exception. The "Germantown" district east of the downtown area was the city's "foreign-born" ghetto. Living conditions there and on the north side (that is, north of the CPR main line) varied from poor to scandalous. Yet prosperous Anglo-Protestant merchants ensconced in the south and west ends felt no compunction in squeezing rents of up to $50 a month from central and eastern European immigrant families for such hovels, this in a city where the average worker's monthly earnings totalled a meagre $71 – when steady work was available.[9] With labour temporarily given the upper hand, the city fathers and their business allies were undoubtedly anxious that "difficulties" might arise. Since even the most optimistic among Regina's better-off classes must have realized that rhetoric alone was not likely to guarantee labour co-operation, council opted for something more tangible.

As early as July 2 there had been vague pronouncements to the effect that some sort of inexpensive municipally arranged residential construction on city-owned land might be in the offing. But as McAra was quick to point out, such a scheme depended "almost entirely on the loyal support of the labour men in the city."[10] Rumours talked of as many as five hundred such workmen's dwellings. However, the threat of labour disturbances was not the sole inspiration of the plan, for the civic administration were also encountering difficulties in attracting sufficient men for their work crews and there were widespread fears among the city's real estate interests that unsightly shack towns might spring up from the debris if the city did not accelerate the construction of inexpensive housing elsewhere. Finally, there was also the Board of Trade's concern that an already chronic housing shortage, now made worse, would drive workers away and frustrate Regina's hopes for "Western dominance."[11]

Council decided to press ahead with two classes of houses on July 4, the same day the city's recently hired carpenters "struck," or more correctly, quit *en masse* to take better paying private jobs. A Trades and Labour Council official pointed out the obvious: "the union men would not work ... at 45 cents an hour when they could get 50 cents."[12] In fact, in excess of sixty cents an hour was easily had during these hectic days. Contracts for five "cyclone houses" and another five "cyclone cottages" were awarded to two local builders. The councillors also decided to have eight shacks quickly constructed at city expense as temporary residences. Monthly rents for the houses were set at $35, though the mayor undoubtedly reflected his colleagues' sentiments in hoping the dwellings would be sold instead. "We must put this on a sound business basis," he reminded them, "for it is outside the regular work of relief."[13] It was agreed, however, that the subcommittee set up to supervise the program should give special consideration to widows with no means of support who might wish to acquire one of the houses and then take in roomers.[14] Opposition from Alderman Cornelius Rink, a self-appointed spokesman for the city's foreign-born population, that the proposed rents were too high for the working class families the initiative was ostensibly designed to aid was dismissed by L. T. McDonald, the secretary-treasurer of the Board of Trade, on the grounds that "it would be too bad to put poorer houses on such excellent property."[15] A confidential report jointly compiled by two of the volunteer relief subcommittees and submitted to council July 13 stated in part:

> The committees cannot press home too much the need for many city houses to be sold on easy terms or to be rented. The surface looks smooth but there is ugly trouble beneath. Scores of families are being temporarily housed by others already too crowded, or in tents or useless shacks and roofless buildings. These people are waiting for the city to make good. They cannot wait long. These committees in touch with people worst effected [sic] believe one hundred city houses ... would do more real good than all the other things combined which the city can devise for relief. If the city has the lots and can get the funds for building, by way of a loan, this is the greatest possible means of relieving the people and keeping them here as citizens of Regina.[16]

Yet work on the various municipal dwellings proceeded at a glacial pace during the remainder of July, in sharp contrast to the rapid progress made in constructing the city's own $30,000 warehouse promised to a clamouring business community as temporary accommodation for wholesalers.

Meanwhile, more labour trouble was brewing, and on July 22 the painters struck. Again, the dispute revolved around the structure of maximum wage rates established by the Builders' Exchange which served to drive down the pay skilled men could earn, and which was about 10 per cent lower than comparable schedules in Saskatoon and Moose Jaw. The Regina unions wanted parity and an end to the structure based on maximum rather than minimum rates. The *Leader* confined itself to praising those non-union painters and other tradesmen who had assisted in the rebuilding of the city, taking "no advantage of the plentitude of work and shortage of men whereon to enforce a claim."[17] The strike lasted ten days, ending in a partial union victory, but this did not bring labour peace. By late September the carpenters were once again threatening to strike and the bricklayers were already out. The latter confrontation ended only after three weeks of valuable construction time were lost and many building sites had been closed down for the winter.

Above: Tornado damage to a working class residential area of Regina north of the CPR tracks. Courtesy: City of Regina Archives, Regina Public Library Collection RPL-B-456.

Below: An upper storey view looking southeast from the downtown. Several schools can be seen in the distance, along with the east wing of the Legislative Buildings at the far right. Courtesy: City of Regina Archives, Regina Public Library Collection RPL-A-905.

In late August, city council decided to contract for an additional fifteen houses, and promised still more if there was a demonstrated need. However, this was the last contract let and even three of these houses were never constructed.[18] A firm decision was also made at this time in favour of sale over renting, and with the exception of the inevitably mentioned widows, all applications had to meet "regular terms."[19]

It was about this time as well that evidence of improprieties in the contracting of the various municipal dwellings came to light. Again the irrepressible Alderman Rink,[20] whose First Ward included the "Germantown" district, sparked the controversy by alleging that the city had never properly tendered the contract for the shacks and that the completion price was too high. He further revealed that the excess profits had found their way into the pockets of both the contractor and the dealer who had sold him the lumber, Aldermen Halloran and Martin, respectively.[21] Several days earlier the city commissioner had offered the weak defence that it had been impossible at the time to get anyone else to do the work unless tenders were called, and tendering would have taken time. Alderman Halloran, he said, happened to have a few men at his disposal, and the special housing subcommittee had decided to give him the work, but when pressed, Thornton was unable to produce any records of Halloran's costs. Rink then turned to the contract for the houses, asking if anyone knew who was really behind this company and why the city had also awarded that contract without tender? Alderman Martin argued feebly that the emergency nature of the situation had prevented the following of "ceremony," whereupon, after vowing to tighten up procedures in any future cases, the aldermen turned to other matters.

By mid-November, only three of the cottages and five of the houses had been placed in the hands of cyclone victims or "widows without any means of subsistence," and no further applications were on file. This left two cottages and twelve houses unclaimed, and on Thornton's recommendation the city advertised these for sale on the regular market in the hope of closing out their chequered scheme on a profitable note.[22]

Just as civic leaders turned primarily to volunteer help in organizing and carrying out cyclone relief, so too they adopted a form of volunteer financing to pay for it – the Regina Cyclone Relief Fund, established by a proclamation of Mayor McAra on July 2.[23] By the end of the summer, contributions from governments, businesses, and individuals across the

Lorne Street immediately south of the downtown, where many of the
city's more substantial middle class homes were located, and which took
the brunt of the storm. Courtesy: City of Regina Archives, Regina Public
Library Collection RPL-B-455.

country would swell the fund to $217,949. With the mayor making a personal donation of $1,000, other leading men of commerce and the professions followed suit until the list of contributors read like a "Who's Who" of Regina society.[24] Of those who contributed $100 or more, eighteen listed their occupations as real estate, finance, or insurance, six more as lawyers and eleven as businessmen. National and regional enterprises were also notably generous, as were the federal, Saskatchewan, and other provincial governments and a long list of cities and towns.[25]

Administered by the Relief Executive, the Cyclone Relief Fund had to provide the bulk of the cash needed to finance non-reconstruction relief expenditures. The community can be thankful that the public responded so generously, since the city fathers showed no inclination to draw on general tax revenues for such purposes, no matter how pressing, and the Scott and Borden governments squabbled over who would or should provide any additional relief financing beyond the city's means. A year-end report indicates that great caution was exercised in disbursing this money. Just over $82,000 remained unexpended, but the committee emphasized that remaining claims, particularly those of the severely injured, would absorb every cent remaining.[26]

The Relief Executive took every opportunity to impress on the public that the fund would be impartially and efficiently disbursed, even going so far as to have themselves incorporated as a limited liability company in order to guarantee by "the closest system of auditing of all accounts and expenditures ... that everything is absolutely above board."[27] Some idea of the manner in which the funds were distributed can be seen in the operations of the Relief Executive's subcommittee for house furnishings. Claimants first presented their financial requirements to the subcommittee. If the request was approved – and it was judged on need rather than loss – the claimant received a purchase order which all Regina merchants accepted, ordering what was needed, up to the authorized amount. The list of the purchases then had to be submitted to the subcommittee for final approval. Once this process had been completed, the claimant would return to the merchant and pick up the goods, returning the bills to the Relief Executive for payment from the Relief Fund.[28] The furnishings committee reported that instances of misrepresentation had been rare, and that in "the vast majority of cases there was a scrupulous care [on the part of the applicants] to keep well within the facts." Indeed, they emphasized that "in many cases it was almost impossible to get relief accepted even where it was absolutely necessary." But perhaps equally telling was their comment that "while a helping hand [is] a great boost, these cases are also opportunities for pluck and spirit in individual citizens."[29]

While the relief fund was sufficient to fulfill its limited role, where, in the absence of insurance, would individual citizens find the money to finance the cost of reconstructing their damaged property – cyclone victims' single most pressing need by the city council's own admission? Newspaper accounts reassured Reginans that local "businessmen and financiers [were] bending their will and brain toward the task of raising the money and outlining the best plan for securing and rendering financial aid to men who have been hit so hard," their efforts no doubt spurred on by the fact that many of city's leading businessmen were themselves among the hardest hit.[30] Any suggestion to utilize a general property tax levy, with its "great advantages of being civically universal, equitable, and effective," was rejected out of hand.[31] The prospect of an outright gift from the federal or provincial government was the hope, but also extremely unlikely.[32] Loans from one or both of the senior governments were a more realistic prospect.

In appreciating what unfolded, one must remember that Saskatchewan was in the throes of a provincial election campaign, with the polling date set for July 11. Thus, there was every incentive for the federal Conservative government and incumbent provincial Liberals to outbid one another on the cyclone relief issue in a blatant attempt to secure Regina's vote. The Conservatives moved first, with Robert Rogers, Borden's Minister of the Interior (and to all intents, of Western elections), wiring McAra that Ottawa would "be prepared in any reasonable way at all to render such cash assistance as the ... circumstances would justify" and promising to dispatch one of his trusted agents from Winnipeg, immigration commissioner Bruce Walker, to make an on-the-spot report.[33] Walker arrived on the 8th, the same day as Rogers' second telegram, which confirmed that if Walker's reports bore out the initial damage reports, he would not hesitate to recommend a substantial loan or loan guarantee for reconstruction purposes.[34] Not to be outdone, that very day saw the premier reveal his government's plan to loan Regina $500,000 in order to speed the city council's own reconstruction loan program.[35] While the staunchly Liberal *Leader* hailed

Scott's pledge as the acme of statesmanship, the exasperated *Province*, the city's Tory voice, could only fume that it was another Liberal trick, masterminded by "the Honourable James Allcrook" (provincial treasurer, James A. Calder) and unfortunate Reginans' contribution to a "reptile fund to buy the rural Grit members."[36]

At that evening's council meeting both proposals were keenly discussed. Walker dismissed the provincial offer, contending that the damage called for at least $1 million in assistance and hinting strongly that the Borden cabinet would approve whatever help he recommended. "Time is the essence of this Dominion relief ... and I will see that we get after it hot foot," Walker assured the eager mayor and councillors. "There must be no delaying until the need for relief has gone by."[37] Judging from his superiors' actions, however, it would appear that the need had "gone by" on July 11, the day Scott's Liberals swept back into office. The silence from Ottawa was broken some days later when Walker informed the mayor by letter that "notwithstanding the Minister's [Rogers'] warm personal interest in this matter ... there are obstacles which are practically insurmountable."[38] Perhaps hoping that they might still salvage something, council decided to dispatch a delegation to Ottawa consisting of the mayor and two leading citizens, A. E. Whitmore and Dr. W. D. Cowan. These gentlemen met several members of the Borden cabinet in early August, with inconclusive results apart from the disheartening news that parliamentary approval might delay federal help for several more months.[39] The delays in reconstruction attributable to uncertainties over the ultimate financing were now becoming a serious matter.[40] At a public meeting called by the mayor, he outlined the status of the various loan proposals in full detail. There was "unanimous" opinion that the city accept the province's offer on the best terms that could be arranged, it being understood that the city fathers should still expend every effort to obtain the "promised" million-dollar loan from Ottawa.[41]

In the meantime, however, the provincial treasurer, whether at the Relief Executive's behest or not is uncertain, had decided to pursue the Ottawa authorities on Regina's behalf. Rogers rebuked Calder's obvious political motives in a stinging telegram. He then went on to outline his version of the events of early July, in essence that constitutionally financial relief was a provincial matter, that he had not known of Scott's pledge when he made his own on July 8, and that if he had, he would not have felt obligated to commit Ottawa to any further assistance.[42] When Calder persisted, Rogers' telegraphed reply was predictably blunt: "I presume Regina does not require duplicate loans."[43] On August 22, the Liberals made the entire correspondence public and it soon found its way into the pages of a gleeful *Leader*.[44] Hard pressed to refute this barrage of allegations, a *Province* editorial entitled "Shameful Misrepresentation" nevertheless made a loyal attempt to cast Ottawa's role in the most favourable light. The "Liberal organ" responded predictably with a salvo of its own, entitled "How Bob Rogers Deceived Regina."[45]

Almost lost in this political din was official word from Finance Minister Thomas White that no Dominion loan for the reconstruction of cyclone damage would be forthcoming.[46] White frankly admitted to the mayor that "not only is there no precedent for such a loan but that similar requests have been declined in the past" and furthermore, that it would be "impracticable for the government to make loans in all cases of catastrophe involving property loss and it was impossible to discriminate between communities." In retrospect it is clear that politics played a major role – indeed, the central role – in this entire loan saga. Whether or not the federal minister knew of the premier's pledge when Walker, a trusted confidant acting on his behalf, made the offer of a million-dollar loan on the evening of July 8 seems academic, since Rogers' decision to revoke the offer had little to do with such chronological hairsplitting. The provincial election results rendered Dominion aid superfluous, at least in a political sense, yet more importantly Rogers' plan would have been an unlikely victor in a cabinet rigorously opposed to the setting of any precedent for more than token Dominion financial assistance in a local disaster.

With the city now committed to accepting provincial aid, its plan for providing reconstruction loans, held in abeyance for the past seven weeks, could at last proceed. For many citizens, the wait had been too long – their patience exhausted and possessing the wherewithal to obtain private financing, they had already made their own arrangements. Moreover, if they had needed any additional encouragement to do so the city had provided it a few weeks earlier by announcing that it would begin to enforce the demolition of all wrecked or partially damaged buildings not under repair, if need be by employing city crews at the owners' expense.[47] In keeping with earlier practice, overseeing the handling of loan applications and ensuring they were dealt with on a "strictly business basis" fell to another committee specially struck for the purpose. Headed by Robert Henderson (still another realtor), it also included the mayor, Aldermen Peart and Martin, and business-man John Reid. The Relief Executive had already decided that the loans would be repaid in ten annual instalments at 6 per cent interest and guaranteed by a second mortgage. Those interested in the loans were given until August 24 to make their applications.[48] Practically all of the initial applicants turned out to be those very persons whom the municipal-provincial agreement had been intended to aid, namely those of more limited means who had lost heavily.[49] By the end of September the committee had approved over eighty loans, the average amount being $2,500, and seemed almost relieved that the summer's delays had driven so many Reginans to make other arrangements.[50] Nevertheless, by the following spring it was apparent that the $500,000 would not be sufficient to cover all the loan applications on hand. This proved the least of the city's difficulties, however, because recession conditions in 1913 rendered the sale of municipal debentures a virtual impossibility and Regina quickly fell behind in its own repayments to the provincial treasury. During the war years the city was fortunate to meet even the interest charges, and by 1917 the provincial government had retaliated by threatening to foreclose on its $2 million mortgage. Negotiations followed, and in December of that year the two parties reached an agreement under which the city agreed to repay the outstanding principal and interest over the next five years.[51] Despite this, arguments between the two governments continued to flare up when Regina's payments periodically lapsed or the city agitated for the right to sell blocks of the mortgaged property. Improving economic conditions in 1922 finally enabled the city to pay off its obligations by the end of that year. For its part, the provincial government had hardly been a paragon of fiscal virtue. Successive provincial treasurers had declined to repay the principal on their original bank loan, preferring to refinance it periodically and divert the city's payments to other budgetary purposes. As a result, it was not until December 31, 1958, that the Government of Saskatchewan actually retired its cyclone loan debt. The total interest paid by the province over the obligation's forty-six-year life exceeded $1 million, clearly making the Bank of Commerce the chief beneficiary of Regina's cyclone encounter.[52]

The difficulties encountered by many of the loan recipients were even more serious than the predicament in which the city fathers found themselves. The same problems of recession and war proved insurmountable for these individuals, and several dozen, including a not insignificant number who had rebuilt damaged properties as speculative ventures,[53] banded together in the Regina Cyclone Association to lobby for a more equitable sharing of the financial losses. Their situation reached its nadir in 1919 when a provincial demand for repayment had led to talk in council of insisting on the rigid enforcement of the city's own mortgage rights. Of course, for the loan recipients in arrears this meant the prospect of losing their homes a second time. Such fears were hardly groundless, since the city did foreclose on several of the "cyclone houses" and "cottages."[54]

So far this paper has shown how both existing and improvised municipal institutions attempted, with varying degrees of success, to meet the relief needs of the people of Regina in the weeks following the devastating cyclone of June 30, 1912, and also how the ensuing provision of relief became entangled in political partisanship. However, it remains to examine the impact of this natural disaster on the local business community and its collective view of Regina's future. In 1912, the business and professional elite of the "Queen City" were thoroughly swept up in "boosterism," that phenomenon of aggressive, chest-thumping civic pride in all matters commercial which they shared with their contemporaries in other prairie centres. With Regina's – and hence their own – future prospects at stake as her rivals strove to surpass her, it is hardly surprising that the calamitous events of June 30 should send shock waves through the city's business community.

In the days immediately following the cyclone, editorials in all three city newspapers attempted to assuage any fears that Regina had sustained a mortal economic blow. "The Greater Regina is as certain as the rising sun," heralded the *Leader*,[55] while the *Standard*, owned by J. K. McInnis, one of the city's more substantial realtors, echoed similarly optimistic sentiments:

> It is the indomitable spirit of the West that leads Regina on to bigger and better things, and by its aid Regina will yet resume her place in the forefront of Western cities.... The houses will be larger and the warehouses more substantial.

No effort will be spared to retain for this city its commercial supremacy. Before the disaster we were all citizens of no mean city; today we are citizens of a devastated city; but tomorrow we shall be citizens of a bigger, better, and greater city.[56]

But it remained to the *Leader* to strike the most exuberant note, reminding its readership in "No Doubters Here" that:

Cities which the world calls great today have passed through their hours of trial. London has known its disasters. Chicago felt the sting of great adversity. San Francisco was virtually blotted out. What are they today? ... Out of their adversity came their greatness. So will it be with Regina.[57]

As the days passed, it became apparent that the property damage, while undeniably severe in some districts, had been exaggerated, thus giving even greater cause for optimism. "Will Regina suffer a tremendous setback as a result of the recent tornado? No! Most emphatically, No!" enthused the *Leader*, and as confirmation, invoked the results of a survey of local bank and trust company managers which showed that "without a single exception the heads of these financial institutions ... express their unbounded faith in the future of the city."[58] The encouraging announcement that a leading – but unnamed – Eastern firm of wholesale boot and shoe men would soon erect a large five-storey block in the city was given much play.[59] Still, it was real estate that had been and remained the index of Regina's prosperity, and in early August the *Leader* printed a lot-by-lot account of the previous month's sales, pronounced "the normal and ... steady increase in the price of property," and predicted that "interesting deals will be closed shortly whereby some big capitalists of the East will become owners of Regina suburbs."[60]

However, in spite of this growing confidence, the city fathers had to maintain a vigilant watch against potentially damaging rumours spread by outsiders. A booklet of disaster photographs circulating in Toronto prompted one of the city's "friends" there to suggest McAra "take some steps toward suppressing this as it is going to have a damaging effect if these books are distributed broadcast over the country."[61] Though he could take no action in this instance, the mayor did not refrain from using his influence when it might be effective, as in writing the editors of *The British News in Canada* to express his

> ... appreciation of the efforts being made by your people to counteract any ill influence that might come as a result of the cyclone.... The Board of Trade will appreciate the unsolicited effort on your part to give Regina at this time the assistance that it would seem she needs.[62]

However, it was not simply outsiders who saw in Regina's calamity a financial opportunity dangling before their eyes. "The Man Who Buys Regina Property Now Will Make Money – This is the day of opportunities," trumpeted one unfortunately timed advertisement the day after the cyclone struck.[63] Yet it proved prophetic enough – for sellers. Real estate interests were among the first, but certainly not the last, to cash in on their city's new-found fame:

> Thousands are visiting the city to see the ruins, and scores of these are buying property as an investment.... Real estate sales are increasing, land values are climbing, and outlying property is coming into prominence faster than anticipated. Now is the time to buy in Regina.[64]

Officially, opportunities for profit did not detract from the fact that the cyclone had brought the community together, and in the process highlighted what was best in the city's spirit. The *Standard* enjoined all citizens to rise above petty self-interest:

> Any attempt to exercise extortion or to take UNDUE advantage, for purposes of personal gain, must be frowned down, checkmated and exposed. Let prices remain as they were. Whether we be land lords, vendors, caterers, carpenters or common labourers, let us not lose sight of the Golden Rule. Thus shall we speedily recover, and be in the end the better for a calamity which has already, in a large measure, checkmated selfishness and strife, giving free flow to the soothing sap of human kindness.... The vigorous rivalry and grasping

Above: The toppled Winnipeg Elevator Company grain elevator. The CPR quickly put the damaged rail yards back into working order. Courtesy: City of Regina Archives, Regina Public Library Collection RPL-B-453.

Below: Looking south along Lorne Street, the direct path of the tornado. Recently constructed brick structures like First Baptist Church, Knox Presbyterian Church, and the YMCA (L-R) stood up remarkably well. Courtesy: City of Regina Archives, Regina Public Library Collection RPL-B-451.

greed of a week ago are today quenched in a calamity that involves the whole community.[65]

Rhetoric aside, there seems little question that the cost of reconstruction was inflated to some degree by the immediate and overwhelming premium placed on both materials and skilled labour, but by how much is impossible to determine. The Regina Cyclone Association, hardly a disinterested body, always maintained that "the price of labour and materials increased tremendously."[66] However, shortly after the storm the *Leader* reported, perhaps in response to rising public suspicions, that the lumber companies were "exhibiting the proper spirit and have kept the prices for all building commodities at the same price as before the catastrophe," after which there was no further comment on the question in any of the city's newspapers.[67] Nor were there complaints in the press that food or clothing prices had risen unduly. Suffice to say that even without raising prices, these would have been very prosperous days for anyone connected with the building industry, July witnessing some $363,000 worth of reconstruction on public buildings and warehouses alone.[68] The year set a long-standing record for the value of construction in Regina, with a total of just over $8 million in building permits issued, a 58 per cent increase over the previous year. It is obvious that the repair or replacement of cyclone-damaged structures was a chief contributor to the capital's vigorous building activity during 1912. However, both Saskatoon and Moose Jaw had shown healthy increases as well, without the benefit of a reconstruction boom.[69] Certainly those building supply merchants who could meet the avalanche of orders were quick to purchase advertisements like the following:

> We wish to express our sympathy to our more unfortunate fellow Wholesalers.... Just received: one carload of plate glass, two carloads sheet glass, one carload ready roofing, one carload tar paper.[70]

Unquestionably, one of the groups which did profit handsomely from Regina's catastrophe was the insurers. Cyclones had been a sufficiently rare occurrence in the region prior to June 30 that only one policy had been in force in the whole city. However, the first weeks of July offered rather improved prospects for sales, with large advertisements trumpeting the offerings of various companies. Nor was Regina alone in this respect, for good ideas had always spread quickly in the Canadian West. In the Manitoba capital, for example, the Ryan Agency was solemnly warning residents within days that "Winnipeg May Be Next!"[71] According to the manager of one of Regina's leading agencies, over $1.5 million in cyclone insurance policies had been written in the first two weeks following the storm, all of them unsolicited.[72]

On July 9, shortly after the establishment of the Cyclone Relief Fund, the executive of the Regina Board of Trade (W. P. Wells, H. G. Smith, C. O. Hodgkins, and L. T. McDonald), swept up in a moment of public-spiritedness, voted to return the unexpended $5,000 portion of their city advertising grant on the condition it be subscribed to the Fund, generosity which was duly credited in the newspapers. However, at a council meeting some weeks later, Alderman Peart moved that the money be returned to the Board on the grounds that there was now plenty available in the Relief Fund. Alderman Rink disagreed, pointing out with some sarcasm – and a good deal of accuracy – that the storm had provided more free advertising for the city than the Board of Trade could accomplish in ten years, and that the moneys should remain where they were. Alderman Peart then rather revealingly interjected that *"as the Board of Trade and the city were practically the same thing"* [emphasis added] – after all each was trying to do everything it could to further the interests of the city – opposition to returning the money was just political quibbling. Yet perhaps sensing a embarrassing issue, the majority favoured following Rink's advice.[73]

It would be appropriate to conclude this account with the most grotesquely commercial and certainly the most bizarre scheme to emerge in the cyclone's aftermath. Disasters invariably attract the curious, and contemporary newspaper accounts were filled with reports of trainloads of "holiday-makers" journeying to see "the spectacle of ruin" and "throngs of curious sightseers coming from Moose Jaw and nearby towns to view the wreckage."[74] Exhibition Manager H. C. Lawson, himself the owner of a $13,000 "heap of ruins," was convinced that still more wanted to come and produced sheaves of letters to support his contention. "People of Regina who have thought upon the subject have no doubt found considerable difficulty in determining the precise benefit that would be reaped by the city as a result of the destruction to property by the cyclone," pondered a writer for the *Province*, but thanks to the fertile mind of the exhibition manager, he now had the answer:

> Many people will be attracted to Regina during the [upcoming] exhibition merely because of the opportunity that will be afforded to see the damage wrought.... Mr. Lawson is very decidedly of the opinion that this unlooked for benefit of the cyclone ... should be taken full advantage of and that every opportunity should be given to visitors to see the ruins are not cleared away at the end of the month by the enterprising owners of property in the devastated area.[75]

This scheme was stillborn, for as we have seen the city fathers were determined to expedite the demolition of all damaged buildings, by court order if need be.

What conclusions can be drawn about the impact of the cyclone on Regina and its population? While substantial financial loss was incurred, it was narrowly defined and even then, with a few exceptions, not long-lasting. The demands for cyclone relief required an immediate response, but decreased continuously as the days passed and were restricted to an easily identified minority of the population. In the Regina of 1912 there existed no mechanism that could respond to the relief needs created by a major disaster, and the municipal authorities admitted as much by calling into being an *ad hoc* organization consisting of the Relief Executive and its many subcommittees which soon completely overshadowed the established organs of city administration. These arrangements involved the transfer of immense responsibility and the associated decision-making power to non-elected individuals. It was done to an extent not readily apparent from a mere examination of formal committee representation, and certainly with no guarantees that the broader public interest would be embraced. This phenomenon was typical of that found in the rest of Canada and the United States when catastrophes occurred during this period.[76] Certainly no one in a position of authority argued that the events of 1912 revealed any need to adopt permanent administrative arrangements to respond to disaster.

In the aftermath of the cyclone the close interrelationship between the city's business and professional elite and its municipal government were made readily apparent. Not surprisingly, both groups found inti-

A postcard image of tornado victims and their damaged home. These advertised the citizens' "grit" and elicited national sympathy. Courtesy: City of Regina Archives, Regina Public Library Collection RPL-A-244.

mate collaboration a natural course in this as in any other matters. But there were two additional factors which played a part in the Regina elite's unified public face during the ensuing weeks. The first was the close relationship between personal and community prospects and all that this implied if the city's commercial future was imperilled. The second was their need to maintain an image of decisive leadership and thus preserve their dominant political position within the community.

In terms of the speed, efficiency, and fairness of its disbursement, the actual provision of relief to those needing it during the cyclone's aftermath was no better than adequate, and this chiefly because people expected so little. Moreover, there is no question that the disparate social and economic conditions prevailing at the time were factors in the quality of the services provided. Indeed, the degree to which relief was provided at all in 1912 was in large measure dependent on the success of the publicly subscribed relief fund, for the absence of significant assistance would not have resulted in more than the personal inconvenience of the relatively small number of seriously affected victims. Furthermore, the municipal response to the cyclone disaster demonstrated that considerable emphasis was placed on a "business-like" relief policy, belying the supposed separation of matters of disaster relief from poor relief, while revealing a municipal proclivity to shirk its social responsibilities. Certainly, even in times of crisis additional funds always seemed to be available if city council perceived a sufficiently pressing and deserving requirement. For instance, council allocated "without the least hesitation" $16,000 toward its share of the expected costs of the preparations for the one-day visit to Regina of His Royal Highness, the Duke of Connaught, two and a half months after the cyclone had cut its swath of death and destruction.[77]

Excepting those most directly affected (and the great majority of Reginans, it must be remembered, did not live in the path of the storm), the catastrophe did not seem appreciably to alter the rhythm of life in Regina. But should this perplex us? The Saskatchewan capital was a community in which the dominant element saw "Acts of God" merely as misplaced cobbles on an otherwise well-paved road to a "Bigger and Better Regina," yet also a community in which a great many others found daily existence itself a sufficient struggle. Under these circumstances, it is really not so surprising that the majority of the citizenry should view catastrophe only as a diversion, and a temporary one at that, from the established order of things, to be endured and then, if they were fortunate enough not to be permanently scarred by loss, quickly retired from their collective consciousness.

NOTES

1 Although the correct meteorological term for the class of storm striking Regina is "tornado," "cyclone" was invariably used at the time and I have followed that practice for the sake of consistency.

2 Frank W. Anderson, *Regina's Terrible Tornado* (Calgary: Frontier Publishing, 1968); Montagu Clements, "Storm Clouds Over Regina," *Saskatchewan History* 6, no. 1 (Winter 1953): 17–23; and Earl G. Drake, *Regina: The Queen City* (Toronto: McClelland & Stewart, 1955), 144–49.

3 July 2, 1912, 1.

4 The northside committee consisted of the Reverend Guy, Mr. Schlester (occupation unknown), and Alderman Halloran (a realtor), while the southside committee membership included L. A. Rounding and D. S. McCannel (both realtors) and lawyer A. G. MacKinnon. Mayor McAra was a leading figure in city real estate and investment circles, W. P. Wells was the president of the Board of Trade, J. A. Allen was a lawyer, and J. A. Reid was deputy assistant provincial treasurer as well as the government printer. The five members of the Finance Committee were the chairman, businessmen Robert Martin; E. B. Andros (occupation unknown); Cornelius Rink (a realtor); businessman M. B. Peart; and E. D. McCallum, who was involved in finance, insurance, and real estate. Clements, "Storm Clouds Over Regina," 23; Regina City Council Minutes (hereafter cited as Council Minutes), City of Regina Archives, July 29, 1912, 175; and *Henderson's Regina Directory, 1912* (hereafter cited as *Henderson's Directory*).

5 In order to provide the same facts to a news-hungry populace, one local daily conducted its own survey, enjoining its reporters to "make a personal canvass of every heap of ruins and secure from the homeless people estimates of their losses." The reception accorded these gentlemen as they journeyed from heap to heap is unrecorded: *Regina Daily Standard* (hereafter cited as *Standard*), July 2, 1912, 1.

6 Ibid., July 4, 1912, 5.

7 *Province*, July 6, 1912, 3. See also ibid., July 4, 1912, 1.

8 Ibid., July 2, 1912, 4.

9 Frank Rasky, "The Tornado That Blew Down Regina," *Liberty* (July 1959): 52–53. The conditions were far from exaggerated. With considerable fanfare the *Leader* published a series of exposés during that summer on the abysmal health and housing conditions that prevailed in Regina's poorer districts, accusing the responsible civic officials of "criminal neglect." See *Leader*, July 3, 1912, July 7 and 31, 1912, 9.

10 Ibid., July 3, 1912, 1–2; *Manitoba Free Press*, July 3, 1912, 1.

11 *Leader*, September 6, 1912, 2; *Manitoba Free Press*, July 8, 1912, 5.

12 *Standard*, July 4, 1912, 1. The city had hired the carpenters the day after the cyclone hit at the "current rate," which the workmen took to mean the hourly rate of fifty cents paid by contractors not affiliated with the Regina Builders'

Exchange. The city, on its part, refused to pay more than the latter organization's maximum rate of forty-five cents per hour: *Standard*, July 4, 1912, 1.

13   *Leader*, July 9, 1912, 5.

14   Council Minutes, September 3, 1912, 194–95. The subcommittee was composed of W. H. Duncan and C. Willoughby (co-partners in a large office block, with the latter also president of an investment firm) and W. T. Mollard, president of a trust company: *Henderson's Directory*.

15   *Leader*, July 9, 1912, 5. At one point during an earlier discussion Alderman Peart had offered a solution to the problem of high rents – a small family of modest means could live in one of the four bedrooms, subletting the remainder, and thus be able to live rent-free: *Province*, July 4, 1912, 3.

16   Report of the House Furnishing Committee, July 13, 1912, Finance Committee of the City of Regina (hereafter cited as Regina Finance Committee), City of Regina Archives, file 68, 1912.

17   *Leader*, July 23, 1912, 2; and *Province*, July 23, 1912, 9.

18   Memorandum from City Commissioner Thornton to the Relief Executive, August 30, 1912, Regina Finance Committee, file 72, 1912.

19   The "regular terms" were as follows: for the houses – a $300 cash downpayment with monthly payments of $35 for the first two years, $40 for the next two, and $45 for the last year, at which time the unpaid balance on the $4,217 purchase price (which included $1,200 for the city lot) was to be paid off by cash or loan. For the "cottages" – the downpayment was the same and the monthly rents $8 less. The purchase price of the cottages was $3,183, including $1,100 for the lot. The "shacks" were to rent for $10 a month: *Province*, August 31, 1912, 9.

20   Rink, a small-scale realtor and "businessman," was a Dutch immigrant who claimed to have fought on the side of the Boers during the South African War. In various ideological incarnations, he would be active in Regina municipal politics as an alderman or mayor well into the 1930s.

21   *Province*, September 4, 1912, 1 and 7; August 31, 1912, 9.

22   Council Minutes, November 18, 1912, 270.

23   *Standard*, July 2, 1912, 5.

24   Ibid., 10.

25   The hard work of clearing debris appeared to have generated some powerful thirsts, with several contributions to the Relief Fund recognizing the fact, among them $2,344 from the Licensed Hotel Keepers and $500 from Hiram Walker and Sons: *Standard*, July 2, 1912, 10, and *Henderson's Directory*.

26   *Leader*, November 26, 1912, 5. Of the $135,845 appropriated from the fund up to that date the expenditures had been: furniture losses, $70,805; clothing losses, $14,372; temporary house repairs, $13,746; surgical assistance and nursing, $13,369; food, clothing, and other supplies to relieve immediate distress, $9,924; clearing the devastated area, $5,041; salvage and property protection by the militia and police, $3,196; administration, $3,067; and undertakers' and burial charges, $2,325: *Standard*, July 2, 1912, 10; and Report of the Relief Committee, November 22, 1912, Regina Finance Committee, file 72, 1912.

27   *Leader*, July 8, 1912, 2.

28 Ibid., July 20, 1912, 1.

29 Report of the House Furnishing and Canvass Relief Committees, July 13, 1912, Regina Finance Committee, file 68, 1912.

30 *Standard*, July 3, 1912, 1.

31 Ibid., July 2, 1912, 4.

32 During the first weeks following the cyclone the city clerk devoted a good deal of his time to correspondence with officials in American and Canadian cities which had suffered some comparable disaster. Of interest was the degree of financial assistance these centres had received from the higher levels of government. The results were disappointing, as they revealed little precedent for more than a token provincial or state response and none at all for a federal one. Typically, these cities had had to rely on their own financial resources, insurance settlements, and generously subscribed public relief funds: Copies of various telegrams and letters, c. July 1912, Regina Finance Committee, file 65, 1912.

33 Rogers to McAra, July 3, 1912, Regina Finance Committee, file 69, 1912.

34 Ibid., July 8, 1912.

35 *Leader*, July 9, 1912, 1.

36 *Province*, July 10, 1912, 4; *Leader*, July 9, 1912, 4.

37 *Province*, July 10, 1912, 1 and 9; *Leader*, August 23, 1912, 1 and 5.

38 Walker to McAra, July 16, 1912, Regina Finance Committee, file 69, 1912.

39 Ibid., McAra report to the Relief Executive, August 8, 1912.

40 *Standard*, August 5, 1912, 1.

41 Council Minutes, August 14, 1912, 186.

42 Calder to Foster, August 9, 1912, and Rogers to Calder, August 15, 1912, Regina Finance Committee, file 69, 1912.

43 Ibid., Rogers to Calder, August 17, 1912.

44 *Leader*, August 23, 1912, 1 and 5.

45 Ibid., August 23, 1912, 4. See also "In a Hole," August 26, 1912, 4; and *Province*, August 24, 1912, 4.

46 White to McAra, August 20, 1912, Regina Finance Committee, file 69, 1912.

47 *Standard*, August 1, 1912, 1.

48 *Province*, August 13, 1912, 9; and *Leader*, August 17, 1912, 16. Negotiations between Calder and the finance committee commenced shortly after the return of the ill-fated Ottawa delegation. Under the resulting arrangements, the province agreed to borrow $500,000, then loan it to the city, which would in turn re-loan it to individual sufferers or retain it "to permit the rebuliding of homes and institutions and to permit the erection of new buildings at minimum cost." The rate of interest paid by the city was to be no greater than that charged the province, and in no case to exceed 5 per cent. The city was to commence retiring its debt as soon as conditions on the municipal debenture market were favourable. The province apparently presumed this was a mere formality since the Act called for retirement to commence in the spring of 1913 with the first of ten equal payments. As a guarantee of repayment, $2,000,000 in unencumbered city-owned land was to be set aside. Moneys were advanced in instalments to the municipality for disbursement by the loan committee with the final

transfer of $81,580 occurring on March 25, 1913: *Statutes of the Province of Saskatchewan* (hereafter cited as *Statutes of Saskatchewan*), 1912–13, An Act Respecting the City of Regina, Chapter 66, 349–59.

49   *Province*, August 27, 1912, 9.

50   *Standard*, September 24, 1912, 2.

51   *Statutes of Saskatchewan*, 1918–19, Chapter 93, 501–3.

52   Jack Schreiner, "Cyclone Account Finally Closed," *Leader-Post*, February 2, 1959, 15.

53   Such was freely admitted from time to time by the individuals themselves. See the Association's submission to city council reprinted in the *Leader*, December 2, 1918, 2; William Martin Papers, Archives of Saskatchewan, Regina Cyclone Association petition c. April 1919, 26413-22.

54   William Martin Papers, letter to P. M. Anderson, lawyer for the Regina Cyclone Association, March 21, 1919, 26409-10; Regina Cyclone Association petition, c. April 1919, 26413-22; letter to Commissioner Thornton, September 15, 1919, 26436-37; and letter to J. J. Renwick, member of the Regina Cyclone Association, October 4, 1920, 26489-90.

55   July 3, 1912, 4.

56   July 4, 1912, 4.

57   July 4, 1912, 4. Saskatoon and Winnipeg newspapers editorialized in a similar vein: *Manitoba Free Press*, July 2, 1912, 4 and *Saskatoon Daily Phoenix*, July 2, 1912, 4.

58   July 3, 1912, 1 and 4.

59   *Province*, July 4, 1912, 9.

60   August 8, 1912, 12.

61   McBain to McAra, July 19, 1912, Regina Finance Committee, file 65, 1912. In an ironic twist, the *Leader* published its own lavishly illustrated "Cyclone Souvenir" later that summer, selling them to the curious for ten cents.

62   McAra to the editors of *The British News in Canada*, July 23, 1912, Regina Finance Committee, file 64, 1912.

63   *Leader*, July 1, 1912, 3.

64   *Province*, July 13, 1912, 7.

65   July 2, 1912, 4.

66   William Martin Papers, Regina Cyclone Association petition, c. April 1919, 26413-22.

67   July 3, 1912, 11.

68   *Leader*, August 1, 1912, 18.

69   *Henderson's Directory*.

70   *Province*, July 2, 1912, 3.

71   *Manitoba Free Press*, July 2, 1912, 14. Similar cyclone insurance ads were prominently displayed in the *Saskatoon Daily Phoenix*.

72   *Standard*, July 15, 1912, 1.

73   *Province*, August 31, 1912, 9; McDonald to city clerk, August 23, 1912, Regina Finance Committee, file 20, 1912.

74   *Manitoba Free Press*, July 2, 1912, 1.

75   July 19, 1912, 3.
76   John C. Weaver and Peter de Lottinville, "The Conflagration and the City: Disaster and Progress in British North America During the Nineteenth Century," unpublished paper, 22–4; and Edward F. Dolan, *Disaster 1906: The San Francisco Earthquake and Fire* (New York: Julian Messner, 1967).
77   *Leader*, September 14, 1912, 4.

"ATLANTIC NO. 3 DISASTER FROM RAGING INFERNO TO BEACON OF PROMISE"

David Breen

Among the events eagerly anticipated by Edmontonians on the Labour Day long weekend in 1948 were the concerts and other activities scheduled to mark the official opening of the Canadian Broadcasting Corporation's new radio station, CBX. Boasting a new, state-of-the-art, 50,000-watt transmitter located at Lacombe, CBX's planned primary broadcast range extended from the U.S. border in the south to the Peace River and Fort McMurray areas in the north. The powerful new station was intended to fill in a critical gap in the CBC's trans-Canada programming network. And, to highlight the importance of the occasion, the corporation's senior officials, including Davidson Dunton, chairman of the CBC board of governors and Dr. Augustin Frigon, CBC general manager, were scheduled to be present.

First to arrive, "complete with cowboy hat and yellow shirt," was the network's acclaimed commentator and much-loved storyteller, John Fisher.[1] He reminded Edmontonians of CBC's mission to bring Canadians together, and in keeping with this mandate, Fisher announced that he was in the city to launch his fall series at the new station. The story he had prepared for the corporation's national audience was about Alberta, its vast resources and promising future. And, as for Alberta's future, Fisher predicted: "a beautiful rainbow will hang over the sunshine province."[2] In his wildest dreams Fisher could not have imagined how nature would upstage and dramatize his message from the West.

On Labour Day Monday, September 6, Fisher and the other CBC dignitaries were assembled for dinner at the home of CBX station manager Dan Cameron. About 7 p.m. there was a telephone call from the Hotel Macdonald in downtown Edmonton, where a CBC crew was busy in the hotel ballroom with the final preparations for the scheduled live broadcast of the ceremonies and concert that were to inaugurate the opening of the new station. Apparently one of the CBC reporters gazing out of a hotel window noticed a vast cloud of black smoke gathering on the southern horizon. The call to Cameron and his dinner guests was to inform them that the Atlantic Oil Company's No. 3 well had caught fire. This was not entirely unexpected; the viewers from the hotel knew the meaning of the towering black clouds almost immediately. The rogue Atlantic well had been running wild for months, spewing gas and oil to create a huge oil lake. From the outset the fearsome prospect of fire had been uppermost in the minds of the men desperately toiling to bring the well under control. Now their worst nightmare had been realized.

With most of the senior CBC brass gathered at the Cameron house, the reporter telephoning from the Macdonald did not have to wait very long for instruction to go get the story. Next morning John Fisher, or "Mr. Canada" as he was known to some, had an Alberta story for his national radio audience that was not part of the corporation's carefully scripted inaugural program. In his newscast Fisher informed Canadians that "last night the wild oil in the Leduc field, 20 miles south of Edmonton, caught fire. Thousands of barrels of oil went up in flame and smoke." Then, to help listeners create a visual image, he transferred to the voice of CBC radio announcer Ralph Horley, who said, "it's the worst oil fire I've ever seen. This brings back memories of the bombing of Berlin." Horley was trying to describe an inferno generated by acres of burning oil. Fisher added that when they got permission to travel beyond the mounted police cordon closer to the site of the "outlaw Atlantic No. 3," they saw "the boiling and the bubbling up from below that sent the flames hundreds of feet into the air; eruptions that sent mud and shale flying in every direction from the centre of the well." The newscast description drew also from a second visit to the raging well by chartered plane the following morning. Referring to the awesome view, Fisher recounted that "at one point in our circuit of the flaming pillar, the flames rolled almost to our eye level as we flew along at 3,600 feet" and the dense black smoke levelled off way above, "somewhere around 9,000 feet."[3]

Edmontonians, who could see the smoke twenty miles distant, learned more about the disaster in their daily newspapers. One who best captured the impact of the conflagration upon those witness to it was *Edmonton Journal* reporter Art Evans. Responding to the comment "Old Nick must be working overtime," Evans added:

This remark was voiced by a grimy oil worker Monday night standing 600 feet from the billowing cauldron that was Atlantic No. 3. The same thought must have occurred to many more. One look and biblical reference to the eternal fires of damnation kept coming to mind.

You can watch a hotel or factory go up in smoke and prophesy the flame's end but this was different. There was something eternal about this fire – the way it reached for the sky like a vast orange mushroom that appeared to cascade outwards and down before climbing again. It was nature, not in her kindest mood but having her own way as usual and with unlimited reserves to state her case. The onlooker knew that all the foamite, firemen and four-alarms in the country couldn't do a thing about it.[4]

The raging inferno at Atlantic No. 3 captured the headlines, making the CBX opening a back page story. Nonetheless, the Canadian Broadcasting Corporation's intention of drawing Alberta to the attention of the nation was achieved in the most dramatic, if unplanned, manner.

The stunning photographs and newsreel footage showing the acres of flame surrounding the oil well and the pall of black smoke that stretched for nearly a hundred miles across central Alberta presented an awesome climax that drew world attention to a story that had been unfolding for six months. Atlantic No. 3 gave first notice of its deviant intent in the predawn darkness of March 8. The graveyard crew drilling the Atlantic Oil Company's third well in the Leduc field had just penetrated the 5,331-foot mark, nearing the expected vicinity of the D3 reservoir, when the ground convulsed and a terrific surge of pressure shot a 150-foot gusher of oil, gas, and drilling mud up through the drill pipe and beyond the top of the 140-foot derrick. Along with the oil and mud came showers of shale and gravel, exiting with such force that, as one crew member recalled, it perforated the corrugated metal sheeting used to winterize the rig drilling floor, "just like you turned a machine gun on it."[5]

The immediate and traditional response of trying to stem the flow by pumping tons of drilling mud into the hole proved futile. After a few days' pause, the tremendous, but now released, reservoir pressure

Aerial view of Atlantic No. 3 looking east. Steam can be seen rising
from the two relief wells to the right and left of the blaze. The well in the
foreground is Imperial Leduc No. 43. Courtesy: Aubrey Kerr.

---

began to force oil and natural gas through the shallower rock forma-
tions to the surface. Miniature geysers of mud, oil, and gas began to
erupt out of hundreds of craters in a wide radius around the drill hole.
The fear of fire now became extreme, and there was the further huge
problem of runaway crude oil production. Although earth and snow
dikes were quickly bulldozed to contain the acres of accumulating oil,
cold winds continued to blow oil spray far from the rig, thereby adding
to the colossal mess and making working conditions more difficult for
relief crews.

On site at Atlantic No. 3. From left to right: Lyle Caspell, Landman, Frank MacMahon, Promoter and Spi Langston, Engineer. Courtesy: Aubrey Kerr.

As March passed, with the rogue well still blowing enough oil to the surface each day to maintain a crude oil lake, the immensity and seriousness of the situation began to sink in. All of the efforts made by the well owners and the drilling contractor to stop the flow had failed, including a last-ditch effort to pump a 10,000-bag mixture of cement slowly down the well. The cement had simply disappeared, just like everything else that had been pumped into the well.

With the failure of Atlantic Oil's drilling contractor, General Petroleum, to bring the wild well under control, it was apparent that something had to be done quickly to counter emerging public and industry unease. To this end, the agency responsible for monitoring the field operations of Alberta's oil and gas industry, the Petroleum and Natural Gas Conservation Board, took the initiative on April 12 to hire the widely known American wild-well fighter Myron Kinley to take charge of relief efforts. Having honed his skills in California's oil fields, Kinley was known as a "shooter," that is, one whose preferred method of "killing" wild wells was to blast them closed with a properly placed charge of dynamite – and his body bore the shrapnel wounds that signalled the hazards of his calling.[6] And on the hazard scale, Atlantic No. 3 ranked high, as Kinley would soon learn first-hand from the weary crew who by this time had been on the frontline for more than a month. On one occasion shortly after his arrival, when he directed his men "to get out there" and get on with the task, he was met with the collective rejoinder "do it yourself, you're getting the big money."[7] From the moment the well had blown out of control there was an awareness that only a spark was required to set off a firestorm. Incineration was a live possibility and if, on occasion, the men hesitated in jumping to the orders of the battle-scarred veteran of California, Texas, and Oklahoma well-wars, it is understandable.

In the end, Kinley's efforts proved as fruitless as those of his predecessor. After failing to clear the drill pipe, as a prelude to lowering and setting off a charge of explosives to block the hole, Kinley tried to seal the wellbore with heavy mud weighted with barite. Not only was this effort unsuccessful, but oil and gas began to erupt from a new band of craters north of the rig and oil production began to increase. Next, in early May, Kinley decided to try to stem the flow by pumping down a mix of "roughage." His exotic recipe of sixteen tons of redwood fibre, forty-three tons of cottonseed hulls, twenty-one tons of sawdust, a quarter ton of feathers, 490 sacks of mud and ten sacks of lime simply disappeared down the hole without effect like all the previous offerings.[8] Although Kinley was convinced that if "not interfered with" he could bring the well under control, what credibility he had on arrival was now largely dissipated.[9]

In fact, as Aubrey Kerr has observed, Kinley's approach to the situation was ill-considered.[10] First, since the well was not on fire there was no need for a dynamite blast. Moreover, a blast to seal the wellhead or casing would not likely have stemmed the flow, when gas and oil were also erupting in small geysers from dozens of small craters in the vicinity of the wellbore.

Given Kinley's inability to bring the well under control, the mood in Alberta began to shift. Albertans had not experienced anything like this before. At first, the blowout was incorporated into the popular excitement that still lingered from the recent Leduc discovery and the hectic development that had fallen in its wake. By early May, however, the excitement had begun to change to unease and impatience, especially in the farm community around Leduc. The "experts" were obviously having no success in bringing the well under control. The press was beginning to suggest the potential for large surface loss claims. As well, apprehension was being raised about oil-contaminated spring runoff reaching the nearby North Saskatchewan River and endangering Edmonton's water supply. The mounting level of worry caused the *Calgary Herald* to caution that although the situation was serious, it did "not warrant the hysteria engendered by highly coloured news reports," which hinted that communities in the Leduc vicinity were likely to be "blown sky high."[11] To dampen the rising anxiety, the Alberta's Petroleum and Natural Gas Conservation Board felt compelled to reassure Albertans that "excellent progress was being made."[12]

The public's emerging restiveness was complemented by growing unease in another quarter. As owner of 80 per cent of the field's production, Imperial Oil was growing increasingly worried that if an effective means to bring the well under control was not found soon the field could be ruined. From the outset, Imperial had monitored control efforts closely at Atlantic No. 3 and had consistently lent whatever material assistance was requested. As the weeks passed, discussion regarding the Atlantic problem took on a more organized form and moved to a higher level within the Imperial organization, and discussions with the Conservation Board regarding what might be done to tame the rogue well also became more focused.[13]

The thought that Alberta's newest and long-awaited oil field might be in jeopardy was just as disquieting to the Alberta government. Premier Manning and his colleagues were contemplating an election call, and the increasing public restiveness in the Leduc-Edmonton area was a concern. Technical, economic, and political circumstances thus combined to demand bold action on the part the province's responsible regulatory authority, the Petroleum and Natural Gas Conservation Board. At this juncture, the Board's credibility also became directly bound to the outcome at Atlantic No. 3.

Pushed to act, the Board's response was swift and decisive. On May 11 it announced that, by authority granted to the Board under the *Oil and Gas Conservation Act*, it was assuming control of the Leduc oil field.[14] The Board ordered that all wells in the field cease production as of 8 a.m. May 13, and it also announced that it was expropriating

Atlantic's wild well and had retained V. S. (Tip) Moroney, Imperial Oil's western Canada operations manager, to supervise operations at the well until it was brought under control. The Board's draconian intervention was immediately noted but not applauded by New York's vigilant financial community.[15] Never before in North America had a regulatory authority shut in an oil field and seized private property.[16]

If the Board's action drew some question, no one had any doubt about the immensity of the job faced by Tip Moroney. *Newsweek*'s description of the well-site spectacle is suggestive.

> Around No. 3 gas and oil were belching from thousands of holes. Eyewitnesses described the mad, green-black sea of boiling and leaping oil, gas, and mud behind 20-foot dikes. There were "bubbles as big as card tables", "oil sprays 10 feet high." The Alberta government estimated that from 8,000 to 10,000 barrels of oil were escaping every day over an area of 10 acres. In places the 75,000-barrel sea of crude oil around the well was 15 feet.[17]

Blair Fraser's description of the spring scene at Atlantic No. 3 is just as vivid.

> ... [as] the ground thawed, the whole 25-acre field became a swamp of live oil dotted with active craters. Sometimes it oozed up quietly, sometimes it came up in geysers 20 to 50 feet high, but always it kept on coming. The whole field bubbled and quaked like a pot of porridge and the oil ran down the ditches to collect in great pools.[18]

Only by shutting in the field could Imperial Oil's Leduc pipeline system be made available to begin draining the growing lake of oil surrounding the Atlantic well.

Moroney came to his assignment with impressive credentials. Tip Moroney was a Standard Oil of New Jersey career man, and had been with the company since 1926 after graduating from Georgetown University in Washington, D.C. His apprenticeship had been served in Oklahoma's Seminole field and in the Brea-Parinas fields in Peru. In late 1947, when Imperial Oil's parent company realized that the Leduc discovery represented a significant oil strike, Moroney was sent from Venezuela to bolster the still limited professional staff that Imperial had in Calgary. A man of broad field experience and some familiarity with wild wells, Moroney was the logical member of Imperial's senior resident engineering staff to be nominated to try to tame Atlantic No. 3. Under no illusion about the difficulty of the situation, Moroney accepted the challenge only on the condition that he be given absolute control.[19] Moroney also insisted upon the inclusion in his "team" of two old Turner Valley hands: driller Charlie Visser and mud man Jim Tod. Taken from Imperial's subsidiary, Royalite Oil Co., the men possessed skills critical to the success of Moroney's plan of action.[20]

His conditions agreed to, he returned a few days later to obtain Board approval for his plan. Moroney proposed a more sophisticated approach than that of his predecessor, Myron Kinley. He advised the drilling of two relief wells to intersect the D-3 producing zone as near as possible to the point where the Atlantic No. 3 wellbore entered the same zone (see Figures 1 and 2).[21] While this was underway, the nearby Imperial No. 48 well would be prepared as an injection well to take water from the North Saskatchewan River to begin an attempt to flood the wild well.[22] In flooding, Moroney's intent was to establish a water-saturated area at the base of the well. The water would then be displaced into the well by natural pressure and its heavier weight relative to oil was expected to result in the "killing" of the well. Moroney also wanted more stringent steps taken to reduce fire hazard. Concerned about the numbers of curious onlookers, he wanted much tighter security around the well site. Guards would be stationed at every access point to ensure that only pass holders entered the area and that matches, cigarettes, and other inflammables were removed from workers entering the danger zone. Also, a permanently staffed first aid and ambulance station was to be set up nearby. The Conservation Board accepted Moroney's plan and his conditions.

With Moroney directing efforts at Atlantic No. 3, Imperial was seen to be in charge and public confidence began to rise.[23] Within the industry, the situation also became less tense, particularly after June 3, by which time much of the accumulated oil lake had been drained and it became possible to reopen the field for production, thereby enabling the smaller independent companies to take advantage of a strong market and to re-establish badly needed cash flow. The now muted concern about the wild well came just in time for the Alberta government. With a provincial election called for August 18, Premier E. C. Manning and his Minister of Lands and Mines were busy enough defending their government's petroleum policy without having to address awkward questions about the six-month-old Atlantic No. 3 blowout.

Drilling of the west and south relief wells proceeded slowly through the summer.[24] After departing from the vertical at about the two-thousand-foot level, directional surveys had to be taken constantly to ensure that the sloping wellbores remained precisely on target. It was not until early September that the west relief well neared its anticipated target. Board Chairman Ian McKinnon arrived for the critical and long-awaited moment. And as though to mock the latest efforts of those who would restrain the well's freedom, serious new eruptions and cratering began to occur in the immediate vicinity of the abandoned Atlantic drilling rig. Braving pieces of rock and loose bits of iron being hurled into the air by the force of the oil and gas escaping from the nearby craters, Imperial's "danger pay" gang tried desperately to prevent the 140-foot derrick from toppling.

Having to contend with the suddenly more active well was not Moroney's only problem. There were difficulties at both of the relief wells. Drilling at the south well had stalled while the crew attempted to remove an obstruction from the wellbore. At the west relief well the planned depth had been reached, but the wellbore was about five hundred feet off target and the error was complicated by the very "tight" formation found at the bottom of the drill hole. The well refused to take the water that could shut off the runaway production at Atlantic No. 3. In a word, Moroney's situation was too-loose rock on top and too-tight rock below.

On Friday, September 3, in the midst of a fifty-five-mile-an-hour gale that lifted a hard-driving oil spray which again soaked the site, crews at the west relief well commenced an "acidization" process that they hoped would improve permeability and allow the water circulation that they required.[25] Efforts at the Atlantic No. 3 derrick site also came up short. Early on Monday the rig finally tipped into the gaping crater that had been building over the previous six months. To this point the rampaging well had thwarted every effort to curb its excess, and among those at the site in the muck and grime, tension mounted.

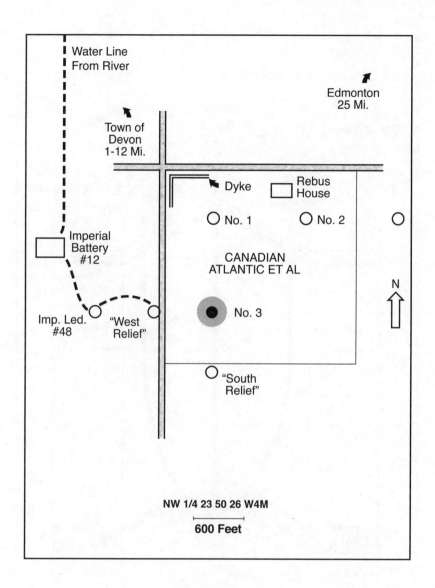

Figure 1
Atlantic Oil Company Petroleum and Natural Gas Lease, Summer, 1948.
Courtesy: Aubrey Kerr, Atlantic No. 3.

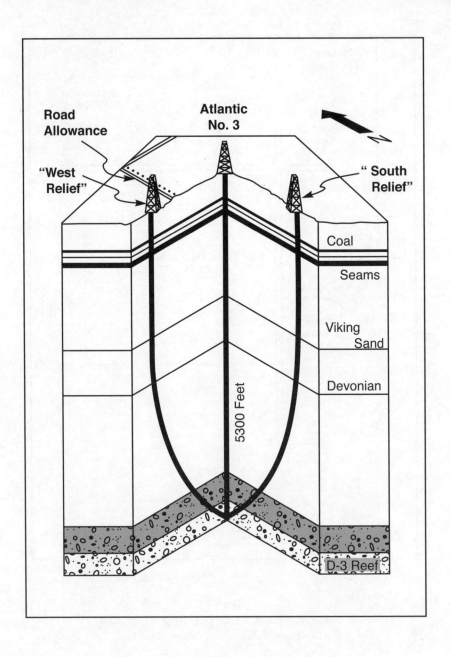

Figure 2
Atlantic No. 3 Relief Wells, Summer, 1948. Courtesy: Aubrey Kerr,
Atlantic No. 3.

Still, Moroney had grounds for some optimism. First, the collapsing oil rig had not set off a blazing inferno that from the outset had been the overriding fear. Second, a further acidizing job at the west relief well appeared to have succeeded in increasing the formation permeability sufficiently to permit effective water access to the No. 3 wellbore. Moroney's trial, however, was still not over. His men had just started pumping water down the relief well when Atlantic No. 3 caught fire. Moroney and Conservation Board Chairman Ian McKinnon were there to witness the huge fireball that at once engulfed the well site. With others they watched transfixed as the fire worked its way out along the oil drainage ditches to the northwest oil pit and spread over the oil-saturated land to create an awesome field of fire.

Also on hand to see the fiery nightmare was John Rebus, a man who had a more personal stake in the unfolding drama than the other watchers. Rebus was the farmer on whose land Atlantic No. 3 was situated and the owner of a one- eighth share of the wild well's production. His witness to the event was described, perhaps with some licence, by *Edmonton Journal* reporter Hal Pawson.

> Dour John Rebus, 38, glanced out his farm kitchen window at 6:20 pm Monday. He stared for an endless moment.
>
> Before his eyes he saw the final horror of a six month-old monetary nightmare that had started out as a rosy dream of riches for himself and nine other members of the Rebus family.
>
> Atlantic No. 3 was on fire. John cursed that magic word "oil" as he scrambled up and ran for the barn. By the time he had his tractor hooked up to a plow, the greedy orange flames were licking at storage sumps 200 feet south of his barn.
>
> Silently, John raced his tractor around his immediate farm home site, plowing up an emergency fire wall. He finished the grim task in record time.
>
> With the same grim silence, he backed his truck up to his house door and loaded his household furnishings." I'm through," he said, as he drove off into the smoky dusk.[26]

What caused the fire remains conjecture. It is probable that a piece of shale hurled by the gas out of the wellbore crater struck a part of the metal rig causing a spark. Such a disaster had always been Moroney's great fear. Still, he was lucky: no one had been killed and, at this juncture, he possessed effective means to deal with the crisis. By the second day, the presence of grey smoke with the flames revealed that the massive injections of water down the west relief well were mixing with the oil and would eventually stem the flow of oil and gas and smother the fire. The fire was quenched on September 10, but the struggle at Atlantic No. 3 was not yet over. The resumption of oil and gas flow was prevented only by the hydrostatic head or weight of the water column produced by the continuous injection of enormous amounts of water. The cavity at the bottom of the No. 3 wellbore had to be plugged, and it was for this reason that Moroney had ordered the drilling of two relief wells. While the injected water flow was maintained at the west relief well, the crew at the south relief well began cementing and plugging No. 3 wellbore. This essential but almost forgotten second part of the Atlantic No. 3 contest took remarkable ingenuity and another two months to achieve.[27]

With the flames extinguished, the cloud of black smoke that had hung over the region quickly dissipated, but only to be replaced by a cloud of a different order that was no less ominous. The *Financial Post* called attention to its presence as Moroney's men were putting out the remaining pockets of fire in scattered surface oil pools. The critical issue was that of liability. The Post pointed out that "almost endless claims for damages are expected to be filed," and uncertainty about who were likely to be winners and losers began to be reflected in share values.[28] It was anticipated that the unknown, but presumed substantial, cost of extinguishing the well would be charged against the Atlantic Oil Company, and that the company would suffer some kind of penalty for overproduction. It was also presumed that there would be royalty claims from the freehold owners of the well site, that there would be claims by farmers for surface damage, that operators forced to restrict production would seek compensation, and that other operators would bring forward the complex question of damage caused to a common reservoir.[29] In short, there was a looming legal tangle that promised to take far longer to resolve than the six months that it had taken to bring the wild well under control.

This was a cause of great anxiety to the Alberta government; it did not want a series of complex interlocking court actions that might stall further development of the Leduc field. As long as Moroney and his crew were still trying to place a permanent seal at the bottom of the Atlantic No. 3 wellbore, the final cost of taming the rogue well could not be determined, and this gave the Conservation Board time to move potential litigants toward an out-of-court settlement.

Farmers' claims, including that of $25 from Mary Yaremko for the damage suffered to the washing hung on her clothesline, were settled with little dispute, and for the Rebus family the runaway crude oil production eventually brought an accelerated royalty payment $352,323.[30] The Leduc operators, however, were not satisfied so easily. Their losses of foregone and unrecoverable production were of a different magnitude, and they were not as readily quantified. By December, after several informal meetings and the continuing exchange of proposals had failed to bring agreement, the government and the Conservation Board began to lose patience. The government's impatience was accentuated by a second oil well crisis. Although the Mercury-Leduc No. 1 blowout of November 15 was brought under control in just four and a half days, it served to remind that decisions made regarding the settlement at Atlantic No. 3 would be recognized as precedents. To bring negotiations to a conclusion, the Conservation Board called representatives of the eleven producing companies in the Leduc field to meet in its Calgary office on January 26. There, with Board Chairman Ian McKinnon and Alberta's Deputy Attorney General, the oil company delegates pounded out an agreement.

At the meeting, with the prospect of an arbitrary legislated settlement hanging over their heads, the oilmen recognized that compromise would have to be the order of the day. At issue was how the money in the Board-administered trust fund that had accumulated from the sale of oil produced by and pumped from the Atlantic No. 3 oil lake should be distributed, and what penalty should be exacted from the Atlantic Oil Company. The agreement reached at the January 26 meeting was then confirmed and reinforced by a special act of the Alberta legislature. Assented to on March 29, 1949, the *Atlantic Claims Act* assured the Conservation Board of whatever additional powers it might need to carry out the terms and the intent of the agreement. More important, the Act shut off the possibility of legal challenge by forbidding anyone who remained dissatisfied from taking legal action against Atlantic or the Conservation Board "unless such a person [had] first obtained the consent in writing of the Attorney General."[31]

The *Atlantic Claims Act* brought to a close what had been a long ordeal for the Alberta government and its Conservation Board. It is apparent that the Atlantic No. 3 crisis caught both the government and the Board unprepared. Both Premier Manning and Board Chairman McKinnon seemed uncertain at first about the kind of leadership they should provide. For the first two months of the wild well's rampage, they mainly stood by in hopeful anticipation that the industry would solve the problem. In good part, this is understandable; both were confronted with a new situation and some time was required to assess the capability of the well owners to deal with the situation. The previous incident from which direct experience could have been drawn was the Royalite No. 4 blowout, but that occurrence was separated not only by different geological and technical circumstances but also by the twenty-four years that had passed.[32]

Given Manning's close relationship with the Board and his personal confidence in McKinnon, his inclination to stand aside is easily understood. The Board's reluctance to intervene, however, was more complex. It was not just a matter of inexperience and faith in industry expertise; the Board's situation was more complicated because it had been party to the flawed decision that precipitated the blowout. Atlantic No. 3 had provided good evidence of its troublesome nature long before the celebrated blowout of March 8. That the Board's most experienced member had given his consent to risk drilling "dry" through the final thirty feet into the anticipated production zone, knowing that this accentuated the risk of a blowout,[33] made it extremely difficult for the Conservation Board to question Atlantic's procedure, and at first offered the Board little alternative other than to stand aside in the hope that the company would be able to assemble the expertise necessary to bring the well under control. Finally, after more than two months of failure and mounting public and corporate pressure, the Board was compelled to act, and by the time the rampaging well was eventually tamed months later, important lessons had been learned. The Atlantic blowout was truly the Board's, and to a lesser extent, the Alberta government's baptism of fire.

The criticism levelled by the *Edmonton Bulletin* was close to the mark:

> The fact that the damage may be restricted is no reason to excuse the fact that the well was permitted to get out of control. The highly competitive nature of oilfield development makes well drilling a race against time. Under these circumstances it is essential that the government exercise strict supervision of the work.
>
> Standards should be set and rigidly maintained with regard to equipment used and precautions taken to prevent a catastrophe in case of trouble such as that which plagued Atlantic No. 3 at Leduc. A proper trained and efficient staff can prevent repetition of the calamity.[34]

Much tighter and more informed field supervision was required – this was the lesson learned.

Atlantic No. 3 shattered the post-Leduc euphoria that was primarily fixated upon counting the number of successful new wells and admiring increasing production statistics. While the blowout gave dramatic confirmation of Alberta's status as a major player in the development of the continent's petroleum resources, it also gave sombre notice that it was time to reflect more seriously upon the manner in which petroleum exploration and production was going to be supervised in the field. With the moral authority conferred by the Atlantic experience and bolstered confidence in assuming a higher profile in the field, the Conservation Board moved quickly to improve the quality and reach of its field inspection system. More and better qualified field staff were engaged, and when the Redwater field just north of Edmonton was discovered in October 1948, a Board field office followed shortly after. The reinforced commitment to field inspection came at the right moment. In the seven months following the Redwater discovery, four new fields were discovered: Joseph Lake, Excelsior, Golden Spike, and Settler. The Atlantic blowout on eve of Alberta's post-war oil boom helped to set a standard of oil field inspection and supervision that was superior to that in most of the American oil-producing states and which ultimately became an internationally recognized model.[35]

The Atlantic No. 3 "show" was also perfectly timed to generate huge and consequential interest beyond Alberta's borders. The weeks of spewing oil and the inferno that distinguished the final stage of the drama underway in the Leduc oil field served as a convincing beacon to the national and international investment communities. Imperial Oil's February 1947 discovery at Leduc had been duly noted in the nation's financial pages and the industry press, but it was the runaway oil production and spectacular fire at Atlantic No. 3 that really delivered the message that a very significant "oil-play" was underway in Alberta. By May, two months after Atlantic No. 3 had set upon its wild course, the struggle underway to subdue the well was known across the continent.[36] The stunning news photographs and newsreel coverage that appeared after the well ignited on September 6 only quickened the mobilization of capital destined for Alberta. Commenting just a little more than a year later on the American presence in Alberta, *Fortune* magazine acknowledged "the continent-wide publicity" generated by the Atlantic blowout and informed its readers:

> The Canadian oil play is overwhelmingly the work of the US industry. Imperial Oil, which holds 70 per cent of the proved reserves, is a subsidiary of Standard of New Jersey. Every other major oil company in the US and every important independent is in the Canadian deal.[37]

The accelerated rush of investment capital not only hastened the pace of development, but the accelerated arrival of so many new players meant a more competitive environment and the faster erosion of Imperial's dominance.

How was it that a burning oil well could so greatly accelerate the rush of investment capital into Alberta? It was more than just the notice that it gave of a major oil strike; it was also a function of the times. Awareness that the oil strike represented a significant find coincided with an understanding that U.S. domestic production had peaked and could not keep up with growing demand. At the same time the raging debate on the partition of Palestine and growing tension in the Middle East underlined the risk of relying upon imported oil from that region. Articles such as "Oil Shortage Growing Worse" and "Middle East Oil for Soviets? Impact on Palestine Policy" in *U.S. News and World*

Report are representative of the barrage of newspaper and magazine articles that confronted Americans through the winter and spring of 1948 and cultivated the climate of concern.[38] Given the convergence of domestic and international factors, the pyrotechnic display at Atlantic No. 3 was assured of a very receptive audience.

The impact of the fire was well understood by contemporary observers. A Toronto stock broker explained to *Maclean's* editor Blair Fraser:

> I don't care what [the fire] cost, it was worth it three times over. Here in Alberta you've got one of the great oil fields of North America, a tremendous pool of natural wealth just discovered. Up to Labor Day, even Canadians didn't know it was here – now everybody's heard of it from here to Mexico.
>
> That fire certainly put Alberta on the map.[39]

Leduc No. 1 is properly remembered as the Leduc discovery well, but Atlantic No. 3 told the world.

NOTES

1   *Edmonton Journal*, September 3, 1948.

2   Ibid.

3   Aubrey Kerr, *Atlantic No. 3* (Calgary: S. A. Kerr, 1986), 188, quoting the CBC radio broadcast retrieved from the CBC Archives in Ottawa. Most accounts describe the flames reaching six or seven hundred feet.

4   *Edmonton Journal*, September 7, 1948.

5   Kerr, *Atlantic No. 3*, 61, quoting Hugh Leiper. Taped interview at Glenbow Archives.

6   Kerr, *Atlantic No. 3*, 81.

7   Paul Bedard, taped interview at Glenbow Archives.

8   M. Kinley to I. N. McKinnon, June 10, 1948, Alberta, Energy Utilities Board (hereafter cited as EUB), Atlantic No. 3 general file.

9   Kerr, *Atlantic No. 3*, 84.

10   Ibid., 81.

11   *Calgary Herald*, May 13, 1948.

12   Ibid., May 19, 1948.

13   Kerr, *Atlantic No. 3*, 95. It is unclear whether Imperial approached the Board with a proposed solution or whether the Board asked Imperial for a specific recommendation about what should be done.

14   EUB, PNGCB, Minutes, May 13, 1948.

15   *New York Times*, May 13, 1948.

16   Believing that a state of insurrection existed, Texas Governor Ross S. Sterling declared martial law on August 17, 1931 and shut in the entire East Texas oil field, but individual properties were not seized and the government did not take over the operation of oil wells.

17   *Newsweek*, May 24, 1948. A very similar description can be found in *Time*, May 24, 1948.

18   *Maclean's*, November 1, 1948.

19   Kerr, *Atlantic No. 3*, 104.

20   From Okotoks, Charlie (The Dutchman) Visser had had more than twenty years' experience and was Royable/Imperial's drilling superintendent. Jim Tod early in his career set about developing better drilling muds, or muds better suited to particular situations, and by 1948 had a reputation of being one of the best of a very select breed.

21   EUB, Minutes, May 20, 1948, including V. S. Moroney to I. N. McKinnon, May 19, 1948.

22   Atlantic's Nos. 1 and 2 wells were also to be prepared as injection wells to accept the excess oil produced by Atlantic No. 3 that could not be handled by existing pipeline facilities.

23   *Financial Post*, May 27, 1948.

24   This difficult task was made even more complicated by the fact that the Atlantic Oil Co. was unable to furnish data that precisely located the bottom of their well.

25 For a description of the situation see *Edmonton Journal*, September 4, 1948.

26 *Edmonton Journal*, September 7, 1948.

27 For an excellent discussion of the technical difficulties and the creative solutions arrived at on site, see Kerr, *Atlantic No. 3*, 142–55.

28 *Financial Post*, September 11, 1948.

29 *Calgary Herald*, September 11, 1948.

30 Farmer's claims, mainly for surface damage, totalled $27,447.45: EUB Library, Atlantic No. 3 file.

31 An Act to Determine All Claims Arising From the Atlantic No. 3 Oil Well Disaster, *Statutes of Alberta*, 1949, Chapter 17, Section 5. $160,000 from the trust fund was set aside for each of the two nearest wells, Imperial-Leduc No. 48 and Leduc-Consolidated No. 2, as compensation for the damage caused. As a penalty for the over-production of its No. 3 well, the Atlantic-Oil Company's Nos. 1 and 2 wells were restricted to two-thirds of the production that they would normally have been allowed. In addition, Atlantic was restricted from drilling further wells on the leasehold where its Nos. 1, 2 and 3 wells were situated. The combined impact of the restrictions had the effect of greatly reducing the production that Atlantic might normally have expected from the leasehold. For a more detailed discussion of the terms and how they were determined, see David H. Breen, *Alberta's Petroleum Industry and the Conservation Board* (Edmonton: University of Alberta Press, 1993), 285–88.

32 EUB, "Oil and Gas Well Blows, uncontrolled Blows and Blowouts: 1924–1983."

33 See Kerr, *Atlantic No. 3*, 55–58, on the controversial decision and the technical issues involved.

34 *Edmonton Bulletin*, May 13, 1948.

35 Breen, *Alberta's Petroleum Industry*, 512–15, 517–24, for a more detailed discussion of Conservation Board field organization and procedures, and for a comparison of the resources devoted to field expectation by Alberta's Petroleum and Natural Gas Conservation Board and the Texas Railroad Commission (the equivalent agency in Texas). Alberta's Conservation Board engineers became well known as oil field management consultants in the Middle East and elsewhere.

36 See, for example, *New York Times*, May 13, 1948; *Newsweek* May 24, 1948, *Business Week* (New York), June 5, 1948 and *Time*, May 24, 1948.

37 *Fortune* (January 1950).

38 "Oil Shortage Growing Worse" *U.S. News and World Report*, January 16, 1948; and "Middle East Oil for Soviets? Impact on Palestine Policy," *U.S. News and World Report*, March 5, 1948. See also "Oil Troubles the International Waters" *New York Times Magazine*, February 22, 1948; "American Security and Foreign Oil" *Foreign Policy Reports*, March 1, 1948; "Oil Crisis: How Long," *Business Week*, February 14, 1948; "Oil Situation, Today and Tomorrow," *Congressional Digest*, October 1948; "Arab League Bars Pipelines while US Backs Partition," *New York Times*, February 22, 1948.

39 Blair Fraser, "The Taming of No. 3," *Maclean's Magazine*, November 1, 1948.

IT COULD HAVE BEEN MUCH WORSE THE 1952 OUTBREAK OF FOOT AND MOUTH DISEASE IN SASKATCHEWAN

Max Foran

> Foot and Mouth crowded Korea peace discussions, the North Atlantic Treaty Alliance and the accession of Queen Elizabeth to the British throne right off the front pages of Canadian newspapers – *Canadian Cattlemen*, April, 1952.

Livestock health issues are considered serious not for their impact on the human condition (Britain's recent outbreak of Mad Cow Disease notwithstanding), but rather for their economic implications. A mild outbreak of any contagious disease can ruin individual stock owners in a very short time. When the disease is more widespread or virulent it can decimate herds and impact negatively on local and regional economies. One disease outbreak in Austria, for example, turned villages into what one observer described as "ghost towns." In the case of a major outbreak involving a highly feared and contagious disease, a whole country's economy can be affected. Loss of exports through prolonged embargoes can have catastrophic effects on a dependent national economy. Although diseases like pleuro-pneumonia and tuberculosis fall into the latter category, easily the most feared of all animal contagions is foot and mouth disease. Its appearance in Saskatchewan in the winter of 1951–52 sent shudders of alarm through Canada's livestock industry. The subsequent successful measures taken to eradicate it revealed a level of official coordination and intensity unrivalled in the annals of Canadian animal health practice. In the aftermath of the battle, the impact of the sustained embargoes and the memories associated with unexpected and paralyzing internecine differences simply underscored the horror of what might have been had the disease not been contained so quickly and effectively.

The international implications of contagious animal diseases were an outgrowth of the escalating global trade in livestock during the late nineteenth century. Animals entering another country often carried infectious diseases which subsequently spread to home herds. In most cases following a disease outbreak, entire containment was impossible, especially in Europe, with its large livestock numbers and its plurality of nationalities.[1] The island nation of Great Britain was more fortunate, and in the second half of the nineteenth century an increasingly watchful Board of Agriculture closely monitored the health of imported animals. Being younger nations, the United States and Canada were even more fortunate. Their live animal imports were largely restricted to purebred stock, and by the time their livestock industries were firmly established, scientific advances in detection and a rigid system of quarantine containment had ensured a level of livestock health immeasurably higher than in Europe and superior to that of Great Britain.[2] Moreover, Canadian herds enjoyed a greater degree of disease immunity than those in the United States, whose susceptibility to disease was increased by her border with Mexico and through the risk factor associated with higher animal inventories. For example, up to 1952, the United States had spent millions of dollars controlling nine major outbreaks of foot and mouth disease.[3]

The methods of controlling a disease outbreak were generally the same in all countries. Following detection, the disease was contained locally through quarantine. Trading nations immediately imposed an embargo on all imports from the afflicted country. Sometimes widespread vaccinations, or dipping in the case of mange, were the main eradication methods. However, while vaccination was employed when feasible or effective, the most popular method, and one followed in Great Britain, involved widespread slaughter. Certainly, Canada with her British legacy followed the mother country's tradition. For example, when an animal from a valuable imported purebred herd of two hundred Galloway bulls showed signs of pleuro-pneumonia in 1886, the entire herd plus another 226 head on adjoining farms were immediately slaughtered.[4]

Canada's meat industry has always formed an integral part of her economy, with exports being crucial to sustain profitability and to control domestic price levels. Exports of live cattle and meat to the United States totalled $130 million in 1951. Yet the dangers of animal health issues with respect to export markets resided almost entirely with cattle, as they comprised the only large-scale trade in live animals. Canada's annual beef surplus had reached the equivalent of over 350,000 head by 1951, and since exports of beef could rarely compete with those of Argentina, Australia, or even the United States on a cost-efficient basis, the surplus had to be cleared largely in the form of live animals. After 1913 the vast majority went to the United States, usually as feeder cattle to the midwest, or as finished animals to the burgeoning markets of the Pacific northwest.[5] Up to and beyond the World War II, this trade in live cattle was of crucial importance not only to the economies of the western provinces but to eastern Canadian farmers, who often finished western-bred cattle on feed from land too expensive and restricted to allow large-scale cattle raising.

Thus it was not surprising that Canada historically followed a path of stringent protection and defence of herd health. Two outbreaks of mange, one in the early 1900s and another in 1918, were swiftly eradicated in a co-operative programme which involved both government officials and participating ranchers and farmers. Tuberculosis, Bangs Disease, and brucellosis were all subject to ongoing control programmes, and in the 1940s a concerted attempt was made to eradicate the warble fly. The point is that herd health was always a crucial matter of concern and pride for the entire Canadian livestock industry. In 1950, for example, only sixteen animals out of ten thousand in an accredited T.B.-free zone showed a positive reaction for tuberculosis, while a testing programme for Bangs Disease revealed an infection rate of one twentieth of one per cent.[6] Indeed, one of the few boasts made by a country not known for expansive self-congratulatory sentiments were those frequent Canadian utterances attesting to the disease-free condition of her livestock. In this respect, the prolonged British embargo on Canadian cattle between 1892 and 1923 on the grounds of suspected pleuro-pneumonia was a cause of perpetual disquiet, not so much for the loss of trade as for the slur placed on Canadian herd health. The embargo, which was in all probability wrongly imposed and unfairly maintained by English producers to exclude competition, required incoming cattle to be slaughtered at the point of entry rather than being taken inland for finishing. In an era of declining British trade its overall economic impact was not substantial. The impugning of a national reputation was another matter entirely.[7]

Of all diseases, foot and mouth, also known as aphthous fever, is regarded by far the most dangerous threat to livestock health. Although considered a disease of cattle, foot and mouth affects all cloven-footed animals. It was first detected in Europe in the eighteenth century and by 1839 had made its appearance in Great Britain.[8] Carried by a barely detectable and highly resistant virus which comes in six diverse forms, foot and mouth is extremely contagious, and its rapid spread to almost all exposed susceptible animals leads to heavy economic losses. Infection may be spread from direct contact with diseased animals that are highly contagious long before they show visible symptoms. Indirect contamination, however, is far more dangerous because of the range of carriers and the fact that the virus can live for extended periods outside an animal's body. According to F. E. Mollin, Secretary of the American Cattleman's Association, foot and mouth virus remained in Californian soil for 345 days following an outbreak there. The virus may reside on manure, hay, utensils, drinking troughs, railway cars, stockyards, barnyards, or pastures. Human beings, although rarely infected, may carry the virus on their hands and clothing. It may also be carried by rats, dogs, cats, chickens, and other birds either on their bodies or in their excretions. Even milk in a raw state may also transmit the disease to animals fed with it.[9] Indeed, the virus endures many of the processes used in dairy products, including high temperature and short-term pasteurization. It also survives in both processed and frozen meats.[10] In the outbreak under discussion, the later infections were caused by viruses in the melting spring snows. The omnipresent danger of the disease is also reflected in the variety of sources to which individual outbreaks have been attributed. Included are garbage washed ashore from ships, a cowpox vaccine, migrants' clothing, imported South American meat, and even migrating birds. Furthermore, vaccines are difficult to prepare, partly because the virus only multiplies in living tissue, and also due to the fact that the six strains are distinct immunological types. An animal made immune to one strain is still susceptible to the other five.[11]

The progress of foot and mouth disease is fairly consistent. Following an incubation period of between three and six days, an eruption of vesicles or blisters occurs on the mucous membrane of the mouth and on the skin between the toes and above the hoof.[12] Udders also become inflamed. These vesicles rupture within twenty-four hours, forming erosions and ulcerations, accompanied by salivation and extreme tenderness in the affected parts. Mortality rates vary. In severe outbreaks, it may be as high as 30 to 50 per cent. An outbreak of a less deadly strain may produce death rate of only 5 per cent. However, regardless of the mortality rate, the secondary effects are devastating to both animal and owner. Abortions, significant weight loss, severe lameness, impairment or complete loss of milk production, and, most appalling of all, unrelenting pain all combine to make death the only merciful solution.

The seriousness of foot and mouth disease is best reflected in the measures taken to contain it. Slaughter numbers in some countries are enough to stagger the imagination. Between 1946 and 1951, Mexico slaughtered over a million head trying to eradicate the disease and regain access to the American market.[13] The Americans themselves slaughtered 175,000 head in 1914 and another 105,000 ten years later trying to contain the disease.[14] The costs of containment were high. The 1914 eradication campaign cost the Americans $9 million, while Texans paid out a million dollars a month in 1929 trying to contain an outbreak in that state.[15] In the five years following the outbreak in Mexico in 1946, the American government spent $122 million aiding the Mexican control programme.[16]

Thus, when foot and mouth disease was officially diagnosed in cattle from a farm near Regina on February 25, 1952, it understandably sent ripples of alarm and fear through the whole industry. *Canadian Cattlemen* editor Ken Coppock, referred to the announcement as a "blue Monday for Canada's cattle industry."[17] Coppock reflected the current consensus when he pointed out to his readers that Canada had never before experienced foot and mouth disease on her soil. He might have been wrong. According to a prominent early Canadian veterinarian, J. G. Rutherford, there had been three detections of foot and mouth disease in the nineteenth century, one in Montreal (1870), another near Toronto (1875) and a third at Point Levis (1884). In all cases the virus was isolated and did not survive the winter.[18] Coppock, however, was definitely wrong in assuming that the diagnosis had been swift and efficient. If anything, the Canadian containment programme had gotten off to a protracted start.

On November 26, 1951, a batch of cattle belonging to Leonard T. Wuss, a farmer at McLean twenty-eight miles east of Regina, became sick. Following standard procedure, a provincial veterinarian conducted the mandatory tests, which indicated that the animals were suffering from infectious vesicular stomatitis, a highly contagious disease which was not unknown in Saskatchewan and, while far less dangerous

An infected animal. Courtesy: The Grant MacEwan Photograph Collection.
Canada Department of Agriculture Photograph.

than foot and mouth, exhibited itself in very similar early symptoms.
All herds showing the vesicular condition were placed under quarantine
and observation, as was the Burns feedlot in Regina.[19] So sure were
seven veterinarians of their diagnosis that they did not forward samples
to the Animal Disease Research Institute in Hull, Quebec for conclu-
sive testing, a decision endorsed by the Veterinary Director General of
Canada, Dr. T. Childs, who felt that the outbreak was too far inland to
be foot and mouth disease.[20] In a seemingly contradictory vein, Childs
later claimed that he felt that it was advisable in any potential risk situation to make the diagnosis in the area where the infection began rather
than chance sending easily breakable vials long distances for laboratory
testing.[21]

The calm continued into December with no further spread of the
diagnosed stomatitis, and in January 1952, Childs, who was in Regina
on an unrelated matter, declared the cattle in the Burns feedlot to be

disease-free and removed the quarantine. By early February, however, the disease began appearing in additional herds in the vicinity which, more ominously, were manifesting the more serious lesions associated with foot and mouth disease. Following a telephone conversation between provincial veterinarians and the Animal Health Branch in Ottawa, samples from infected animals were received at the Hull laboratory on February 16. Childs interrupted his holidays and arrived in Regina on the 17th and a day later quarantined the entire area of suspected infection. Although early reports from Hull indicated that test animals were developing the disease, it took a week before the dread diagnosis was confirmed. On February 25, it was formally acknowledged that foot and mouth disease had arrived in Canada.

From this point on, the official action was quick and concerted. Although federal Agriculture Minister James Gardiner arrived in Regina to take personal charge of the situation,[22] the task of coordinating the eradication and containment programme was put under the direction of Dr. Ken Wells, Associate Chief Veterinarian in Ottawa, and Dr. N. D. Christie, District Veterinarian at Regina. Headquartered on the third floor of the Post Office building in Regina, a team consisting of as many as fifty veterinarians from five provinces plus agriculturalists, engineers, administrators, and Mounted Police personnel used their enhanced powers in round the clock operations to counter what was readily acknowledged as the greatest crisis ever to confront the Canadian livestock industry.[23] Areas of focus included diagnoses, investigation, animal and farm inspection, transportation, quarantine enforcement, burial pit excavation, slaughtering operations, records and finance, and disinfectant measures.

Containment was effected within the quarantine area, which comprised a rough band surrounding Regina to a depth of about fifty miles. The outer edges of this band included a buffer zone of modified quarantine regulations. The main quarantine area took in eleven rural municipalities, including South Qu'Appelle, Edenwold, Sherwood, Pense, Lumsden, part of North Qu'Appelle, Lajord, Bratt's Lake, and Redburn plus all livestock delivery points in Regina and Moose Jaw. All movement of livestock was prohibited to and from and within this area, as was personal travel between farms.[24] Regular inspections took place on all farms in the quarantine area, and were intensified in instances where new infections were detected. Infected premises were thoroughly cleaned and disinfected and possible sources like straw and hay burned. All food stocks which might have come into contact with infected animals were also burned. Elevators in the quarantined area were not allowed to accept or move grain out.

Because of its virulence, the disease had spread readily. For example, it was believed that visiting farmers to the Wuss farm had carried the virus to their own herds on their clothing. The original twenty-two infected premises were located in three main areas. The first was in the McLean district, where the disease was originally detected. The second and main area was north and west of Regina, while a third was isolated to two farms near Truax, the owners of which had purchased cattle from the McLean area. A later outbreak at Ormiston was traced to meat bought in the original infected area in late January and subsequently frozen. Two other outbreaks occurred in the Weyburn area in late April. By the time the disease had been fully contained, it had been observed in more than thirty separate locations.

The slaughter policy of containment did not include all animals within the quarantine area as popularly imagined. Only those animals within an infected area were slaughtered. These included cloven-footed animals and poultry. The disposal was generally carried out by marksmen from the Mounted Police, and extraordinary efforts were taken to ensure that the virus did not survive the creatures it had infected.

Under the direction of L. B. Thomson, noted agriculturalist and Director of the Prairie Farm Rehabilitation Administration (PFRA) in Regina, seven disposal sites were chosen near Regina, McLean, and Truax. Huge bonfires were built to soften the ground, which was then blasted to prepare it further for the PFRA bulldozers. The pits so created were two hundred feet long, thirty feet wide and fifteen feet deep. The animals were driven to their burial ground in vans specially treated with an inner coating of tar. Once inside the pits they were shot by Mounted Police marksmen who, like all others in the area, had to wear a protective rubber suit. Footbaths containing a 20 per cent solution of lye were also compulsory components of the slaughter operation. After the animals had been dispatched their carcasses were covered with slaked lime and the pits then filled in.[25]

Accurate statistics on the precise numbers of animals slaughtered vary. The official number given on March 15 was 1,069 cattle, 129 swine, 97 sheep, 1,610 poultry 13,192 eggs, two test horses, and one luckless goat that was a former mascot for the Saskatchewan Rough Riders Football team.[26] A later figure given in early May set the number of cloven-footed animals destroyed at 1,742.[27]

Compensation for loss of animals received prompt attention in the House of Commons. Under an amendment to the Animal Contagious Diseases Act, stock owners were compensated at market value for the loss of their animals. For cattle this ranged from $40 up to $700 for purebred stock. In all, the federal government paid out about half a million dollars in stock loss compensation. However, efforts by the Saskatchewan Government to seek compensation for workers who had lost their jobs as a result of the outbreak were unsuccessful.[28]

Control measures extended beyond the quarantine area. Animals were admitted but not allowed out except for immediate and inspected slaughter at Moose Jaw, Prince Albert, Saskatoon, Winnipeg, and St. Boniface. Modified quarantines were also placed on stockyards, packing plant stockyards, and feedlots in Alberta. Livestock known to have left the quarantined area for other points in Canada were traced and inspected for the disease. Individuals going to town from an infected area had to disinfect their shoes with lye before leaving and returning.[29] Central checkpoints for milk and stock trucks were set up in Regina where milk cans were steamed and the trucks disinfected. Even milk being pasteurized from the quarantined area was subjected to higher than normal heat levels. Movement of other animal products were prohibited. For example, over seven thousand cattle hides and $70,000 worth of furs were held in Winnipeg and Regina respectively.

Two examples convey the seriousness of intent which characterized the entire programme. The federal government halted all immigration to Canadian farms from countries known to have foot and mouth disease, while those not going to farms were subjected to thorough inspections for the disease. Even the latter's heavy luggage, which was normally allowed to go through to destination, was forwarded in bond to be inspected by a customs official and veterinarian. In early March, following the discovery of two new sources of infection, an order was issued prohibiting the importing of all livestock or fresh meat into the quarantine area.[30] The order in effect meant that Regina, a city of some 75,000, was deprived of meat completely.

The control programme was an outstanding success. Although secondary outbreaks occurred outside the quarantine area, the disease did

Animals in Pits prior to Slaughter. Courtesy: The Grant MacEwan
Photograph Collection. Canada Department of Agriculture Photograph.

not spread beyond southern Saskatchewan. Though the last recorded outbreak was an isolated case within the buffer zone at Weyburn on May 1, the campaign to stamp out foot and mouth disease in Saskatchewan continued unabated through the summer months. It was not until August 19, 1952 that an announcement was made proclaiming the elimination of the disease from Canadian soil. In a dramatic editorial, Ken Coppock summed up the general admiration for a task well done:

> With the proclamation there comes to a close a period in which the Health of Animals Branch carried on an epic fight in disease control and at the same time overcame the handicaps of the cold winter months and the muck and mire of a spring thaw. The job which was done without fanfare will long stand as a major undertaking accomplished efficiently and thoroughly.... The Health of Animals Branch has achieved an enviable reputation among the veterinarians of the world.[31]

The foot and mouth outbreak ended in August. The U.S. embargo did not. At first, the American authorities said they would wait the traditional year after the last occurrence of the disease before resuming normal trading relations. The dismay at hearing this news was compounded by the ending of the U.S. embargo against Mexico on September 1. The western Canadian cattle economy continued to lose millions of dollars in export sales through the fall of 1952. However, a good fall meant more pasture and a greater level of stock retention. The subsequent limited and more uniform marketings kept domestic prices surprisingly firm and, more importantly, gave producers some light in what had been an extremely dreary year. Then came the truly unexpected. On November 29, 1952, the United States, faced with a feed shortage in New England,[32] smaller than expected import volumes from Mexico,[33] and buoyed by the energies of the new Eisenhower administration, broke with tradition and announced the removal of its sanitary embargo only three months and ten days after the last recorded outbreak in Weyburn. It could be argued that while the Canadian government declared the foot and mouth outbreak over on August 19, 1952, Canadian livestock producers would likely place the date at March 1,

1953, the day the United States lowered its barriers to the admittance of livestock from Canada.[34]

Despite its quick and efficient containment, the foot and mouth outbreak caused widespread disruptions which generated intense political debate and controversy. Typically, fingers were pointed and factional interests emerged. Solutions were sought, some traditional and ill-founded, others more imaginative, and fortunately a few with lasting implications for animal health security in Canada.

The most serious problem, and the one which primed the pump for other related issues, concerned the United States, with its absorption of 98 per cent of Canada's surplus livestock production. Following desperate importunities by Canadian authorities for a temporary or selective regional embargo, a sympathetic but adamant United States followed international practice and imposed a wide-ranging embargo on a host of Canadian livestock and livestock-related products. Included were cattle, sheep, goats, and hogs, as well as fresh, chilled or frozen beef, veal, mutton, lamb or pork. The embargo extended to straw, hay, hides, skins, and bone meal. Hams and bacon were accepted provided that all bones were removed at place of origin, the meat left in an unfrozen condition for at least three days following slaughter and then thoroughly cured through two separate salt-based processes.[35]

The U.S. action removed the market for Canada's surplus meat production. The resulting glut of 360,000 head of live cattle and about one hundred million pounds of meat products meant a total collapse in domestic prices and potential ruin for large segments of the nation's livestock industry. The federal government originally tried to counter the situation by restricting the import of all meats into Canada, a move that did little to redress the situation given the existing imbalance between imports and exports. A further measure was the encouragement given to farmers not to market their cattle. This voluntary measure was not successful since it offered little incentive beyond free feed for quarantined farmers unable to move their herds to summer pastures. Furthermore, farmers were accustomed to selling their stock after seeding. They were also aware that animals retained for a longer time than was necessary would be marketed at a heavier weight, and given the current Canadian consumer preference for lighter carcasses, would bring discounted prices.[36] Thus heavy marketings continued through the spring and early summer. Prices began to fall. The April

Saskatchewan Rough Rider Mascot being led into slaughter pit. Courtesy:
The Grant MacEwan Photograph Collection. Canada Department of
Agriculture Photograph.

Opposite page above: PFRA Director L. B. Thomson inspecting animals in slaughter pit. Courtesy: The Grant MacEwan Photograph Collection. Canada Department of Agriculture Photograph.

Opposite page below: A Look of Despair. A farmer whose herd was destroyed because of the disease Courtesy: The Grant MacEwan Photograph Collection. Canada Department of Agriculture Photograph.

Above: Grant MacEwan left with Dr Ken Wells, Associate Chief Veterinarian, Ottawa centre, and L B. Thomson, Director Prairie Farm Rehabilitation Administration, Regina. Courtesy: The Grant MacEwan Photograph Collection. Canada Department of Agriculture Photograph.

Pit burning of slaughtered animals. Courtesy: The Grant MacEwan
Photograph Collection. Canada Department of Agriculture Photograph.

---

price of steers in Toronto was $25.10 per cwt. A year earlier they had
been $32.66. Farmers in Saskatchewan saw prices dip by 50 per cent.
Livestock by-products were equally affected. Hides dropped from 43.5
cents to 16.5 cents, and tallow from 22 cents to 6 cents per lb.

The seriousness of the situation was compounded further by the
provincial governments of Manitoba, Ontario, and British Columbia,
which by the end of February had closed their western/eastern borders
to all meat products. This unexpected move isolated Canada's two
largest beef exporters (Alberta was affected equally by these restrictions) from all trading options beyond their borders.[37] Responding to
a provincial loss of $14 million in livestock revenues from February to

May, the Alberta Government began preparing a court challenge to the British Columbia restrictions. *The Western Producer* slapped the wrists of the three provinces by calling their leaders "sergeants and lieutenants" who should be leaving the battle to "the generals."[38] Similar sentiments were echoed by the Canadian Beef Council, the Western Stock Growers Association, and the *Canadian Cattlemen*. The latter Calgary publication gave Alberta the high moral ground by referring to her "duty to her sister province" and to her abiding confidence in the federal disease containment measures.

Clearly, the federal government was caught by surprise by these provincial actions. Agriculture Minister Gardiner fully expected national approval of the extensive measures being taken to control the disease and that the provinces would tender their best service through co-operation and deference to federal control in a disaster of national scope. He argued further that any provincial ban was unnecessary and ran counter to announced federal policy which did not compel any province to accept out-of-province meat. He also stressed the point that the interprovincial restrictions only fuelled the fires of those in the United States who wanted the embargo against Canada retained.

A harried federal government faced with alarming meat surpluses in Saskatchewan and Alberta and the mounting hostile lobby from the five affected provinces brokered the impasse at a federal-provincial conference in early April. Manitoba, Ontario, and British Columbia agreed to remove their restrictions if the federal government guaranteed a $25.00 per cwt floor price for good steers.[39] On April 9, it was announced that a federal Prices Support Board purchased surplus beef from inspected packing plants at the agreed-upon floor price. Though originally projected to end in July, the floor price policy was maintained until the ending of the American embargo. Thus, by the middle of June shipments within Canada had returned to normal.[40] There can be no doubt that this measure saved the Canadian livestock feeding industry from bankruptcy.[41] According to J. S. McLean, President of Canada Packers Limited, the steps taken were the only ones possible and "the expected heavy losses would be only a fraction of that which would have followed had the situation been allowed to drift."[42] It seems unarguable in the face of their actions in making the lifting of their restrictions contingent on the floor price arrangement that the three provinces had based their restrictions at least in part on economic grounds. Protection of local industry from a national glut was clearly a priority.

The opposition Conservatives tried to profit politically from the disease outbreak by demanding a Commons Committee of Inquiry into the reasons for the delay in diagnosing the disease as foot and mouth. This sixty-member committee first convened on April 30, and took evidence on two occasions before being "adjourned indefinitely." It was obvious that public opinion overwhelmingly endorsed the actions taken to stamp out the disease, and saw the committee's existence as blatantly political. As M. L. Schwartz commented in the *Canadian Cattlemen*, "it is in the best interests of justice to officials involved, to leave 'politics' out of this national problem."[43] Dr. N. D. Christie, one of the directors of the eradication campaign, bluntly told the investigative committee that the only dissatisfaction with the handling of the disease came from Ottawa, a statement neither challenged nor denied by James Gardiner.[44] An irate producer put it another way when he maintained that the adverse publicity engendered by the investigation committee was tantamount to spending a million dollars a day "helping Yank cattlemen in their quest to keep the embargo on."[45]

The foot and mouth outbreak placed national restrictions on the agricultural industry by denying access to seasonal agricultural workers from other countries. H. H. Hannan, the President of the Canadian Federation of Agriculture, in referring to the loss of twenty-five thousand European seasonal workers, stated in March that Canada would face the worst year of its history in labour shortages.[46] Yet, in the marketing and processing components of the industry, particularly in Saskatchewan and Alberta, hundreds were thrown out of work.

The removal of the U.S. market because of the disease resurrected old debates about the natural outlet for Canada's surplus meat production. The spectre of the long-abandoned British market loomed again as a possible alternative. In a highly unusual three-way deal struck in April, New Zealand beef originally destined for the United Kingdom market was sold in the United States so that 60 million pounds of Canadian beef could replace it in Great Britain. It was a temporary respite only, and one which fell below U.S. exports by 70 to 80 per cent. As Canadian cattlemen well knew, any current attempt to renew the British market on a permanent basis would inevitably prove as futile in 1952 as it had been since 1913, despite the persistent federal attempts to demonstrate otherwise. The following quote from an industry expert in July 1952 is reminiscent of similar utterances in 1923, 1931 or 1945 when referring to a then-restricted American market: "… it is the most desirable market and all other arrangements may be only temporary expedients to tide over the present threat of a glut on the Canadian market."[47]

The foot and mouth outbreak brought into focus another long-standing source of concern to the Canadian livestock, and in particular the cattle industry. For years Canada's per capita meat consumption had lagged well behind other producing countries like Argentina, Australia, or New Zealand. Although the reasons were linked more with production costs than dietary preferences, the lag in domestic meat consumption had bothered the industry since the late 1920s. When Burns and Co. told Canadian producers in an open letter in July 1952 that "the richest and most comfortable nation in the world is that which eats the most meat," it was displaying more encouraging rhetoric than a conviction born of experience.[48] After a surge in meat consumption during the war, a more familiar pattern had begun to exert itself by 1950. Per capita consumption was below 50 lb. in 1951 and lower than it had been in depression-ridden 1933. Also, the detriments of a meat diet had been long paraded to the public through school textbooks and popular magazines. Not surprisingly, then, the threat of disease, especially a notorious and infectious type like foot and mouth, could scarcely be described as a public confidence builder for increased meat consumption.

The fact that a relatively restricted outbreak of foot and mouth disease could so easily cripple national and international trade in livestock led to some soul-searching on the part of both government and industry. The latter felt that future outbreaks should be treated on a regional rather than a national basis, and that with proper coordination with the United States at the government level, no major trade disruptions need transpire. It was naive thinking, and one doubtless influenced by the American admiration for the Canadian eradication programme as well as the co-operation that had been extended by U.S. animal health officials. It did, however, fly in the face of previous livestock-related trade practices between the two countries. That the United States would risk enraging its own producers by deferring to an industry in another country which supplied about 2 per cent of its cattle marketings was inconceivable. Certainly those cattlemen who could remember their bitter and unsuccessful tariff battles of the 1920s would agree.

The federal government was more practical. Almost as soon as the outbreak ended it established new and closer disease monitoring practices. One was the removal of foot and mouth experimentation from Hull to a safer location on an island in the St Lawrence River. The second was the establishment of an Animal Health Emergency Organization to deal with any emergent disease-related problem within the livestock industry. Organized on three levels, federal, provincial, and local, and under the direction of the Veterinary Director General, the programme involved veterinarians and volunteer participants in the very early identification of diseases, as well as follow-up and treatment procedures. Also, it was probably no coincidence that the U.S. House of Representatives appropriated $10 million in May 1952 to establish a foot and mouth experimental laboratory on Long Island. With an annual budget of $3–4 million, a capacity for four hundred animals, and a staff of fifty scientists and 250 assistants, the new facility was expected to do much toward developing vaccines and more effective early control methods.

When measured against other disasters or even against outbreaks of the disease elsewhere, the foot and mouth epidemic in Saskatchewan was not a major catastrophe. It did, however, cost the Canadian taxpayer millions of dollars to eradicate it, and caused diminished revenues close to $100 million in lost export sales. It was estimated that the total loss in livestock values and the capital value of farms and ranches was somewhere between one and two billion dollars.[49] It is undeniable that the outbreak clearly demonstrated the Canadian ability to mobilize substantial resources in order to counter a national threat. More significantly, however, the presence of foot and mouth disease on Canadian soil shattered any preconceived notions about the country's imperviousness to global animal disease incursions. It can and did happen in Canada. In this sense it was fortunate that the disease broke out in an area where effective containment was possible. It is a sobering thought to ponder the economic and environmental implications of a foot and mouth outbreak in the ranching areas of central British Columbia, where rough terrain and the abundance of wild and susceptible ungulates would have made containment an expensively prohibitive and environmental nightmare. It could have been much worse.

How did foot and mouth disease come to Saskatchewan? Despite pains-taking efforts, the source of the outbreak was never fully ascertained. Canada's Chief Animal Pathologist, Dr. C. A. Mitchell, was convinced that the virus had not entered Canada through a live animal but had been transported in a settler's effects, possibly those of a European seasonal agricultural worker.[50] In fact, authorities originally thought that they had isolated the source in the person of Willi Brunjen, a German immigrant from Westphalia, where a foot and mouth outbreak had recently occurred. Bruntjen was located in Vancouver and taken to Hull for exhaustive testing of his clothes and belongings.[51] Eleven days of laboratory tests showed no trace of foot and mouth disease, and officials were forced to admit further that even if traces of the virus had been discovered on Bruntjen there was no possible way its origin could be ascertained. And so the original source of the outbreak slipped into apocrypha, with the most popular explanation blaming an anonymous recently-arrived migrant unwittingly feeding infected meat to hogs.

NOTES

1   In 1952 alone, Denmark had 3,071 outbreaks and France, 304,901. See Frank Manolson, "Research on Foot and Mouth," *Canadian Cattlemen* (December 1952).

2   Apparently, however, Britain had 112 outbreaks of foot and mouth disease in 1952.

3   *The Western Producer* (Saskatoon), March 6, 1952.

4   Canada, *Sessional Papers*, No. 12, 1887, "Department of Agriculture Annual Report."

5   The number of Canadian cattle entering the United States annually was influenced by the latter's tariff. For example, high tariff and low prices inhibited Canadian cattle movements to the United States during the periods 1921–24 and 1930–35.

6   Western Stock Growers Association Papers, Box 3, file folder 13.

7   For greater detail in this fascinating interlude in imperial relations, see Max Foran, "The Politics of Animal Health: The British Embargo on Canadian Cattle, 1892–1932," *Prairie Forum* 23, no. 1 (1998): 3–17.

8   J. G. Rutherford, "Foot and Mouth Disease, 1902," on microfiche, University of Calgary.

9   For good information see E. E. Ballantyne, "Foot and Mouth Disease," *Canadian Cattlemen* (April 1952).

10 *Outbreak Alert: Foot and Mouth Disease*, Agriculture Canada, Publication 1792/E, 1985.

11 Manolson, "Research on Foot and Mouth."

12 Incubation periods may last up to fifteen days or as little as twenty-four hours.

13 *The Western Producer*, March 6, 1952.

14 Ibid.

15 Ibid.

16 *The Western Producer*, April 3, 1952.

17 "With Your Editor," *Canadian Cattlemen* (March 1952).

18 Rutherford, "Foot and Mouth Disease, 1902."

19 T. Childs, "Foot and Mouth Disease in Saskatchewan," *Canadian Cattlemen* (April 1952).

20 *The Western Producer*, February 28, 1952.

21 *The Western Producer*, May 22, 1952.

22 Gardiner enjoyed special powers during the fight against the disease and could make personal decisions which normally would have needed government approval.

23 The Province of Saskatchewan freed veterinarians who were currently working on projects to eliminate Bangs Disease to help the foot and mouth control program.

24 For information on the quarantine area and restrictions, see Norman Wright, "Foot and Mouth Disease and Infectious Stomatitis," *Canadian Cattlemen* (April 1952).

25 See "Battle Against Foot and Mouth Disease"; and "Co-ordinated Team Fights

Foot and Mouth Disease," *The Western Producer*, March 13 and 20, 1952.

26   Childs, "Foot and Mouth Disease in Saskatchewan."

27   *The Western Producer*, May 8, 1952.

28   "Compensation Bill Passed," *The Western Producer*, March 13, 1952.

29   "Foot and Mouth Disease Hits Livestock in Southern Saskatchewan," *The Western Producer*, February 28, 1952.

30   "New Restrictions in Quarantine Area," *The Western Producer*, March 13, 1952.

31   "With Your Editor," *Canadian Cattlemen* (September 1952).

32   The New England States traditionally looked to Canada for much of their feed, which of course had been unavailable to them since the embargo.

33   Mexico had tried to augment domestic meat consumption by building several packing plants after 1946 when she had been embargoed for foot and mouth disease. Not wanting to jeopardize this investment, the Mexican government was initially cautious about resuming large scale cattle shipments to the United States.

34   It should be noted that Canadian livestock were still subject to a modified tariff under the Geneva Agreement of 1947. It was not horrendous, though, and quotas were unlimited.

35   "U.S. Embargo is Clarified," *The Western Producer*, March 6, 1952.

36   "From the Nation's Capital," *Canadian Cattlemen* (June 1952).

37   "Provincial Ban Disrupts Trade," and "Embargo on Livestock Meats Disrupts Normal Marketings," *The Western Producer*, March 6 and 13, 1952.

38   *The Western Producer*, March 13, 1952.

39   An earlier deal had been reached in March when a heavy run was setting in on hogs. See "Canada Packers Limited. Annual Report to Shareholders," *Canadian Cattlemen* (September 1952). With respect to the beef floor prices, Alberta producers maintained that it should have been set at $28.00 per cwt if the real impact of the embargo was to be factored in.

40   British Columbia removed its restrictions in late April and did not re-impose them when the outbreak at Weyburn was detected in early May. It took until early June for the other two provinces to follow suit.

41   *Canadian Cattlemen* (September 1952).

42   "Canada Packers Limited. Report to the Shareholders," *Canadian Cattlemen* (September 1952).

43   "From the Nation's Capital," *Canadian Cattlemen* (June 1952).

44   *The Western Producer*, May 22, 1952.

45   *The Western Producer*, May 8, 1952.

46   "Halt Entry of Farmers Where Cattle Disease Exists," *The Western Producer*, March 6, 1952.

47   *Canadian Cattlemen* (July 1952).

48   *Canadian Cattlemen* (July 1952).

49   *Canadian Cattlemen* (January 1953).

50   "Search Source of Infection," *The Western Producer*, February 28, 1952.

51   *The Western Producer*, March 6, 1952.

PUTTING DOWN ROOTS THE HISTORICAL ORIGINS OF THE ONGOING WEED DISASTER ON THE CANADIAN PRAIRIES

Clint Evans

"Disaster" is a term that normally conjures up images of sudden and dramatic events – events marked by chaotic movement, loud noises, loss of life, and destruction of property. Most are over in a matter of minutes, hours, or days and most are localized incidents that can be attributed to human error, to "acts of God," or to a combination of both. There are, however, some disasters that display few of these features but which are potentially even more catastrophic: ecological disasters. A product of human interactions with the environment over time, ecological disasters have contributed to the loss of countless organisms and priceless biodiversity. They have led to the collapse of entire ecosystems and the civilizations that depended on them and, if current predictions are to be believed, they may even threaten our very existence as a species. The latter is not likely to happen any time soon but, even in a relatively young country such as Canada, ecological disruptions are already having a profound impact on our society.

Consider, for example, the impact of foreign weeds on prairie agriculture. Inadvertently introduced to the Prairies by early settlers, imported weeds soon became the most important class of crop pests in the region. By the time of World War I, weeds were dictating many farming practices and they had eclipsed "soil drifting in the spring, the ravages of the gopher [and] the not remote possibility of drought, hail, rust and early autumn frosts" as the number one production problem facing farmers on the western plains.[1] Two decades later, cultivation to control weeds was implicated as one of the main factors behind the Dust Bowl.[2] By then, weed infestations were essentially out of control. Farm profits were declining, the cost of rehabilitating weed-infested land was beyond the reach of most farmers, and many leading agriculturists believed that the days of extensive grain monoculture were numbered.[3]

Extensive grain farming has survived thanks largely to the post-war development of selective herbicides such as 2,4-D, but the weed disaster has not been averted – it has merely been prolonged. Weeds continue to cause greater economic losses in Canada today "than the combined losses produced by animal diseases, plant diseases, and insect pests."[4] The annual cost of controlling and not controlling these unwanted plants must run into billions of dollars on the Prairies alone, and grain farmers are now entirely dependent on herbicides for the success of their harvests.[5] Low grain prices combined with the cost of weed control are the major causes of the current prairie farm crisis, and nobody knows what the future may hold. Pesticide companies envision a future where crops are genetically engineered to withstand the ravages of broad-spectrum herbicides; farmers face the prospect of utter dependency on these companies for both chemicals and seed. If low grain prices continue, however, prairie farmers will not be able to afford the cost of these expensive inputs. They will then have to abandon extensive grain production altogether unless weeds miraculously disappear.

The seeds of the current weed disaster were literally sown by the earliest pioneers. Foreign weeds probably first arrived on the Prairies as contaminants of crop seeds during the fur trade era. By the early nineteenth century, gardening was flourishing around Hudson's Bay Company posts such as Cumberland House, and immigrant weeds were almost certainly flourishing there as well.[6] One particularly troublesome species, stinkweed (*Thlaspi arvense* L.), was said to have been "brought to the Prairies in the old fur-trading days."[7] A native of Western Europe, where it was called "La Violette" by the French and "pennycress" by the British, *T. arvense* came to be known as "French weed" in Manitoba because of its associations with French Canadians and the fur trade. A herbarium specimen of stinkweed was collected at Fort Garry in 1860, and in the early 1880s botanist John Macoun described it as "abundant in many parts of Quebec; scarce in Ontario; but a real pest in Manitoba and around all the Hudson Bay Co. Posts in the North-west Territory."[8]

The unusual success of stinkweed in Manitoba within a decade or so of the beginning of "fully-commercial agriculture" was an ominous portent of things to come.[9] Prairie farms provided an ideal environment for immigrant weeds to take root and multiply. Centuries of co-evolution with agriculture had beautifully adapted these plants to living under arable conditions, and they found the rich prairie soils much to their liking because of a lack of the predators, pathogens, and competitors that had naturally checked their populations back home. More importantly, prairie farms tended to be large, labour was scarce, and most farmers concentrated on the production of a single crop: King Wheat. The first two factors precluded careful cultivation; the last meant that farmers were not practising crop rotation, the most important "cultural" method for suppressing the growth of unwanted vegetation. Crop rotation was further discouraged by an absence of markets for other agricultural produce. When combined with a lack of seed-cleaning facilities, inexperienced farmers, and an open, wind-swept terrain, the results were unprecedented weed infestations that spread at unprecedented rates.

The rate at which foreign weeds established themselves and spread in Manitoba caught most observers off guard. The botanist John Macoun, for example, seems to have been blithely unaware of the potential for dis-aster when he wrote in 1882 that the soils of the Red River Valley were "practically inexhaustible" and that "bad husbandry has little effect on the crop for many years."[10] By the close of the decade, however, it had become clear that it was "time to look out for the noxious weeds that the carelessness and culpable neglect of past years have contributed very much to make a certain and unfailing crop for long years to come."[11] In 1889, the editor of the Nor'-West Farmer noted that the "prevalence" of weeds in many parts of the province "has become a question of some importance and the best means of exterminating and keeping clear of them is a problem which the farming community as a whole does not appear to understand."[12] A year later he reported that stinkweed "alone has for all practical purposes of cultivation lowered the value of the old river lands at least one half, often very much more."[13]

The situation in Manitoba had become positively alarming by the late 1890s. Stinkweed had spread to such an extent that "fears have been expressed that, in consequence, the cultivation of the land there may yet have to be abandoned on account of them."[14] Government offi-cials noted that "the peculiar greenish yellow colour of the unripe pods in infested crops in many parts of the province [were] at once attracting attention of travelers on the railway" and newspapers were describ-ing it as "the curse of Manitoba."[15] Even experts at the Dominion Experimental Farm at Brandon were finding "it impossible to clean the land from this pest as long as a grain crop is grown."[16]

Other weeds were also making their presence felt. Canada thistle (*Cirsium arvense* [L.] Scop.), the bane of the farmer's existence in Ontario, had long held "possession" of farms in the vicinity of old Fort Garry, and by the late 1880s it threatened "to pollute" the whole Red River Valley "if not checked."[17] Pigweed (probably lamb's-quarters, *Chenopodium album* L.) was even more widely distributed. In extreme cases, over 20 per cent of the "grain" harvested from individual farms consisted of the seeds of this prolific annual species, and during dry years it caused serious losses to inexperienced and expert farmers alike.[18] To make matters worse, farmers had to cope with the steady arrival of new weeds. Cow cockle (*Saponaria vaccaria* L.), for example, was effectively unknown in Manitoba prior to the early 1890s, and yet by 1896 it had spread throughout much of the province with its "pretty porcelain-pink flowers sometimes occurring in such numbers as to give a reddish tinge to many acres of crops."[19]

Manitoba was literally awash with immigrant weeds by the turn of the century. As one farmer observed, close to three decades of poor husbandry had left their mark on the land. The rich black soils were no longer considered inexhaustible, yields were declining, and in "the matter of noxious weeds, Manitoba is generally conceded to be the dirtiest province in the Dominion."[20] The root cause of this rapidly developing crisis was equally well known: "continuous wheat growing" or a "tendency to crop the land for all that can be got out of it, leaving posterity to shift for itself."[21] By the early 1900s the federal government, Manitoba's fledgling Department of Agriculture, and the farm press had launched a massive publicity campaign to draw attention to the scale of the problem. Unfortunately, there was no avoiding the inescapable fact that while the "question of weed destruction and control is the all but universal problem in Manitoba ... it helps nothing toward the mastery of the situation that grain-growing is the most popular branch of farming in this Province."[22]

Manitoba had passed its first anti-weed legislation in 1871, but in spite of rave reviews from outside observers, frequent amendments, and a growing army of officials charged with enforcing the law, it had become something of "a dead letter" by the 1890s.[23] S. A. Bedford, the first Superintendent of the Dominion Experimental Farm at Brandon, summed up the situation in 1905 when he stated that the eradication of weeds was ultimately the responsibility of the farmer: "You cannot clean farms by legislation."[24] A lack of markets for commodities other than wheat also meant that farmers were unable to clean their farms through crop rotation and the intensive cultivation normally associated with this practice. This left farmers little choice but to depend on a single technique – summer fallow – for keeping weed populations in check.

Summer fallowing had long been used in Western Europe for suppressing the growth of unwanted vegetation, and it provided adequate control of annual weeds when performed in combination with more complex rotations and preventative techniques such as sowing clean seed. The main drawback to summer fallowing was that it resulted in the loss of a crop from the land for one or more seasons. Consequently, it was primarily used as the first step in rehabilitating heavily infested fields or in situations where crop rotations were not practical. Summer fallowing was widely used in nineteenth century Ontario, but it truly came into its own on the large farms in the prairie West. As one Manitoba farmer remarked in 1899:

> There is no rotation of crops that I have heard of that can take the place successfully of summer-fallowing. Things are very different here from what they are in Ontario and in many other countries. There the farmer on fifty or a hundred acres has a piece of land in hay, some in pasture, some in wheat, oats and barley, and a considerable acreage in potatoes, turnips, and corn; then they may do without summer-fallowing; but when we consider that many of us have more summer-fallow than many an Eastern farmer has land altogether, it will be easily seen that while that system of rotation may do for the East, it is not adapted for this country.[25]

By the late 1890s summer fallowing had become central to most prairie farming operations, and it remained the farmer's basic defence against weeds until the advent of effective herbicides at the end of World War II.[26] Fields were usually fallowed every three to five years, during which time they were repeatedly ploughed and harrowed in order to promote the germination of weed seeds and to destroy the resulting vegetative growth. Over 15 per cent of all the cultivated acreage in Manitoba was under fallow in any given year during the late 1890s and the opening decade of the twentieth century.[27] Grain accounted for most of the rest while forage and row or "intertilled" crops represented a tiny fraction of the total (less than 3 per cent).

During the opening decades of the twentieth century it became clear that use of summer fallow alone was not able to stop weeds from multiplying and spreading. These were the years of the great settlement boom on the Prairies, and immigrant plants took advantage of inexperienced farmers to spread to the furthest limits of the agricultural frontier. The situation in Manitoba went from bad to worse. New weeds such as wild mustard (*Sinapsis arvensis* L.) continued to arrive with alarming regularity. Dubbed the "yellow peril" by the editor of the *Farmers' Advocate*, wild mustard was still considered uncommon in the west as late as 1898, but within a few years it had become a serious problem throughout the province.[28] The rapid spread of another annual species, wild oats (*Avena fatua* L.), led the same editor to reflect that the "proverbial trait in young men to sow wild oats, seems to have a parallel instance in young countries, and Manitoba is, unfortunately, no exception."[29]

A similar degree of light-heartedness cannot be found in the paper's editorials dealing with an even greater menace: perennial sow thistle (*Sonchus arvensis* L.). Slower to spread but virtually impossible to eradicate by summer fallowing and cultivation, perennial weeds such as *Sonchus arvensis* gradually eclipsed stinkweed and other annuals as Manitoba's worst weeds. Perennial sow thistle was first observed near Cartwright in 1895, and by the start of the next decade this robust cousin of the common dandelion had established a secure foothold in the Red River District.[30] A few years later farmers were reporting that they were "up against it.... The sow thistle must be kept down or we will soon be run off our farms."[31] Their plight led to predictions that the "spread of sow thistle through any district will, sooner or later, usher in the day of systematic 'mixed farming' or usher out the man who is determined to live on straight grain growing," and by the end of World War I sow thistle was being described as "the worst weed that has been introduced into the Province of Manitoba ... the spread of the weed is rapid and seemingly out of control."[32] Estimates of crop losses from sow thistle on heavily infested lands ranged from 50 to 75 per cent and farmers were being warned that in the worst hit districts "loan companies have refused to loan money on farm lands."[33]

When the losses from all weeds were taken into account, the situation looked even bleaker. In 1905, an estimated $20 million worth of grain was rejected by elevator operators in Manitoba because of smut or contamination by weed seeds.[34] This figure, of course, does not begin to measure the true loss due to weeds as it does not include the cost of reduced crop yields, cultivation, and land lying fallow. As early as 1908, reports began to circulate "that many farms in older Manitoba were being abandoned on account of weeds," and by the early 1930s many believed that Manitoba's grain industry had reached much the same crossroad that had marked the end of wheat production in Ontario some forty to fifty years earlier.[35] There was one major difference, however, as *Country Guide* columnist R. D. Colquette explained:

> The causes lie not so much in reduced fertility as they did in Ontario, though the soil of Manitoba is not performing as it once did.... More serious is the weed problem. For this indictment can be laid at the door of the pioneer farmer of Manitoba, that he found a piece of territory free from weeds, and he left it as foul a piece of land as the sun shines on in the course of 24 hours. The weeds are all imported. There isn't a weed worth sneezing at that is native to this western country. The day is past in over seven-eighths of Manitoba when the farmer can plow his summerfallow, give it a couple of strokes with the spring-tooth and get away with it. I know some men who last summer were over their land from five to seven times, and over the thistle patches ten to a dozen times. There isn't a crop that can be grown in these latitudes that will stand such a charge as that injected into its cost of production. Here, then, you have them in the order of their importance: weeds, rust and reduced fertility. They are skimming enough of the cream of the agricultural income of the province to leave the milk a little too thin to sustain a prosperous agriculture.[36]

Manitoba agriculturalists may have been the first to confront a weedy disaster of unprecedented magnitude, but by the early 1930s their counterparts in Saskatchewan and Alberta were struggling with a problem that was every bit as severe. The story of the introduction and spread of immigrant weeds in Saskatchewan and Alberta is, in many ways, even more dramatic than in Manitoba. Large-scale agricultural settlement did not truly begin in the North-West Territories until the late 1890s – some twenty years after the start of the wheat boom in Manitoba – by which time the Territories had noxious weed legislation in place and farmers were in a position to benefit from the experience of farmers in Manitoba.[37] Summer fallowing had been an approved practice on the Prairies for close to a decade and the farm press and government agencies were fully alert to the danger of weeds.

As was the case earlier in Manitoba, the first pioneers encountered little trouble from weeds. William Fream, a highly respected agricultural expert from England, for example, reported that apart from a problem with native prairie rose in one newly broken field, the only weed he observed during his September 1884 visit to the massive Bell Farm near Indian Head was "one solitary plant of corn-cockle, and that, too, in a field of wheat measuring seven miles from corner to corner."[38] Similarly, 161 respondents to a 1954 questionnaire sent to Saskatchewan old-timers (pioneers who had settled in the province before 1914) stressed the "absence in the early years of settlement of a later hazard, the noxious weeds."[39]

The first clear indication that the Territories were on the verge of a disaster similar to that already gripping Manitoba was an outbreak in the early 1890s of tumble mustard (*Sisymbrium altissumum* L.) near Indian Head. Capable of rolling before the wind in the same manner as native tumble weeds, tumble mustard was thought to have been introduced to the Prairies from eastern Europe during the construction of the Canadian Pacific Railway.[40] In 1889 it began to attract the attention of farmers near Indian Head, and soon some fields were so thick with the annual weed that when a mower or other "conveyance was driven into them, it caused them to sway to and fro even several rods distance."[41] Angus MacKay, Superintendent of the Dominion Experimental Farm at Indian Head and the man often described as the "father" of summer fallowing on the Prairies, sounded the alarm in the fall of 1893 when he wrote:

> We were almost buried yesterday with a neighbour's tumble weed [tumble mustard]. A hurricane blew all day from the north-west, and the edge of the field adjoining the farm is

now 10 feet deep with this weed. The trees are full and fences cannot be seen for bank [*sic*] of weeds. The result of yesterday's blow will be to give us many extra days' work next summer, for millions of seeds have been left on the farm. Looking between here and the town while the weeds were galloping along, the prairie seemed like the ocean with a big storm blowing.[42]

McKay's prediction came true the following year. Fields that had been free of tumble mustard in 1893 were now "a mass of flower, and the plants were so thick that every foot was covered with the weed. The tree plots, garden plots and all places of that nature were filled up, and continued so till the frost came."[43] By 1899 tumble mustard had spread east from Indian Head to Manitoba and west to the interior of British Columbia, and it remains a common, aggressive weed throughout the region to this day.[44]

From the 1890s onward, the weedy invasion of Saskatchewan and Alberta followed the pattern established in Manitoba. Annuals such as tumble mustard were the first to arrive. Blown on the wind, hiding in inadequately cleaned seed, and imported in forage from Manitoba, they took advantage of the settlement boom and inexperienced farmers to consolidate their hold on the rest of the Prairies. One species in particular, wild oats, spread so rapidly that by the time many farmers became aware of its presence in their grain fields they were already facing a catastrophe.

The Committee on Lands for the federal Commission of Conservation began collecting statistics on wild oats in 1910. That year 100 per cent of farmers surveyed in Manitoba, 71 per cent in Saskatchewan, and only 3 per cent in Alberta reported the presence of wild oats.[45] Three years later the number of infested farms in Alberta had jumped to 83 per cent, clear evidence that wild oats "was traveling westward with a vengeance."[46] By then the situation had deteriorated to such an extent that on "many farms they [wild oats] leave little if any profit for the farmer."[47] The 1912 report of the Committee on Lands observes that in a few places in the West (probably Manitoba) farms were actually "being abandoned owing to wild oats and the stink weed."[48] By the late 1920s such reports had almost become common-place. Wheat crops in the vicinity of Saskatoon were said to be reduced

The weed problem portrayed as a natural disaster. Source: *Nor'-West Farmer*, May 20, 1929.

by "one half or more by the presence of wild oats" and in other parts of the province farmers were "nearly all bankrupt ... the principal cause of our decline is weeds. Wild oats."[49]

Unfortunately for farmers in Saskatchewan and Alberta, *Avena fatua* was not the only weed vying for control of their land on the eve of the Great Depression. A decade earlier the Alberta Department of Agriculture had noted:

> The condition of the Province with respect to weeds today is much different from what it was nine or ten years ago. In the early days such weeds as Stink Weed, Tumbling Mustard, Russian Thistle, Ball Mustard and Wild Oats, which are classified as either annuals or winter annuals, were the only weeds that appeared to trouble the farmers in their agricultural duties. Today these weeds are of secondary consideration, while such weeds as Canada Thistle, Perennial Sow Thistle, Couch Grass and Poverty Weed have come to the front. True they did not come as quickly as the first weeds

but neither will they disappear as quickly because they are vicious perennial plants.[50]

These "vicious perennial plants" slowly consolidated their hold over Saskatchewan and Alberta, and they were still "on the increase" in the late 1930s despite massive government publicity and education campaigns and the best efforts of farmers.[51]

A growing proportion of farmers now had access to new technology in the form of gasoline tractors and improved tillage implements such as discs, rod weeders, and the famous Noble blade.[52] The impact of these new technologies, however, appears to have been slight. Gasoline tractors first became popular in the late 1920s but, as one Alberta District Agriculturalist predicted, the "tendency towards power farming, we think, will not assist in weed control ... efficient cultivation and weed control is inseparable from a diversified system of farming."[53] True to the expert's prediction, power farming did not revolutionize the war on weeds. Tractors slowly replaced horses as the main source of power on prairie farms over the next two decades, but farmers generally used them to farm more land rather than to farm their land more intensively.[54] In the words of one *Country Guide* columnist: "Nowadays, especially in areas such as western Canada, where land is comparatively cheap and where one man would like to take care of as much crop as he can see, many bad annual and perennial weeds are becoming established in spite of all our fine power equipment."[55] Innovations in tillage implements also failed to give farmers the upper hand in their struggle with unwanted vegetation for the simple reason that they were designed to make the practice of summer fallowing less harmful rather than to replace summer fallowing as the primary defence against weeds.

These new implements were developed in response to a growing awareness of the shortcomings of traditional fallowing techniques. Traditional methods rapidly depleted the soil's organic matter content and left vast expanses of prairie soil bare and exposed to the wind. To make matters worse, many farmers worked the top layer of soil on their fallows to a fine tilth in the belief that pulverizing the soil reduced evaporative water loss. The "dust mulch theory" was widely promoted by advocates of improved dry farming techniques from the late 1890s onwards. By the late 1920s, however, the theory had been "exploded" by scientific testing which showed that a dust mulch was no "more

Joint Dairy and Weed Meeting and Demonstration, Seven Persons, Alberta, 1907. Courtesy: Glenbow Archives NC 4-7c.

effective in conserving soil moisture than where the surface has been untouched."[56] Most farmers needed little convincing by then. A series of droughts during the war years and early 1920s convinced many that over-working fallows and summer fallowing in general offered little more than an open invitation for the soil to blow. Summer fallowing had become "a necessary evil" and soil drifting "caused mainly by too frequent fallowing" was now seen "as great a problem as moisture supply."[57]

The Dust Bowl of the 1930s punctuated the need for change. Designed to reduce soil drifting by preserving a layer of stubble and dead weeds on the surface of fallows, implements such as the Noble blade soon soared in popularity. Farmers began to practice a new technique variously known as "ploughless tillage," "stubble mulching," or "trash farming," and bare or black fallows gradually became a thing of the past. By the mid-1940s the prairie landscape had been transformed,

A Weed class at Olds Agricultural College 1920–21. Courtesy: Glenbow
Archives ND 3-934.

the threat of soil erosion was greatly reduced, and tillage methods had
undergone a revolution. The fallow-grain system of agriculture, however, still remained entrenched and weeds continued to benefit as a
result.

Fallowing as a method of weed control was no more effective in
1945 than it was in 1916, when a prominent Saskatchewan farm leader
and politician, W. R. Motherwell, observed: "It is true that fallowing
done properly and [at] the right time is a wonderful controlling factor
in weed growth, but our growing season is so short and the growth of
weed seeds in the fall to be killed by the following winter's frosts is so
very limited, that weeds are increasing in spite of fallowing every third
year according to the best known methods."[58] Similarly, the rise of
power farming and ploughless tillage simply reinforced the centrality

of fallowing in the "straight grain growing farming system" – a system that one editor of the *Nor'-West Farmer* described as "the best ally weeds have."[59]

Straight grain growing must have been a very good ally indeed, for by 1921 John Bracken, Principal of the Manitoba Agricultural College and soon to be Premier of Manitoba, estimated "that the weed crop of Saskatchewan costs her farmers $25,000,000 a year, and probably this item does not cost the average farmer in Saskatchewan more than it does the average one in either of the other Prairie Provinces."[60] Fourteen years later a member of the National Research Council's Associate Committee on Weed Control placed annual crop losses through weed competition alone at nearly $40 million for the three prairie provinces.[61] He added that the true cost of weeds would be many times higher as it also included factors such as the cost of cultivation, the loss of crops during fallow years, greatly added expenses in terms of harvesting, handling and seed cleaning, the cost of dockage or hauling an estimated 4,526 car loads of weed seed to the major grain terminals, and significant reductions in the market value of contaminated grain.[62]

Anecdotal evidence provides an even clearer picture of the scale of the disaster. In 1937, for example, another member of the Associate Committee on Weed Control lamented that the tide of weedy invasion had now reached the outer limits of the prairie agricultural frontier: the recently settled Peace River country. There, weeds such as wild oats and stinkweed had already become "serious and menacing," while others such as perennial sow thistle were present and destined to cause problems in the near future.[63] He added:

> Since the opening of colonization in the Canadian West, the settler has carried his weed problems with him. All too little attempt has been given to preventing him from fouling the new homestead with the weed filth of the old. In the gear of his machinery, the bowels of his animals, the feed sacks and fodder that he carries with him, is the seed of future trouble, and it multiplies fast. Thousands upon thousands of settlers driven out of Manitoba, Saskatchewan and Southern Alberta, by weeds, have blithely loaded up their second-hand machinery and other effects and headed north without cleaning the weeds out.[64]

Further to the south, in the older portions of the Prairies, agricultural experts were suggesting that the cost of eradicating perennial weeds was "often more than the value of the land itself."[65] Weed infestations had, in other words, "developed to such an extent that the farmer is unable to rehabilitate the land out of his own resources."[66] By the early 1940s, weed control represented "the largest cost required in producing crops," weeds had eclipsed drought, soil drifting, and insect pests as the "main factor in reducing crop yields" and, in the wetter portions of the Prairies, it was "conservatively estimated" that weeds were causing crop losses in the neighbourhood of 25 per cent.[67]

In 1955, H. E. Wood, Chairman of the Manitoba Weeds Commission, opened the 8th Western Canadian Weed Control Conference in Regina with the statement:

> That present-day farming in Western Canada should be confronted with a colossal weed problem, while unfortunate, was probably inevitable. In the 50-year period 1901–51 the number of farms established throughout the three Prairie Provinces increased by 4 ½ times, the cultivated acreage by nearly 13 times – 65,000,000 acres of virgin land coming under cultivation. Moreover this land has been cropped almost exclusively to small grains under what for a better term might be called extensive mechanized farming. Row crops and the seeding of grasses and legumes, basic in most countries to a sound agriculture and to checking the inroads of weeds, is not to this day practiced to any significant extent in Western Canada.[68]

Wood was speaking in an era of renewed optimism some ten years after the release of the first truly effective "selective" herbicide, 2,4-D, which, along with the bewildering array of equally potent herbicides that followed, revolutionized weed control on the Prairies so that by the early 1950s prairie farmers were using chemical weed killers "on a larger proportion of the crop land than any other comparable region of the world."[69] Herbicides remain one of the mainstays of grain production on the Prairies today, but they have not ended the war with weeds as early proponents predicted. They have instead become yet another prop for the grain-fallow system of farming that very nearly brought about its own destruction in the 1930s and 1940s.

Prairie soils continue to harbour vast reservoirs of dormant weed seeds, and noxious weeds still abound on poorly managed crop land, on the margins of fields, in ditches, along roadsides, and throughout urban areas. Weeds have suffered a setback but they are far from vanquished, and as soon as farmers ease off on their spraying, weeds return with a vengeance to reclaim the land they colonized during the first half of the twentieth century. Another way of looking at the situation is to say that weeds have found their niche. Unfortunately, as plant ecologist Don Gayton explains, this poses a serious problem because the "traditional chemical herbicide industry is based on ignorance of the ecological niche concept."[70] He continues: "These chemical 'silver bullets' kill undesirable plants all right, sometimes whole fields of them, but they do not destroy the niche. Unless other, more desirable plants are primed and ready to spring immediately into the empty niche, a new flush of weeds will simply occupy it again."

Gayton's observation underscores the point that the weed disaster has not disappeared, it has simply adopted a new guise. Direct crop losses no longer provide a reasonable measure of the disaster, although they remain significant. Rather, the true measure of the scale of the disaster today is the billions of dollars spent on the purchase and application of herbicides without which most prairie farm operations could not survive. This places a huge burden on the prairie economy and a crippling tax on farmers facing grain prices as low as in the 1930s. It also places a huge burden on the environment in the form of chemical residues, a loss of biodiversity and habitat, and potentially disastrous genetic transformations resulting from the unknown consequences of bioengineering and the development of herbicide resistance in weeds.

Like most other disasters, the one positive note to the weedy disaster on the Canadian Prairies is that it has considerable educational value. It demonstrates that our grasp of the relationship between people and the environment is far from complete and that modern society is still enmeshed in the "natural" world that surrounds it. Our ongoing struggle with weeds on the Prairies highlights the danger of seeking technological quick fixes to complex ecological problems; of seeking to cure the symptoms of a disease rather than the disease itself. It also reminds us that even seemingly minor ecological disasters have the potential to disrupt vital sectors of a nation's economy. Ecological disasters lack the drama of a bridge collapse, a tornado, or a catastrophic

Planes used for weed spraying, Drumheller area, 1951. Courtesy: Glenbow
Archives NA 4186-27.

---

flood, but their effects are often more far reaching and profound. They
have destroyed entire civilizations in the past and they have the potential
to do so again. Modern technology can shield us from the worst effects
over the short term, but without fundamental changes to the way in
which we interact with the environment, technological answers to
ecological problems simply pass the burden of seeking a solution on to
future generations. By then it may be too late.

NOTES

1 Saskatchewan, Department of Agriculture, *Annual Report*, 1918, 90.

2 E. S. Hopkins, "Weed Projects on the Dominion Experimental Farms in the Prairie Provinces," *Proceedings of the Associate Committee on Weeds* 5 (1939): 8.

3 Alberta, Department of Agriculture, *Annual Report*, 1940, 12.

4 Clarence Frankton and Gerald A. Mulligan, *Weeds of Canada* (Ottawa: Minister of Supply and Services Canada, 1993), 1.

5 In the first printing of *Weeds of Canada* (1955), the author estimated that the annual cost of controlling and not controlling weeds in Canada alone exceeded $500 million: Clarence Frankton, *Weeds of Canada* (Ottawa: Department of Agriculture, 1955), 1.

6 For a quick overview of fur trade era farming, see Lewis H. Thomas, "A History of Agriculture on the Prairies to 1914," *Prairie Forum* 1, no.1 (1976): 31–35.

7 Manitoba, Advisory Board, *Our Canadian Prairies* (Toronto: C. Blackett Robinson, 1895), 88.

8 K. F. Best and G. I. McIntyre, "The Biology of Canadian Weeds. 9. *Thlaspi arvense* L.," *Canadian Journal of Plant Science* 55 (1975): 283; John Macoun, *Catalogue of Canadian Plants*, Part 1, *Polypetalae* (Montreal: Dawson Brothers, 1883), 56.

9 Stanley N. Murray, "A History of Agriculture in the Valley of the Red River of the North, 1812 to 1920," Ph.D. dissertation, University of Wisconsin, 1963, 153.

10 John Macoun, *Manitoba and the Great North-West* (Guelph: World Publishing Co., 1882), 197, 201.

11 *Nor'-West Farmer* (Winnipeg), July 1890, 548.

12 Ibid., August 1889, 215.

13 Ibid., August 1890, 576.

14 Thomas Shaw, *Weeds, and How to Eradicate Them* (Toronto: J. E. Bryant, 1893), 7.

15 Canada, Department of Agriculture, Dominion Experimental Farms, *Annual Report*, 1895, 181; *Regina Leader*, July 13, 1899.

16 Dominion Experimental Farms, *Annual Report*, 1895, 181.

17 *Nor'-West Farmer*, September 1888, 237.

18 *Nor'-West Farmer*, January 1886, 12–13; Dominion Experimental Farms, *Annual Report*, 1894, 333–34.

19 Dominion Experimental Farms, *Annual Report*, 1896, 275.

20 *Nor'-West Farmer*, April 1898, 169.

21 *Nor'-West Farmer*, May 1897, 154; Manitoba, Department of Agriculture, *Annual Report*, 1900, unpaginated introduction. For an excellent summary of the weed problem arising from the late nineteenth century wheat boom in Manitoba, see Murray, "History of Agriculture in the Valley of the Red River," 253–76.

22 *Farmers' Advocate–Western Edition* (Winnipeg), March 8, 1905, 329.

23   *Nor'-West Farmer*, August 1890, 576.

24   *Farmers' Advocate–Western Edition*, December 6, 1905, 1767.

25   Ibid., July 5, 1899, 346.

26   For a useful summary of the history of summer fallow on the Prairies, see Thomas D. Isern, "The Discer: Tillage for the Canadian Plains," *Agricultural History* 62, no. 2 (1988): 80–81.

27   Joseph H. Ellis, *The Ministry of Agriculture in Manitoba, 1870–1970* (Winnipeg: Manitoba Department of Agriculture, 1970), 143–44.

28   *Farmers' Advocate–Western Edition*, May 25, 1904, 756; Dominion Experimental Farms, *Annual Report*, 1899, 187. Wild mustard remains a common problem in cultivated fields throughout the Prairies: G. A. Mulligan and L. G. Bailey, "The Biology of Canadian Weeds. 8. *Sinapsis arvensis* L," *Canadian Journal of Plant Science* 55 (1975): 175.

29   *Farmers' Advocate–Western Edition*, November 8, 1905, 1620.

30   Manitoba, Department of Agriculture and Immigration, *Noxious Weeds and How to Destroy Them* (Winnipeg: Department of Agriculture and Immigration, 1897), 22; *Farmers' Advocate–Western Edition*, October 6, 1902, 721, and June 15, 1904, 866.

31   *Nor'-West Farmer*, March 20, 1911, 347.

32   Ibid., March 20, 1911, 347, and June 5, 1919, 831.

33   Ibid., June 5, 1919, 831.

34   *Farmers' Advocate–Western Edition*, December 6, 1905, 1,767.

35   Ibid., September 9, 1908, 1213.

36   *Country Guide*, April 1931, 3.

37   *Revised Ordinances of the North-West Territories*, 1888, Chapter 21.

38   William Fream, *Canadian Agriculture–Part I. The Prairie* (London: William Clowes & Son, 1885), 66.

39   Allan R. Turner, "Pioneer Farming Experiences," *Saskatchewan History* 8, no.1 (1955): 53.

40   Shaw, *Weeds, and How to Eradicate Them*, 186.

41   Ibid.

42   Dominion Experimental Farms, *Annual Report*, 1893, 192.

43   Ibid., 1894, 225.

44   Ibid., 1899, 185.

45   J. W. Robertson, "Work of the Committee of Lands," *Report of the Canadian Commission of Conservation* 3 (1912): 61.

46   F. C. Nunnick, "Agricultural Surveys and Illustration Farms," *Report of the Canadian Commission of Conservation* 6 (1915): 213.

47   F. C. Nunnick, "Agricultural Survey, 1912," *Report of the Canadian Commission of Conservation* 4 (1913): 157.

48   Robertson, "Work of the Committee of Lands," 62.

49   *Country Guide*, November 1, 1928, 7, and October 1, 1929, 5.

50   Alberta, Department of Agriculture, *Annual Report*, 1918, 105.

51   Ibid., 1939, 12.

52   See Isern, "The Discer," 80–87, for a succinct history of the evolution of tillage

on the Prairies. Readers desiring further information on the development of the Noble blade can consult Grant MacEwan's *Charles Noble: Guardian of the Soil* (Saskatoon: Western Producer Books, 1983).

53 Alberta, Department of Agriculture, *Annual Report*, 1929, 68.

54 Over 60 per cent of prairie farmers were still using horses in 1941. A decade later almost all commercial farms were operating with tractors: Robert E. Ankli, H. Dan Helsberg, and John Herd Thompson, "The Adoption of the Gasoline Tractor in Western Canada," *Canadian Papers in Rural History* 2 (1980): 33, 35.

55 *Country Guide*, July 1944, 20.

56 *Grain Growers' Guide*, September 15, 1927, 15.

57 F. H. Reed, "The Summer-Fallow," *Dominion Experimental Farms Sesonable Hints – Prairie Edition* 22 (March 1922): 10–11.

58 *Nor'-West Farmer*, January 20, 1916, 60A.

59 Ibid., February 5, 1924, 96.

60 John Bracken, *Dry Farming in Western Canada* (Winnipeg: The Grain Growers' Guide, 1921), 361.

61 E. S. Hopkins, "Losses Caused by Weeds," *Proceedings of the Associate Committee on Weeds* 2 (1936): 31.

62 Ibid., 33–34.

63 W. D. Albright, "The Weed Problems of the Peace," *Proceedings of the Associate Committee on Weeds* 3 (1937): 12.

64 Ibid., 13.

65 E. S. Hopkins, "Weed Projects on the Dominion Experimental Farms in the Prairie Provinces," *Proceedings of the Associate Committee on Weeds* 5 (1939): 10.

66 Alberta, Department of Agriculture, *Annual Report*, 1940, 12.

67 Alberta, Department of Agriculture, Field Crops Branch, *Weeds of Alberta: Their Identification and Control* (Edmonton: Department of Agriculture, 1941), 2.

68 H. E. Wood, "Fifty Years of Weed Control in Western Canada," *Proceedings of the Western Canadian Weed Control Conference* 8 (1955): 2.

69 J. Stan Rowe and Robert T. Coupland, "Vegetation of the Canadian Plains," *Prairie Forum* 9 (1984): 245.

70 Don Gayton, *The Wheatgrass Mechanism: Science and the Imagination in the Western Canadian Landscape* (Saskatoon: Fifth House, 1990), 47.

THE TOLL OF TWO IMAGES[1]

David C. Jones

INTRODUCTION

The images that humanity generates from deep beliefs are not just images. They are creations of the mind that manifest themselves in reality and that bear their own inherent consequences. And sometimes, they come in sequences that magnify a sense of harm, even devastation.

Doubtless, the worst of Palliser's dry Triangle is in southeastern Alberta, embraced by a line linking Lethbridge, Bassano, and Hanna to the Montana and Saskatchewan borders on the south and east. Extending into Saskatchewan, this arid core, as one observer said, is still the size of an empire.[2]

Throughout its history, this empire was conceived variously, and each conception manifested itself on the landscape. Two conceptions, or images, are of lasting import – that of the agricultural settlement boom and that of the post-World War I settlement disaster.

In the last generation of the nineteenth century, this dry belt region was held over for ranchers. Tragically, the policy was overturned after 1896, and sodbusters were allowed to inhabit the area and oust the cowmen.

Following ruin on the parched fields that did exist between 1889 and 1896, the climate seemed to change. In the twelve years before 1897, only four registered precipitation over ten inches, and the average was 8.9 inches. In the ensuing five years, the precipitation ranged from 15.9 inches to a whopping 22.3, and the average was 19.5 inches.[3] Not only had nature smiled, but also the government had changed. In the hands of the domineering Clifford Sifton, the lasting wariness of the Department of the Interior about the wisdom of inhabiting the dry areas reached its nadir. The new orthodoxy was reflected in a Sifton promotional cartoon which said plainly: "There is no desert country."[4]

In early 1905, Frank Oliver, the vituperative editor of *The Edmonton Bulletin*, succeeded Sifton, and the dry belt came under the plough.

After an inauspicious start in the extensive homesteading of the region from 1908 to 1912, the farmers harvested two mammoth crops in 1915 and 1916, and then disaster struck. From 1917 to 1926, smitten by a plague of evils, headed by drought, they were all but wiped out.

THE GARDEN

There were at least four levels to the image creation of the ebullient settlement period – the promotion from outside, from agricultural experts, from the burgeoning regional centre of Medicine Hat, and from the new tributary towns. At each level, the flavour and fervour of the new image strengthened.

"Magician's wand never produced more striking effect than did the placing of a pair of steel rails over the stretch of prairies southwest from Saskatoon," Frank Oliver's pamphleteers blared in *Canada West: The Last Best West* in 1910. In 1908 there were no towns, no elevators, and few wheat fields. A year later, there were seven villages, three incorporated, and dozens of elevators. "Nearly all of the wheat went No. 1 Northern, bringing 80 cents or more a bushel." Thousands of acres yielded thirty or more bushels each, and everyone made money.[5] Once the land of great ranches, southwestern Saskatchewan and southern Alberta, the CPR chirped in, were now the domain of King Wheat.[6] "The one thing about Alberta," a reporter nodded, "is that the rain falls when it is needed."[7] Southern Alberta, said a writer for the *Canada West Magazine* was "a land blessed of the Gods – a land over which bending nature ever smiles and into whose cradle she emptied her golden horn."[8]

In time, a dominant investor in Alberta lands would be the Associated Mortgage Investors of Rochester, New York. Focusing over-long on the fabled drylands, Kingman Nott Robins, the company's treasurer, stressed: "It is a matter of common observation that the rainfall in a newly settled prairie country increases with settlement, cultivation and tree planting." He cited Professor Agassiz, who theorized that the building of railroads and settlements invariably disturbed the electrical currents in the winds and brought the inevitable – rain. "As the area of cultivated land is increased," Robins advised, "the danger from early frosts diminishes."

Zeroing in on the demands of his own capitalistic profession, Robins noted that there were no irksome usury laws to limit the dictates of the lender, no messy dower rights to confuse the title, no irritating exemptions or prior liens to impair the sanctity of the first mortgage, no maddening hitches or delays in foreclosure proceedings should the borrower submerge.[9]

A second source of the promotion originated from the outside too, from the professional agriculturists bent on eradicating any remaining fears about the desert. Between 1908 and 1910, the "wisdom" of Professor H. W. Campbell was trumpeted across the dry areas. The basic assumption of most dry farm mentors was that one had only to know how to conserve moisture, and no crop would fail.[10] A supporting assumption was that a crop could be assured if enough moisture resided in the soil at seeding. "Summer rain is not an essential to the raising of good crops," said the aptly named Professor Surface, "nor is drought necessarily fatal to high productiveness of the soil."[11]

A third phase of promotion originated from the major regional centre in the heart of the dry belt – Medicine Hat. John T. Hall, the ultimate booster, directed the city department of publicity. Aided by the local *News*, Hall pumped out several pamphlets, the most notable of which related the observations of Rudyard Kipling after his famous visit to the gas city "with all hell for a basement." Kipling was the poet of the empire, and on his trip through western Canada in 1907, he was the master of hyperbole.

Waxing evocative, Kipling described his tour of a show farm near the Hat one warm Sunday. The owner, M. A. Zahnizer, had taken his fold to church, but the visitors nonetheless "slipped through the gates and reached the silent spic and span house, with its trim barn, and a vast mound of copper-coloured wheat, piled in the sun between two mounds of golden chaff. Everyone thumbed a sample of it and passed judgment," said Kipling, " – it must have been worth a few hundred golden sovereigns as it lay out on the veldt – and we sat around on the farm machinery, and in the hush that a shut up house always imposes, we seemed to hear the lavish earth getting ready for new harvests."

At a picnic, the locals talked of the projects in the town that was "born lucky." Deeply impressed, Kipling saw them as the strong arm of resolve that would refashion the countryside a hundred miles around. Together they talked of projects first in their own city and then in the numerous tributary towns. Said Kipling, referring to a wonder of the ancient world, "I felt as though I were assisting at the planning of Nineveh."[12]

As settlers poured into the dry belt, they and those immediately following were subjected to another round of intense boosterism, centring on the mushrooming trade hubs which were the new towns. Augmented by the enthusiasm, the frenzied occupation of the territory west of the Hat, near Carlstadt, took place. Mammoth farm outfits rolled their steam engines out onto the flats and began working some of the largest acreages – between twelve and twenty sections – in the history of the West.[13]

Local newspapers appeared, irregularly at first, until 1911, when the *Carlstadt Progress* began. Editor Calvin Goss was a classic extension of the propaganda of the Department of the Interior, the railways, the mortgage interests, and the large regional papers. He reckoned fortunes could be made in real estate in the new towns between the Hat and Calgary. "Three years ago Bassano was nothing," he wrote in early 1912, "two years ago Brooks was nothing; but look at them today. This year is Carlstadt's."[14]

"Watch Carlstadt, the Star of the Prairie," Goss intoned.[15] "Let us have faith in this Land of Opportunity, and make it the garden and granary of the world."[16]

By 1916 the growth of the outlying Alberta dry belt was astounding. The population had bounded from 4,415 in 1901 to 101,679; the number of farms had increased from roughly 2,000 to 30,883; and the area in crop had spread from 80,700 acres to 2,690,230 acres in 1915.[17] No less than 45 per cent of all farms in the province in 1916 were in the dry areas, and the wheat crop came to 75 per cent of the provincial total. In 1900 the dry belt wheat harvest had been a drop in the bucket; by 1915 it stood at 50 million bushels.[18]

THE WASTELAND

Following the bumper crops of 1915 and 1916, the desert reasserted itself, and in the worst-hit sub-regions, there was not a crop of consequence until 1927. No fewer than five commissions of inquiry examined the wreck centred on Carlstadt, renamed Alderson during the war. Wandering through the ruined civilization of southern Alberta, beginning in 1921, pollsters counted bodies – those still abiding and those gone. By 1921, losses were terrible, over the next three years, horrendous. From 1921 to 1926, the best off of 138 townships across 3.2 million acres lost 55 per cent of its population. Part-way through the debacle, in late 1924, Russell and Snelson, officials of the Department of the Interior, examined these same townships – one that had 65 resident farmers six or seven years before and now 11; another 55, now 14; another 40, now 2; another 93, now 10; another, 12, now none.[19]

Long before the Great Depression, most of the damage had been done. Farm abandonment in Alberta would never be as severe as it had been in 1926. In fact, in the vast region south of the Red Deer River where it turns sharply eastward – all the way south to Montana and east to Saskatchewan – abandonments in 1926 were over *four times* those of 1936.[20]

Another way of measuring the calamity is by standing it against the legendary evacuation of southern Saskatchewan in the Great Depression. With roughly twice as many operating farms in Saskatchewan in 1936 as in Alberta in 1926, the latter had very nearly as many abandonments. In fact, the three Alberta dry belt census divisions had more abandonments in 1926 than the five most heavily vacated Saskatchewan census divisions in 1936.[21]

Only in the northern third of the Alberta dry belt were abandonments worse in the thirties than the twenties. In Census Division 5, between the southern shores of brackish Lake Sullivan, north of Hanna, and the Red Deer River to the south, there were over 3,700 abandonments by 1936 – two and a half times that in the worst-pummelled census division in all Saskatchewan.[22]

By 1925 rural municipalities were in debt to their eyeballs and were owed a fortune in seed grain and relief extended to farmers now gone. In towns like Alderson, Suffield, Grassy Lake, Youngstown, Jenner, Retlaw, and Richdale, the local treasury was open and bare, village lots were vacant by the hundred, owners wishing to repudiate ownership, and weary reeves and village secretaries not knowing who was still on the tax rolls, where they all were, or even how to find out.[23]

Apt testimonies of the devastation and loss overswept the land. One observer in 1926 reported the whole of the Goose Lake line from Hanna to Oyen along with the line south to Steveville, sown to tumbling mustard, Russian thistle and Russian pigweed.[24]

There was a valuable demonstration by the government show farms that year – Robert Montgomery of Sunnynook abandoned his altogether.[25]

Like hundreds of others, James Roebuck of Whitla was finished. "My money and children have gone, and now my wife says this is her last year on this desert," he told Premier Greenfield in 1922. "Six years in succession without a crop, and only two crops since the country was settled up in 1909. I think that has been a fair trial."[26]

"We'll all be buried down here in this dry belt if we wait for the government to get us out," said H.G.C. east of Lethbridge. "And parts of it are pretty desolate places to be buried in."[27]

Annie Edwards had grown up in the Lomond district. Recalling the blazing summers and scorching winds from 1916 to 1923, she wrote, "these long, hard years absorbed all the pioneer spirit from most of us. I can still see my mother out beside the house leaning against the siding, which was rough for want of paint and looking out across the sand-covered stubble, weeping in silent desperation."[28]

"Any man of ordinary intelligence who has been on the job here since 1917," Thomas Lannan of Ingebrigt, near the Great Sand Hills, told Saskatchewan authorities, "knows what this country is and knows that it will never do for farming."[29] Dust storms rose in fury, facilitated by the destruction of the natural grasslands, topsoil took to the winds, and blowouts denuded thousands of acres.

William G. Wenbourne of Taber summarized the general experience when he labelled himself "a man that came, saw and has not conquered."[30] Speaking of the farm, one lady in this region said, "I swear it was the last thing God ever made, and he didn't finish it."[31]

Between 1934 and 1938, Lois Valli lived south of decaying Alderson. Life in the barrens on the edge of Alberta's first Special Area amounted to captivity.

Using labels off flour sacks and bits of paper, Valli began to write poetry. Her whole world was a great "Empty Land":

There it lies, stretched flat under the bleached sky, looking
    innocent, almost benign.
Burnt light brown, no color relief in the scorched miles of empti-
    ness.

It holds my gaze, though it offers no solace for my need.
The silence is broken only by the whirr of the windmill.
When the snowy blanket covers all, it appears to sleep in the sun.
During the long dark hours the mercury shrinks, timbers groan and
   crack.
The feeble glow of the oil lamp casts a meager ring of comfort on
   the table,
The dim unfriendliness reigns beyond.
When the savage wind lashes the sand or the snow, all bend, turn,
   seek shelter.
Some find it and those who do not are swept away like leaves.
None dare defy such power.
Why must man pit his silly feeble wit against its elemental strength?
Why am I in this merciless place?
The windmill is the only reply I hear. [32]

Silence oppressed her, and depression gripped her, and she fought a
mortal battle for her own self-respect. In "Nine Bar Ranch – 1935,"
she penned:

December, and dark comes early
Loneliness fills my heart,
I think of my friends and parents,
We are many miles apart.
I busily tend to the fire,
The men will expect a hot meal,
But my mind is not on the cooking.
I can't stifle the sadness I feel.
I am not alone in this ranch house.
My husband and children are near
But now I hear no more music,
That's over for me now I fear.
No piano for me to play on.
My fingers are roughened and sore.
What music is the choir singing?
I want to play for them once more.
But I know those times are over.
The crew expects to be fed.

Above: Drybelt Boomers England and England, Railway Avenue and Broadway Street in Carlstadt (later renamed Alderson), c. 1911. Courtesy: Medicine Hat Archives P3519-24.

Below: Ruins at the very same site, 1996. Courtesy: David Jones.

I must concentrate on the present
From now till I go to bed.[33]

Eight miles from doomed Alderson, she could hear the silk trains roaring through on the main line of the CPR. Bearing raw, Oriental silk which deteriorated rapidly, they tore from Vancouver to Fort William fifteen hours faster than the speediest passenger train. En route to eastern markets, their precious cargo had priority over all other rail traffic. Said Lois, "They didn't stop, and they went at a great fast rate, and they whistled frequently. It almost tore my heart out to have to stand there to hear that train going. And there I was – no way to get away, and I was going crazy there almost by myself."[34]

It is hard to capture how far Alderson and its agricultural hinterland had fallen, but one incident in one family symbolized it well.

In spring 1938, Ace Palmer of the Dominion Experimental Station in Lethbridge asked Tracy Anderson, fresh from high school, to supervise some crested wheat grass seeding experiments in the badly eroded dustlands of the southeast. The assignment required living with selected farm families.

East of Alderson, near Bowell, Anderson stayed with a Scandinavian couple who appeared elderly to his youthful eyes. The haystack for the horses was Russian thistle, not unusual, for the thistle if green made passable forage. One supper-time, they discussed the hardships imposed by soil drifting, drought, and depression.

The woman invited him to their food cellar dug into the basement. Through a trap door, they crawled into an earthen compartment, the walls of which were lined with shelves of preserves.

She fingered a dozen quart jars on one level, smiled, and stated: "They ate our crops. We had to eat them."

The jars were filled with pickled grasshoppers.[35]

THE TOLL

The rape of the drylands by promoters and ploughmen alike led to the desecration and despoliation of an empire. Some of it had been unintentional, much of it unforeseen, but what humanity had done here was to ruin eight to ten million acres, to incur unprecedented debt, to exact unparalleled agony, and to so cripple an environment that its only use could be seen as a perpetual wasteland.

There is a correlation between the material and spiritual value attached to any piece of land. If the land is seen as a field of former wrongs and failings, as a theatre of maladjustment and mistreatment, a repository of painful memories, so shall it be. It will attract its own essence in ever-greater concentration and can actually become host to even vaster desolation.

Retreating on every front early in World War II, Winston Churchill determined to stop German landing forces in England with poisonous gas, if necessary.[36] The decision affected Canada.

In 1941, the Canadian government, abetted by Edmonton, expropriated the survivors northeast of Alderson in a two-thou-sand-square-kilometre area known as the Suffield Block. The Block became a chemical warfare base, later euphemistically called Defence Research Establishment Suffield (DRES). Naturally, a shroud of secrecy descended over the compound, lifted occasionally by revelations, some startling, many disturbing.

Suffield's first field experiment was with cadmium. Mixed with explosives, it produced a fume, insidious and odourless, much like any smoke, save that victims could not tell for a day that their lungs were destroyed. On the commandeered dustlands, experimenters fired twenty-five-pound shells, cadmium-laced. At one hundred yards and at three hundred yards from impact, two lines of rats waited in cages.[37]

Later, researchers tested special incendiary bombs, "improved" with cadmium and meant to slay enemy firefighters. In the Suffield burst chamber stood goats. No sooner were they frightened than they were mortally wounded. As their lungs transformed into furlongs of fibrous connective tissue, one expired in two minutes, and four, somewhat less efficiently, in five minutes.[38]

Soon after arriving, scientists conducted open-air tests with deadly botulism. One-twelfth of an ounce, authorities guessed, was enough to kill the entire population of Canada.[39]

Canadian scientists discovered "Compound Z," a derivative of fluorine gas which was three or four times as lethal as phosgene and which killed mice instantly. Said one impressed experimenter, "the damn things just laid down and died." Many field trials were conducted at Suffield.[40]

Above: This abandoned farm in southeast Alberta in 1937 showed just how wrong the early optimists had been. Courtesy: Glenbow Archives 2223-7.

Below: Wheat crops like this one in Suffield in 1915 reinforced the belief that the short grass country was ideal for agriculture. Courtesy: Glenbow Archives NA 2003-40.

As John Bryden notes, Canada actually led in human experiments with toxic agents.[41] Sometimes we are not given enough credit internationally.

The military greatly fancied mustard gas. So they directed two thousand volunteers into the fields and dropped a mustard gas bomb on them. They didn't think the effects would be serious, but burns on some were massive.[42]

George Richardson was one of those told to disrobe and don mustard-contaminated uniforms. "It was a nice day, nothing unusual about it," said he, "... until the middle of the next night. I woke up covered with blisters. They were on my rear end, my private parts. All over."

Once a mustard bomb failed to drop, and when the plane landed, a young electrician tried to disentangle it. "But it blew up," said Richardson. "The gas blew right into his skin, and his leg had to be amputated." He died later.

"What I saw was pathetic," said Richardson. "People were scarred, some were left half blind. Others had terrible coughs."[43]

Another time, thirty troopers meandered into a field wearing white capes and respirators, and a crop duster sprayed choking phosgene gas on them.[44]

Almost incomprehensibly, these guinea pig posts were coveted, at least at first. Said one soldier, "Mostly, it was done to get out of the monotony of day-to-day training in the regiment, and to get a week off at home – that was like utopia."[45]

In the infirmary, utopia was hell. Those with eyes seared and lids crusted shut "were unusually silent, depressed and introspective at the height of the eye effects," said a report.[46] Doubtless some sensed the degree to which their choice had reflected so profound a disrespect for themselves.

A generation after the tests began in 1941–42, thirteen volunteers received $2 extra a day to have diluted measures of the deadly nerve agent Sarin sprayed into their eyes. Traumatized, their pupils contracted to pinholes, and radiant prairie sunlight appeared as dusk and dusk as night.[47]

A fortune was spent on thousands of laboratory animals – mice, rats, guinea pigs, horses, cattle, sheep, goats, dogs, monkeys.[48] The animal experiments were often similar: find some devastating agent

– corroding, poisonous, lethal – which might be applied by or to an opponent; immerse some being down the chain of creation (including man) into the agent; then record the terrible effects, noting nuances occasioned by different dosages and applications.

Experimenters shot sheep in the hind legs with poison bullets at close quarters, and the gentle beasts died in thirty minutes. At two hundred yards, the bullets tore through flesh all right, but the impact was less, and they failed to release their balm.[49]

Sometimes attention focused on countermeasures. Experimenters would hypothesize concerning an antidote, then test if it forestalled horrific pain, crippling injury, or worse, in animals. If it failed, they would repeat the process in variation, making judgments about expected levels of discomfort, disability, and death, in humans.

Scientists became interested in the nerve gas antidote HI-6. They tried some low dosages on expectant mothers, rats, and rabbits, and several offspring were born with "ghastly deformities" – some without brains, without legs; others without jaws, or with orifices misplaced.[50]

In 1990, a representative of the Alberta Society for the Prevention of Cruelty to Animals visited the Suffield facility and complained that, given the guidelines on animal care of the Canada Council, the cages of a dozen Rhesus monkeys were 25 per cent undersized. For some reason the project was cancelled, though the simians in their own way perhaps preferred the small accommodations to the experiments they were slated for.[51]

In 1994, officials decided to evict the herds of wild horses on the Block. Descended from strays released when the last farmers were deported in 1941, these animals had miraculously survived winter and war for half a century. But authorities had recently created a preserve, and the horses were disturbing the delicate ecological balance – a disturbance admittedly mild considering that wrought by tanks, mortars, and bombs.

The irony halted nothing. As the horses were herded away, the recuperative power of nature sagged, and the life force of the stricken region ebbed again.[52]

The uses to which an area may be put are directly related to humanity's treatment of the area heretofore. If the short grasslands had been misused and abused until all around was ruin, if the land was then seen as unloving and unforgiving, destroying happiness and hope, if it persistently conjured up trauma and tragedy – then, if it should call into being an installation such as the Suffield experimental warfare base, who should wonder?

Regarding the deadly work of the Suffield base, there is at certain times only the ugliest of response to the ugliest of challenge. This is not a vindication, but a statement of fact.

The toll of the two dominant images was inherent within them. Images are not just fanciful, artistic constructions of social scientists – they are first beliefs in the mind, then artifacts of reality. Concentrate on them, expect them, and they are born. By virtue of an incongruous, almost laughable contrast, the Edenic image of the settlement period intensified the wasteland image of the subsequent disaster. Nothing could be further from truth than to have called the region "Nineveh." Nothing could have disconcerted more than to have found the best experts so wrong. Errors in judgment of such inconceivable dimension always spawn cynicism. And once cynicism, caustic and collected, was added to the baleful brew of beliefs about the region, inspiration vanished.

Deep, terminal cynicism is a condition of near lifelessness – it is the massive power of the mind turned against itself, focusing on its own false hopes, its own stupidity; it is futilitarian in outlook, despairing in action. And it represents a state in the mind that perfectly replicated the state of the grasslands, that mirrored the inert, barren, and abandoned landscape, particle by particle. The spirit of each was poisoned, polluted, pockmarked, shelled, and cratered – silenced and subdued.

As for our extrication from this sadness, in large measure, it is the human consequences of the error-ridden use of a natural resource that alert us to the need for conservation of that resource. The degree of regret is proportionate to the impulse for reform and the dedication to renewal. It is a ravaged spirit that finally draws attention to itself, to its own need for life and love. However distant or tardy, the final harvestof the flagrant abuse of humans, beasts, or grasslands is inevitably progress.

NOTES

1   Two-thirds of this essay appears in various chapters of D. C. Jones, *Empire of Dust – Settling and Abandoning the Prairie Dry Belt* (Edmonton: University of Alberta Press, 1987), and D. C. Jones, *Feasting on Misfortune – Journeys of the Human Spirit in Alberta's Past* (Edmonton: University of Alberta Press, 1998). An earlier version of the essay was presented to the International Grasslands Conference, Regina, Saskatchewan, 1991. The sections "The Toll" and "Conclusion" have never appeared in print. A new issue of *Empire of Dust*, with a new preface, was published by the University of Calgary Press (2002).

2   W. R. Babington to W. Harvey, December 19, 1920, Saskatchewan Department of Agriculture, Deputy Minister's Papers, xxiii.i, Saskatchewan Archives Board.

3   David C. Jones, *Empire of Dust – Settling and Abandoning the Prairie Dry Belt* (Calgary: University of Calgary Press, 2002), 19.

4   *Canada: The Granary of the World* (Ottawa: Department of the Interior, 1903).

5   *Canada West: The Last Best West* (Ottawa: Minister of the Interior, 1910), 17.

6   Canadian Pacific Railway, *Western Canada* (1909), 27.

7   J. D. "Taber Will Double Wheat Yield," *Calgary Herald*, July 23, 1908, 1.

8   "The Warm Chinook in Sunny Alberta," *Medicine Hat News* (hereafter cited as *MH News*), March 19, 1908, 6.

9   Kingman Nott Robins, *The Province of Alberta* (Rochester, N.Y., 1910), 13, 17, 15, 28–30, 38–39.

10   See W. MacDonald, *Dry Farming: Its Principles and Practice* (New York: Century, 1911); T. Shaw, *Dry-Land Farming* (St. Paul: Pioneer, 1911); E. R. Parsons, *Parsons on Dry Farming* (Aberdeen, S.D.: Dakota Farmer, 1913); J. A. Widtsoe, *Dry-Farming: A System of Agriculture* (New York: Macmillan, 1911, 1920).

11   "Summer Rains are Not Needed," *MH News*, September 16, 1909, 9.

12   "Kipling Visited Medicine Hat," *MH News*, October 1907.

13   Interview of Nels Anderson by David C. Jones, May 24, 1984, Brooks, Alberta.

14   "Climate and Resources," *Carlstadt Progress*, February 22, 1912.

15   "See Carlstadt," *Carlstadt Progress*, February 29, 1912.

16   Editorial, *Carlstadt Progress*, March 7, 1912.

17   *Prairie Census*, 1936, 840–67; *Prairie Census*, 1916, 288–90, 292–95. The number of farms calculated include all of Bow River, Lethbridge, Macleod, and Medicine Hat districts; one-quarter of Red Deer and Battle River districts; and one-third of Calgary East district.

18   *Prairie Census*, 1916, 292.

19   David C. Jones, *"We'll All Be Buried Down Here" – The Prairie Dryland Disaster, 1917–1926* (Calgary: Historical Society of Alberta, 1986), 136–37.

20   *Prairie Census*, 1936, 722; *Prairie Census*, 1926, 702.

21   Ibid.

22   *Prairie Census*, 1936, 722, 1174.

23   Jones, *Buried*, 131.

24   Ibid., 143.

25   Jones, *Empire*, 146.

26   Ibid., 204.

27   Ibid., 205.

28   Ibid., 204.

29   Ibid., 205.

30   Ibid., 86.

31   Interview of Mrs. Leah Slater by Arlene Cooper, Medicine Hat, Alberta, September 30, 1984.

32   Lois Valli, "Empty Land," in *Prairie Wool* (St. Joseph, Illinois: L & L Printing, 1991), 9.

33   Lois Valli, "Nine Bar Ranch – 1935," *Prairie Wool*, 45.

34   Interview of Lois Valli by David C. Jones, Brooks, Alberta, July 11, 1989, in author's possession. For Lois's recovery from this despair, see Jones, *Feasting on Misfortune*, 67–71, 258–59.

35   Tracy Anderson to David C. Jones, November 23, 1989, in author's possession.

36   John Bryden, *Deadly Allies: Canada's Secret War, 1937–1947* (Toronto: McClelland & Stewart, 1989), 60–61.

37   Ibid., 62.

38   Ibid., 217.

39   Richard Helm, "DRES Confirms Tests of Deadly Toxic Agent," *Medicine Hat Daily News* (hereafter cited as *MHD News*), August 21, 1980; *Medicine Hat News* clippings (hereafter cited as clippings).

40   Bryden, *Deadly Allies*, 64–65.

41   Ibid., 166.

42   "Mustard Gas Tales Televised," *MHD News*, September 26, 1989; clippings.

43   Wendy Dudley, "Vet Has Mustard Scars," *Calgary Herald*, February 13, 1991, A1.

44   Denise Helm, "NDP Knew of Gas Testing – ex-Researcher," *MHD News*, September 21, 1988, clippings.

45   Denise Helm, "Harmless Tests, Says Hat Doctor," *MHD News*, September 26, 1988; clippings.

46   Bryden, *Deadly Allies*, 170.

47   Helm, "NDP Knew...."

48   Peter Hays, "'Silly' Test Suggestion Rejected," *MHD News*, September 15, 1989; clippings; Bryden, *Deadly Allies*, 167.

49   Bryden, *Deadly Allies*, 216.

50   Paul Strickland, "Antidote Shakes Nerves," *MHD News*, January 30, 1986; clippings.

51   Paul Melnychuk, "Monkeys to Leave in Weeks," *MHD News*, December 15, 1990; clippings.

52   "Horses ran – but they couldn't hide," *Calgary Herald*, January 26, 1994, A1.

FLOODING IN THE RED RIVER VALLEY OF THE NORTH

J. M. Bumsted

The drainage basins of the Red and Assiniboine Rivers represent two of the regions of North American most susceptible to regular springtime flooding. The Red River flows from about 550 miles south of Winnipeg to Lake Winnipeg, draining an area of 48,000 square miles, only 8,640 of which are in Canada. The Assiniboine River rises in southeastern Saskatchewan about 650 miles west of Winnipeg. It flows to the Forks in Winnipeg, where it meets the Red River. The Assiniboine drains a region of 63,000 square miles, all of which is in Canada.

The Red River flows across the bed of an ancient glacial lake into which it has not managed to cut deep channels. The shallowness of the channels of both the Red and Assiniboine Rivers, combined with the surrounding flat topography, means that when excess water overflows the banks of these rivers, it spreads quickly across the surrounding area. The relative absence of winter precipitation has prevented flood danger from becoming an annual occurrence. The Red River also flows north, which means that springtime flows, often originating in the United States, run into ice blockages on their way to Lake Winnipeg and Hudson Bay. Over the years, removal of the ice has proved easier than rerouting of the excess water.[1]

From time to time. weather conditions have combined with topography to produce major inundations on both sides of the forty-ninth parallel. Those major floods do not necessarily occur in the same year in the United States and Canada. Data on flood elevations on the Canadian side are reasonably accurate since 1826. They indicate that the worst Canadian floods have occurred in 1776, 1826, 1852, 1861, 1916, 1950, 1979, and 1997. On the American side, where records began only in 1873, major flooding came in 1882–3, 1893, 1897, 1916, 1947–8, 1950, 1952, 1965–6, 1969, 1975, 1978–9, 1989, and 1997. The greatest recorded American flood occurred in 1897. The cost of flood damage has constantly increased in both countries as development persists within the flood plain area.

For Manitoba, the conditions for extreme flooding include – usually over several years – heavy snowfalls, late melts, and quick runoffs, often exacerbated by substantial spring moisture.[2] In Manitoba, cyclical periods of wet and dry weather within historical times have occurred in alternation but not in symmetry. Thus three of the highest floods in history occurred between 1826 and 1861, while the period between 1916 and 1948 (the "Dust Bowl" years) was extremely dry. The average period of time between major floods has been 18.4 years, but there is no discernible pattern. The notion that the incidence of flooding has increased in recent years because of changing land use patterns and man-made interventions is a controversial one.

In any event, when the waters do overflow their banks in the valleys of southeastern Manitoba, they create a species of "disaster" quite different from those experienced by most people around the world. Most natural disasters – flash floods, fires, earthquakes, hurricanes, tornadoes, even blizzards – happen extremely suddenly without giving much warning. Many people die because they cannot get out of the way, while the survivors can do nothing but clean up the mess. Manitoba has flash floods, but Red River flooding – on one of the world's major flood plains – is different. It gives weeks of warning, so evacuation is possible. Loss of life is therefore low, and there is some opportunity, even encouragement, for people to attempt to hold back the water with earthen dikes and sandbags. The result has been a cliff-hanging situation that can extend for weeks while the water inexorably rises. Such an event is very capable of exploitation by the modern media, which is drawn to the drama like moths to a flame.

Before 1950, the residents of the river valleys of southeastern Manitoba could do little except to accept stoically whatever Nature unleashed. Flooding was an Act of God and no human attempted to interfere in His divine plan. Everyone met the rising waters on equal terms. All that mattered was the elevation of property and the height of the water. Beginning in 1950, however, people in the valleys – led by their governments – became involved in various schemes of disaster mitigation. They threw up temporary dikes. They planned and ultimately built permanent structures which contained or diverted the water. They began to assist flood victims with both private and public funds.

After 1950, two parallel developments occurred which could be plotted on separate curves. One was an increase in the incidence and extent of flooding. The other was a rise in the level of human expectation for protection and assistance. These two rising curves would finally meet in the spring of 1997.

1. FLOODING BEFORE 1950

The Red River Valley was extremely fertile and easy to farm. But one drawback more unpredictable than a capricious climate and periodic invasions by insect pests was its potential for serious springtime flooding. The first devastating flood in the post-settlement Red River basin came in 1826, just at the point when Lord Selkirk's settlement was beginning to prosper. But an exceptionally severe winter, with heavy snowpacks, was followed by a sudden thaw at the end of April. By May 3 the water was overflowing the banks of the Red, still held in restraint by ice. When the ice gave way around 2 p.m. on May 5, a wave of water carried away everything in its path. Not until May 22 did the waters begin to recede.[3] According to later engineering calculations, the flood of 1826 would have created a water flow of 225,000 cubic feet per second, a maximum elevation in feet at the Forks of 764.5 and an elevation in feet above city datum (ice level) at James Avenue of 37.3.[4]

Loss of life was surprisingly light given the rise of the waters as much as forty feet above ice level and the production of a lake seventeen miles wide extending from Pembina to Lake Winnipeg. Damage to property was extensive but loss of life was light. Nevertheless, despite the fears of the settlement's leaders, Red River sprang back to life very quickly. Crops recovered and the 1826 harvest may even have been better than average. The most important result of the flood was to drive off to the United States most of the European settlers (Swiss and Germans) who lived along the river's banks, many of whom had been unhappy for years.[5] An entire ethnic component of the settlement virtually disappeared overnight. The remaining settlers soon resumed the occupation of low-lying riverfront, and no serious efforts at flood protection were undertaken. The 1826 flood was taken to be an unusual occurrence.

The next serious flood did not occur in Red River until 1852. The water did not crest as high or remain quite as long as in 1826. Later calculations were that the maximum discharge of the 1852 flood was 165,000 cubic feet per second, the maximum elevation at the Forks was

762.5 feet, and the elevation above datum at James Avenue was 35.2 feet.[6] The colony was better developed and settled, however. Hence, property damage was more extensive, particularly affecting certain poorer elements of the population who tended to cluster in the low-lying areas.[7] The loss of fencing was extremely serious. Red River experienced only one death, however. Flooding had become another one of life's many afflictions, to be added to drought, epidemic, grasshoppers, and prairie fires as threats to human happiness. Such disasters could only be endured. As one old Métis who had lost his home remarked, "C'est le bon Dieu qui afflige."[8]

Although twenty-six years had elapsed between the Great Flood of 1826 and the Flood of 1852, the Red River next overflowed its banks only nine years after the last inundation. By 1861 the settlement had its own newspaper, *The Nor'-Wester*, which covered the flood in some detail. A heavy snowpack was followed by a late thaw at the end of April. There was an ice jam, and some even believed that all flooding on the Red was caused by the ice. The *Nor'-Wester* reported, "At last came the winter *finale*. With a loud crash the ice was rent; and driving it before them in wild confusion, the liberated waters rushed down."[9] The 1958 royal commission estimated the maximum discharge of this flood at 125,000 cubic feet per second, the maximum elevation at the Forks at 760.5 feet, and the elevation above city datum at James Avenue of 32.3 feet.[10]

The rising waters drove all the settlers along the Red north of Upper Fort Garry as far as Middlechurch from their homes. No life was lost, however, and damage – apart from fencing – was confined chiefly to the usual layer of muddy slime on floors and walls of the inundated buildings. The flood did not prevent the mails from carrying on, and loss of livestock was low because experienced settlers led their animals to safety in advance of the water.[11]

Despite the experience of 1861 and its predecessor years, recent arrivals in the settlement began from 1862 to build on the low-lying land along the Red River the houses and shops that would become the village of Winnipeg.[12] Incorporated in 1873, Winnipeg flourished and even experienced a substantial boom in the early 1880s. The community was powerful enough to overcome a recommendation of 1874 by Sir Sandford Fleming that the CPR cross the Red twenty miles north of the Forks (at the site of the present town of Selkirk), where flooding was not a menace.[13] A metropolis was rapidly being constructed on a flood plain. The best way to deal with the risks from flooding was with denial. Weather conditions had been on the dry side for years, with winters less severe than earlier in the century. Prime building lots were being exchanged for thousands of dollars, and no one wanted to mention aloud the possibility of flooding. In 1881, construction was started in Armstrong's Point – an area along an oxbow in the Assiniboine River – of "Ravenscourt," a huge mansion built for Winnipeg merchant A.G.B. Bannatyne. This was an early example of the new breed of expensive riverfront housing that would eventually line the riverbanks both within and without the city.

The first threat from the Red River to the thriving little city came in 1882. Despite heavy snows and blizzards in March, the Manitoba *Free Press* assured new immigrants that the weather conditions were "unprecedented," adding, "It may be and probably will be, a long time before we are again troubled in the same way...."[14] Contemporaries advised that rash warnings of possible flooding would lower real estate prices and might well collapse the boom market in the city. As the waters rose in North Dakota, the *Free Press* editorialized, "there are the usual number of people who annually predict a flood, but it is tolerably safe to say that their predictions will not prove any more correct than usual."[15] The city was spared a serious disaster, and most of the problems were regarded as being the result of ice jams. Many Manitobans agreed with their newspaper that flooding was a feature of the past. The extent of human development along the river banks had not increased the danger, but somehow had mitigated it.

Another fifteen years passed by before flooding on the Red again became a serious business. There had been flash floods up the valley – Emerson had been inundated in 1893, for example – but nothing serious had occurred in a constantly developing Winnipeg. In 1897, however, the water rose rapidly in April, totally inundating both Emerson and Morris.[16] Damage was serious south of Winnipeg, and a relief expedition was sent by boat to dole out emergency supplies to the poor.[17] In the city, however, the rise of the river was an opportunity for sightseeing. The favourite point for crowds to gather was between the Pacific Bridge and the Norwood Bridge. Once again, the water in the city's rivers remained mainly in their channels.

As the nineteenth century came to a close, neither the concept of disaster relief nor that of flood protection had made much of an appearance. After 1897, the province continued with earlier efforts to drain the wetlands adjacent to the Red River south of Winnipeg. Provincially organized drainage districts reclaimed large amounts of land previously unusable by laying huge pipes that ran off the water into the Morris and Red Rivers. There was no concern that this water management might increase spring flooding. As a letter to the *Free Press* put it at the time of high water in 1904, "Time changes flood conditions – the flood phantom is becoming a tradition."[18]

The next major flood did not strike southeastern Manitoba until 1916. By this time the nation was at war, and the front pages of the local newspapers were dominated by military actions in Europe. Into a semi-hysterical public consciousness focused around the war, flood threats could only with difficulty make their way. But by 1916, Winnipeg was the "Chicago of the North," a city of 163,000 which was the third largest in Canada and the largest west of Toronto. The city had naturally expanded physically to accommodate population growth, and many new residential neighbourhoods had been developed on or near the city's two major rivers. The city had also increased its amenities, including the construction of sewer lines that drained – like the wetland pipes and ditches to the south – into the Red River.

Not until April 17 did the rapidly rising height of the Red to the south come to be taken seriously in the local newspapers. Most residents took the view that flood threats were, as usual, greatly exaggerated. Even as basements in the low-lying areas of the city began flooding, one Marine Department official assured the city that since the ice was out at Selkirk, there would be no flooding.[19] This time the crisis was more serious, however. As the water rose over the level of the sewer outlets, many houses experienced sewer backup. Realizing the danger, the street commissioner of Weston actually ordered the construction of a four-foot-high dike, one of the first in the province. On April 22 the river jumped its banks at River Avenue, and soon thousands of homes were under water. More than ten thousand residents were forced to leave their homes, hampered by crowds of sightseers, and the cleanup went on for weeks. Homeowners were not only expected to restore their properties at their own expense, but to pay the annual property taxes on them as well. Once the crest was passed, most of the city returned to its anxious watch over the battle casualties in Europe.

In the wake of the 1916 flood, a few voices of concern could finally be heard. In the April 1920 edition of *The Canadian Engineer*, Douglas McLean (of the Manitoba Drainage Commission) warned that unless flood protection measures were begun, the next flood in Winnipeg might cost millions of dollars.[20] McLean insisted that Winnipeg had been protected for more than half a century by a meteorological cycle of dry weather, which was probably soon to end. He denied that ice jams caused all the flooding, and warned that floods of early-nineteenth-century proportions could again strike the city. He advocated a combination of methods of flood control, including reservoirs, improvement of the river channel, diversion, and diking.

No money could be found before World War II to carry out McLean's recommendations, although money continued to be spent on construction of drainage ditches. By 1935, two million acres of land had been reclaimed in the province, and the debentures for drainage – which stood at nearly $7 million – had to be taken over by the province at the height of the Depression.[21] A few dikes were constructed, although most were not intended as flood control measures. Some work on diking along the Assiniboine River was conducted by the Prairie Farm Rehabilitation Agency (PFRA) during the Depression, but the coordination of water management was still well in the future. People would have to recognize the need for coordination in the face of multiple jurisdictions. In Manitoba, moreover, the lengthy struggle between the Dominion and the province over natural resources in 1930 had been ended with an agreement in 1930 by which Ottawa surrendered control over resources – including water. Ottawa's somewhat sulky attitude after 1930 was that resources were now totally a provincial responsibility.

The possibility of serious flooding had been virtually forgotten by 1948. Over thirty years had gone by without trouble from the rising water. In that year, however, a cold winter and heavy snowpack met a sudden rise in temperature in mid-April. As well as causing high water on the Red and Assiniboine, the weather conditions created flash flooding on many streams in the province. Railway and telegraph lines were washed away. Despite constantly rising water, the city engineer of Winnipeg refused to be panicked, apparently hoping that the reality would follow the wish. It did not. The situation to the south of the city became the worst since 1916. On April 20, Mayor Garnet Coulter advised the residents of Winnipeg that the city might be flooded within three days. Seed companies remained open on Sunday to provide linseed to homeowners seeking to plug their drains against sewer backup. St. Boniface began the emergency construction of a number of large earthen dikes, and Kingston Row and Kingston Crescent were already underwater.

As the waters crested in Emerson on April 25, the provincial cabinet finally met in emergency session to talk about flooding. It was possible to wait so long because the government had no plans for active intervention. It agreed to call in the Canadian military. That same day, an emergency meeting was called by the Red Cross Management Committee of representatives from all sectors affected by the flooding.[22] The meeting confirmed what everyone knew at the time, since the Red Cross was the principal agency expected to deal with disaster relief. The Red Cross would be responsible for the supervision of evacuation and other flood relief efforts. Perhaps to its surprise, the Manitoba chapter also found itself responsible for coordination of all flood activities as well. Agriculture Minister Jimmy Gardiner made it clear in the House of Commons that flooding was not a federal responsibility, but a provincial one. The province had insisted on gaining control of resources in 1930, Gardiner noted, and one of those resources was water.[23]

In truth, despite Gardiner's statements about provincial responsibility, flood-fighting was actually being carried on solely by the local municipalities and the victims, who were hastily throwing up dikes and sandbags from one end of metropolitan Winnipeg to the other. In an editorial on April 28, the *Winnipeg Tribune* sympathized with the flood victims, but held out no hope of aid beyond private charity and neighbourliness. The Winnipeg city council voted to ask for an investigation of flooding by the International Joint Commission, which supervised waterways shared by the United States and Canada. Many people, including the *Tribune*'s editorial writers, insisted that the IJC was the principal route to a long-term solution of the problem of flooding.[24] Meanwhile, the Greater Winnipeg Emergency Flood Relief Fund was formally opened on May 4 to provide a central focus for private charitable activity.[25]

The dikes did not always hold, but in 1948, mainly they did. On May 6, announcements were made from every church pulpit in the city of an appeal for emergency funds in the form of a door-to-door canvas. On May 14 the employees of Eaton's donated $2,000 to the Fund, and four days later fifteen hundred volunteer workers collected sixty thousand contribution envelopes across the city. The fund stood at $11,500, and grew a bit beyond that figure before it was wound up.

In fits and starts, the reaction to the 1948 emergency produced a number of breakthroughs with regard to flooding in the Red River Valley. Attempts to coordinate flood fighting and relief appeared for the first time in Manitoba history, albeit by a private agency rather than by government. A large-scale campaign for financial assistance, admittedly of a private rather than a public nature, was also begun. Equally important, there was the beginning of recognition of the importance of flood control. In 1949, Winnipeg city engineer W. D. Hurst addressed the civic bureau of the Winnipeg Chamber of Commerce on the subject of the "age-old flood threat."[26] He observed that the Americans had invested considerable money and energy in flood control, and discussed the various methods of flood control available to Manitoba. Dredging would be too expensive, but dikes would be temporarily effective to protect the lowest ground. Hurst also outlined a scheme of local protection which had been developed by the city engineering department and submitted to the city finance committee. The scheme called for a series of levees and flood walls, several small dikes, and the construction of eight pumping stations to prevent sewer backup. The plan would be initially rejected by the council as being too expensive, but was later in 1949 adopted in principle. Funding was not immediately available, however.

The 1948 emergency provided a bit of a wake-up call to Winnipeg and the communities of the Red River Valley. It was clear that serious flooding was an expensive and disruptive business, but not enough people were convinced that a recurrence of high water was an immediate danger. The flood of 1950 changed a good many minds.

2. THE 1950 FLOOD

By 1950, Winnipeg had gone nearly a century without major flood damage. In that year, however, a virtually defenceless city and valley faced high waters described at the time as "the most catastrophic ever seen in Canada."[27] At its height, the flood water covered an area seventy miles long and five to thirty miles wide, forcing the evacuation of most rural communities in the valley south of Winnipeg and coming within a few inches of producing the complete evacuation of the city's population. Except for a handful of dikes, Manitobans were utterly physically unprepared against the high water. No systematic flood control measures had been put in place north of the forty-ninth parallel. Moreover, none of the levels of government had given any serious thought to either flood-fighting or flood relief. The lack of advance preparedness, perhaps more than the height of the water, was what made the 1950 flood such a disaster.[28]

As had always been the case, the standard response to the threat of flooding in the spring of 1950 was to deny the possibility. But the professionals were worried from the beginning, particularly when the situation deteriorated south of the border.[29] By April 21 it was clear that flooding would be worse than in 1948, and volunteer organizations got on with the business of preparing for the impending disaster. Not until Friday, April 28, were Manitobans officially informed as to just how serious the situation had become, although anyone who read the daily newspapers could see the deteriorating direction in which things were moving. From early April to May 5, the growing menace of flood conditions had been handled as normal operations by the agencies of government, assisted by volunteer organizations coordinated by the Red Cross.[30] Premier Douglas Campbell refused to declare a state of emergency until a meeting late on the evening of May 5, which carried over into the early hours of May 6, told him that centralization of resources and a declaration of emergency was absolutely essential. The Canadian Army was called in, in accordance with an earlier agreement which called for the province to pay the costs of the intervention.[31] Brigadier R.E.A. Morton of the Canadian Army assumed control of flood operations.

Premier Campbell formally wrote Prime Minister St. Laurent on May 7 to request a declaration of national emergency and assurance of federal funds "commensurate with our needs."[32] In a cautious press release, Campbell warned Manitobans not to expect assistance with their private losses.[33] That same day, Prime Minister St. Laurent told the House of Commons that federal aid would be based on the principles of the Fraser River Valley Flood in British Columbia in 1948. Under this earlier arrangement, the Dominion had assumed 75 per cent of the cost of flood fighting and 50 per cent of the cost of immediate relief. Rehabilitation costs would be negotiated later.[34] Thus were the basic Dominion-provincial relationship and the basic principles of Canadian disaster relief well on their way to becoming institutionalized. Before the post-World War II period, Canadian disaster relief had not been based on any well understood policies, and had been both casual and chimerical in its operation. The assumption of any financial responsibility for rehabilitation by federal and provincial governments was part of a new public attitude which was broadly related to the growth of the "welfare state" in Canada, although it has received little attention from those who have studied this growth. In this respect, Canada was clearly ahead of the United States.

The declaration of a state of emergency energized the volunteer effort, as increasing numbers of Winnipeggers joined rural Manitobans in leaving their homes. In terms of neither loss of life nor extent of property damage was the Manitoba flood of 1950 a class-one disaster by international standards. On the other hand, the flood was great theatre. It was highly visual, full of human interest, and produced a series of cliff-hanging escalations in which the drama built over many weeks. The victims could be seen battling courageously against Mother Nature in very photogenic ways, particularly through the ubiquitous sandbagging of the dikes and the riverbanks. The world had time to hear of Manitoba's plight, and was able to follow its determined battle to hold back the rising waters.

One of the outstanding features of the 1950 flood was the creation of the Manitoba Flood Relief Fund, which collected the largest amount any peacetime Canadian charitable effort had ever raised in a single year.[35] A public target of $10 million, originally intended as an impossible goal, was very nearly reached. Money was raised all across Canada, the United States, and Great Britain. Although the extent of international contributions was impressive, over half the final sum recorded came from Manitobans who heeded the injunction to help others "hit harder" than themselves. Related to the extent to which Manitobans helped one another financially was the way they helped one another in other ways. Thousands of volunteers across the province fought the rising waters, and even more assisted with the cleanup. Thousands of houses had been flooded, often over the first floor level, and the biggest structural problems were caused by water, mud, and sewer backup.

Many appliances were damaged and much furniture was ruined. Victims did not know about the financial implications of cleanup until midsummer.

Along with the cleanup came a major effort of rehabilitation, financed in part by senior levels of government, which provided a precedent both for Manitoba and for Canada. On May 17 a joint federal-provincial commission was created to sort out the extent of flood damage and the amount of the federal contribution. It reported in early June, estimating the total costs of the flood at $26 million, which produced a federal grant of $12,500,000.[36] Manitoba complained that this greatly underestimated the real costs.[37] The main process of rehabilitation (never "compensation") ultimately took three forms: the provision of short-term necessities of life for flood victims, which was the responsibility of the Red Cross; the rebuilding or repairing of domestic and farm buildings, which was the responsibility of the senior governments; and the provision of domestic furnishings and furniture for flood victims, the responsibility of the Manitoba Flood Relief Fund. This rough division of responsibility among private charitable agencies, the senior governments, and the international flood fund would continue in existence in Manitoba throughout the remainder of the century, and would greatly influence disaster rehabilitation in other Canadian provinces as well.

The restoration of buildings was the responsibility of the Red River Valley Board, established on May 31. The RRVB appraised damage to domiciles to restore them "reasonably to the same condition as existed prior to the flood."[38] Very few flood victims had private insurance against flooding, and building rehabilitation was almost entirely in the hands of the RRVB, which inspected 2,371 premises in the Red River Valley and 9,342 buildings in greater Winnipeg. The Board did not operate on a replacement cost basis. Including garages and "unusual situations," a total of 11,499 cases were eventually processed by the RRVB, for a total outlay of $11,007,697, an average of $957 per case. While many victims were unhappy with their settlement, most understood that before 1950 they would been left completely to their own devices.[39]

The success of the Manitoba Flood Relief Fund in raising money made it possible for the fund to become increasingly generous in its assistance. The fund's Restoration Committee began modestly, but

The Lyndale Dike, Winnipeg Flood, 1950. Courtesy: Provincial Archives
of Manitoba, Floods 1950 3–1

gradually expanded the scope of its efforts. Initially the fund primarily
assisted the needy, but it was soon replacing all articles of household use
and ornament for all flood victims without insurance. Reimbursement
levels were raised to replacement cost, and the difference between insurance company awards and the appraised value of personal goods was
also made good. Further expansion added extraordinary expenses,
damage to private automobiles, and damage to residences not covered
by the RRVB. Although its efforts were most generous, by mid-August
the committee had paid off nearly all the domestic claims applicants
for less than $2 million. Despite the fund's best efforts to spend its
money, it was eventually left with a $2 million surplus which became a
"Canadian Disaster Relief Fund."[40] Although governments had become
involved, private humanitarianism was the difference between a very
limited rehabilitation and a fairly generous one. Nobody talked about
"compensation" for victims in 1950.

Winnipeg Street, 1950. Courtesy: Provincial Archives of Manitoba, Floods
1950 7

3. THE DEVELOPMENT OF A FLOOD CONTROL CULTURE

After the Great Flood of 1950, Manitoba began to take public steps to
protect against high waters. The first step was taken on July 8, 1950,
with the creation of the Greater Winnipeg Diking Board by the province, with the co-operation of the federal government and the flooded
municipalities.[41] The Board decided to extend to greater Winnipeg the
flood control measures approved by the city of Winnipeg in 1950 but
not yet implemented. The plan called for the construction of thirty miles
of elevated boulevards, high enough to protect against a 1948 flood but
not a 1950 one, and twenty-two pumping stations to lift sewage waste
over the boulevards and thus prevent sewage backup. The schemes created a good deal of controversy, led by citizens whose homes had been
excluded from the new diking arrangements, thus presaging continual
conflicts over the equity of flood protection.[42]

In 1953, an Act of Parliament established the Canadian Disaster
Relief Fund, with the remains of the 1950 Manitoba Flood Relief Fund
contributions as its base. That same year, a huge engineering report was

Emerson in 1950 Flood. Courtesy: Provincial Archives of Manitoba, Floods

released by federal engineers in the Canadian Department of Resources and Development.[43] This report concluded that the new diking system was inadequate, and pointed out that most proposed remedies would have little affect on a flood as big as in 1950. Only three major schemes were deemed worthy of support. These were: (1) a detention basin at Ste. Agathe formed by a twenty-five-mile dike across the Red River Valley south of greater Winnipeg; (2) a diversion of the Assiniboine River around Portage la Prairie with a seventeen-mile channel cut north to Lake Winnipeg; and (3) a Greater Winnipeg Floodway, a gigantic twenty-six-mile "ditch" to divert flood water at St. Norbert back into the Red River at St. Andrews, thus bypassing metropolitan Winnipeg completely. The combination of all three projects was essential to provide maximum protection, said the engineers, who had not attempted to cost their recommendations.

Nothing was done about the federal engineering report until 1956, when greater Winnipeg was again threatened with major flooding, averted only at the last minute.[44] Despite the crisis, there were reports that the Campbell government found the proposed flood protection schemes too expensive. Nevertheless, Manitoba appointed a Royal Commission on Cost-Benefit Analysis to investigate the situation. While the royal commission was conducting its research, the cost-conscious government of Douglas Campbell lost its majority, and the commission reported in December 1958 to a minority government headed by Duff Roblin.[45] The report recommended a floodway, the Portage diversion, and a storage reservoir near Russell, Manitoba. These measures would protect Winnipeg against a maximum flow of 169,000 cfs, or all but one flood every 160 years. It also recommended that ring dikes around the major communities south of Winnipeg were the most cost-effective protection for the upper valley. As well, the commission reported that a self-sustaining flood insurance programme was impracticable, but favoured the establishment of a permanent assistance fund. Another flood of 1950 proportions, predicted the commission, would cost the province over $114 million, and one six feet higher would cost nearly $1 billion.

The flood protection report was one of several policy documents – another was on health insurance – examined by the Roblin government over the winter of 1959–60. The government went to the polls in March 1959 with a platform of major activity. High on its shopping list was a floodway for the city of Winnipeg. Although the voters gave Roblin a decisive majority, the government dragged its heels on the floodway, chiefly because of the expense. Roblin made sure that he had full federal support from Prime Minister John Diefenbaker before proceeding.[46] When debate on the bill approving the proposed flood control measures finally occurred in March 1962, financial considerations were the important focal point, particularly the cost of borrowing for such a massive project.[47] Critics forced the government to concede that the measures being discussed would not protect against a flood of 1826 proportions, and would do nothing for the people living above St. Norbert on the Red River. Nevertheless, when the final vote was taken, both the Tory majority and the NDP voted in favour, and only the Liberal-Progressives against it. The province – and behind it the federal government – was committed to massive expenditures for flood protection.

A bulldozer turned the first sod on the Red River Floodway Project at St Anne's Road just south of the Perimeter Highway on October 6,

1962.[48] Before it was finished, more than a hundred million cubic yards of earth had to be excavated over a length of 29.4 miles, more than had been moved for either the St. Lawrence Seaway Project or the Panama Canal. The heart of the floodway was at St. Norbert, where the two floodway gates were located. In the summer these gates disappeared, but when needed, they could be raised hydraulically to prevent further water from continuing into the Red and thus diverting some of the flow into the floodway. At its peak in 1965, the floodway project employed more than a thousand people. Ultimately it cost $62 million, 58.5 per cent of which was provided by the Dominion. The Manitoba government paid its share out of operating revenues, thereby forestalling complaints about financing costs.

Although the Roblin government was responsible for much of the initiative on flood protection – including the floodway – the Portage Diversion and the Shellmouth Dam were actually completed under the Schreyer government, the former in 1970 and the latter in 1972. The NDP government also negotiated a federal-provincial agreement which led to the construction of a series of ring dikes around Dominion City, St. Jean Baptiste, Morris, Rosenort, and St. Adolphe. The first round of these dikes was completed in 1972.

While the various flood protection projects went forward, both province and Dominion were working on improving their ability to respond to disasters. Earlier floods had been dealt with largely through ad hoc measures, but the Manitoba disaster response during the 1960s became both institutionalized and formalized, to a considerable extent integrated into a national emergency response system. The Emergency Measures Organization (EMO) was in 1965 given the task of coordinating federal involvement in peacetime disasters, and one of its first mobilizations occurred during the flood threat of 1966 in Manitoba. By comparison with the response to earlier disasters, flood response in Manitoba seemed to work like a well-oiled machine.[49]

Along with the measures of flood protection and coordinated flood-fighting also came a series of efforts to provide improved rehabilitation programmes for flood victims, especially in the rural areas. In 1970, a federal Disaster Financial Assistance Program was inaugurated which established a complex formula for federal financial assistance on disasters. In theory, at least, the formula meant that there was no need for jockeying for position between province and Dominion at every emergency and that flood-fighting could be coordinated.[50] In 1976, the federal government and the province of Manitoba signed three agreements to reduce the possibility of flood damage in Manitoba by considering "all practicable structural and non-structural alternatives."[51] The governments agreed to attempt to reduce future flood assistance payments by discouraging development in flood-prone zones of the province. The response to the 1979 flood was generally regarded as evidence of the degree of careful planning.[52]

Despite the successful elaboration of an elaborate flood response system in Manitoba, signs of potential difficulties kept emerging. One was the increasing frequency with which the floodway had to be used, with high water occurring far more often than the history of the previous hundred years had suggested. Another problem involved repeated charges of misoperation of the floodway gates. In one case, the charges denied by the professional water managers in 1974 were subsequently confirmed in 1980 by outside consultants.[53] Furthermore, there was continual development on flood-prone land outside the flood control system, with little attempt at enforcement of standards.[54] By 1997, more than three thousand homes stood in the rural districts just south of the floodway gates, many on land lower than that required by 1979 provincial legislation. By the early 1980s, moreover, many residents of the upper Fraser Valley were convinced that the water engineers were part of the problem rather than the solution; land use changes, road construction, and drainage were responsible for the increased incidence of flooding, not Mother Nature[55] The many hairline cracks in the seemingly seamless web of Manitoba flood management were opened considerably wider by the flood of 1997.

4. THE FLOOD OF 1997

All the experts knew that the potentiality in the Red River Valley was high for a flood substantially higher than anything known to humankind since the first half of the nineteenth century.[56] The question was not if, but when. The recent history of flooding in the valley suggested that the "when" was soon. The average flow of water through the Red River's channel was higher than ever previously recorded, and eventually would produce The Big One. The winter of 1996-97 provided all the necessary preconditions for unprecedented flooding, and a record blizzard in early April deposited huge amounts of wet snow in Manitoba and adjacent regions of the United States. Manitobans were told on Friday, April 11 that water levels would be higher than at any point since 1861, and the situation could only get worse. On neither side of the border was there any practical experience with water so high. "We've never lost the battle before," remarked one American farmer just before his fields went under the rampaging water.[57]

Any complacency that Manitobans may have developed because of the province's flood control engineering was destroyed by April 19, when the Red had left Grand Forks virtually in ruins. Sandbag dikes were easily overrun by the river, much of the downtown area was under-water, and a massive fire was burning out of control in the downtown area. Most of the population of Grand Forks had been evacuated. In Winnipeg, fear suddenly became the order of the day, particularly since the flood forecasters were constantly revising their estimates upward. Reporters from the international media began checking into Winnipeg hotels. While the authorities sought to prevent panic by minimizing the extent of the emergency, television and radio coverage by implica-tion tended to overestimate the extent of the chaos. For most Winnipeg residents, the major risk was from basement sewer backup, no longer covered by homeowner insurance policies after a round of basement flooding in 1994. For those in the Upper Valley, mandatory evacuation from their homes was the order of the day. Many refused to leave.

The Canadian military was ordered to the province in mid-April to assist with the flood-fighting. The province was slow to request military assistance and equally slow to declare a state of emergency, still fearful that it would be left with the bill by the federal government. Despite all the agreements over the years, nothing really had changed since 1950. Fortunately for Manitobans, the military recognized this emergency as an opportunity to repair a public image tarnished by disastrous peace-keeping operations in the Balkans and Somalia, and the Dominion government, which had been extremely generous to Quebec in the Saguenay floods of 1996, could hardly do less for Manitoba. At the same time, Prime Minister Jean Chrétien angered many in the province by refusing to postpone a federal election because of the emergency. Chrétien made the obligatory visit to the city on April 26 to survey the situation, threw a single ceremonial sandbag for photographers, and returned to Ottawa to request the dissolution of Parliament.[58] The election call, purely by accident, marked the end of act one of the drama of 1997. At the point of the call, the water was moving inexorably north, and everyone wondered whether the dikes would hold.

The greatest conceptual problem for Winnipeggers in late April was in recognizing that the floodway would not necessarily save the city in 1997. The water coming in could well have exceeded the capacity of the floodway to carry it away, and was so great in volume that authorities feared that the spreading water would enter the LaSalle river system to the west of the city, thus bringing the flood to Winnipeg by the "backdoor." Construction was started on an emergency dike twenty-four kilometres long at Brunkild, to the south of the city, to prevent this eventuality. Despite the inundation of the tiny town of Ste Agathe on April 29 – the water came in on the opposite side from the dike – much of the evidence at the end of April seemed encouraging.[59] As it turned out, what saved the city was that the Brunkild dike worked, the waters of the Red crested just within the capacity of the floodway, and the entire flow from the Assiniboine River was successfully diverted to Lake Manitoba. The Portage diversion had finally proved its worth. By early May it was clear that large-scale evacuation within Winnipeg would not prove necessary, although a second community south of the floodway – Grande Pointe – disappeared under the flood waters on May 2, leaving its residents as more aggrieved "victims" of flood control measures.[60]

As was usually the case with major floods, the arrival of the crest began to turn attention away from flood-fighting toward cleanup operations. Normally, media interest in cleanup was minimal, but in 1997 post-flood operations took on a political edge, fuelled by concerns that rehabilitation money would not be sufficient to do the job and that the provincial government was dragging its heels on arranging for payment. As in previous floods, the major responsibility for the short-term problems of victims was borne by private charity. Perhaps as much as $50 million was collected for private flood assistance – by the Manitoba Flood Relief Fund, various charities such as the Red Cross and the Salvation Army, and by the churches. As for the provincial government, it made itself increasingly unpopular with flood victims, especially those who insisted that their communities had been sacrificed to protect Winnipeg. Premier Filmon refused to waive a large deductible in the flood assistance programme, and the bureaucratic response to claim adjustment was slow and insensitive. A large part of the problem was that experienced adjustors had been lost in a major government budget cut, something the government could hardly acknowledge. Filmon instead insisted that those who built on the flood plain had to take some responsibility for their losses. On the other hand, the victims south of the city were grieved that Winnipeg escaped almost scot-free – because of the expensive flood protection schemes – while they had to face the water in all its fury. The government had not protected *them*, and at the very least, many argued, there should be swift and total compensation for victims. The province tried to dampen the furor by announcing reviews of government flood-fighting beyond those already set in motion by the International Joint Commission.

5. EPILOGUE

In the end, three commissions would report on the 1997 performance in Manitoba.[61] All of them found weaknesses in both the flood control culture and the 1997 response, but none were devastating in their critiques, and more to the point, none of the reviews really came to grips with the problem of public expectations and perceptions of inequality built into flood protection. One commission caused a bit of a ripple in the press in the summer of 1999 when the provincial ombudsman rapped its knuckles for illegally destroying the records of its hearings.[62] What this probably best demonstrated was the disdain felt by the flood control culture for the historical record. The recommendations for improved flood control made by the various commissions would probably reduce to some extent future controversy in the event of another flood of 1997 proportions or greater, although complaints were voiced in late 1999 that the promised improvements, especially to the ring dikes protecting smaller communities, were still not in place.[63] A Valley divided into those protected by the floodway and those not protected remained unchanged.

Premier Filmon and his government went down to defeat in 1999. Its handling of the flood was not a major issue in the campaign, which was dominated by a debate over health-care coverage and earlier electoral hanky-panky. Most voters have conveniently short memories. But one Valley riding south of Winnipeg which had previously supported the Tories rejected them in 1999, and it was of such swings that the NDP majority was made.[64]

In the United States, rehabilitation and reconstruction were much slower to get organized than in Canada. But by 1999, it was clear that Grand Forks could look forward to a totally reconstructed downtown area, thanks to the absence of protection against the 1997 flood.[65] The new construction included a new football stadium, a new ice arena, and a new arts centre. At the same time, Winnipeg's downtown and inner core – completely defended against flooding at great expense – continued to deteriorate at a rapid rate. Construction of a new football stadium and new ice arena in Winnipeg was the subject of much public debate, and might well not be funded.[66] Grand Forks' downtown rejuvenation and Winnipeg's downtown stagnation were arguably the final irony of Red River flooding as the old millennium ended. In the new millennium, those south of the city were not surprised to learn that the old scheme of the 1950s for a Ste Agathe dike and detention basin – so damaging to the southern Valley – was resurrected by some engineers seeking to provide further protection for Winnipeg. Manitobans also discovered that Red River flood control had little or no effect on flooding of other rivers around the province, which occurred in 2002. All in all, flooding and flood control continued to be political footballs in the province.

NOTES

1 R. H. Clark, *Notes on Red River Floods with Particular Reference to the Flood of 1950* (Winnipeg, 1950). This essay is based partly on my books: *The Manitoba Flood of 1950: An Illustrated History* (Winnipeg: Watson and Dwyer, 1993); and *Floods of the Centuries: A History of Flood Disasters in the Red River Valley 1776–1997* (Winnipeg: Great Plains Publications, 1997).

2 Elmer R. Nelson, "Red River of the North Basin Flood, April–June 1950," *Monthly Weather Review* 79 (September 1951): 169–78.

3 Bishop Provencher to Bishop Panet, July 15, 1826, in Grace L. Nute, ed., *Documents Relating to Northwest Missions, 1815–1827* (St. Paul, 1942), 443; Francis Heron, "Journal of Occurrences, Kept at Fort Garry, in Red River Settlement, from 1st June 1825, until 31st July 1826," Hudson's Bay Company Archives, B.235/1/7/folios 32d-46.

4 *Report of the Royal Commission on Flood Cost Benefit* (Winnipeg, December 1958), 15, based on *Report of the Red River Basic Investigation*, vol. 1 (Ottawa, October 1953), 25.

5 E. H. Bovay, *Le Canada et les Suisses 1604–1974* (Fribourg: Editions Universitaires, 1976), 22–40.

6 *Report of the Royal Commission*, 15.

7 Our best account of this flood is Bishop David Anderson's *Notes of the Flood at the Red River in 1852* (London, 1873). This account had obviously begun as a diary, but was intended for literary as well as historical effect.

8 Ibid., 44.

9 *The Nor'-Wester*, May 9, 1861.

10 *Report of the Royal Commission*, 15.

11 Samuel P. Matheson, "Three Red River Floods," *Transactions of the Manitoba Historical Society*, series 3, no. 3, 1947.

12 Alexander Begg and W. R. Nursey, *Ten Years in Winnipeg* (Winnipeg, 1879).

13 Alan Artibise, *Winnipeg: A Social History of Urban Growth 1874–1914* (Montreal: McGill-Queen's University Press, 1975), 64–66.

14 *Manitoba Free Press*, March 31, 1882.

15 Ibid., April 19, 1882.

16 *Winnipeg Daily Tribune*, April 24, 1897.

17 Journal of George Black, 1897, University of Manitoba Archives.

18 *Free Press*, April 16, 1904.

19 Ibid., April 19, 1916.

20 Douglas McLean, "Flood Prevention Projects to Protect Winnipeg," *The Canadian Engineer*, April 1, 1920.

21 *Report of the Land Drainage Arrangement Commission Respecting Municipalities Containing Land Subject to Levies under "The Land Drainage Act"* (Winnipeg, 1936).

22 "Minutes of an Emergency Meeting of Representatives from Provincial Government, City of Winnipeg, adjoining municipalities, transportation

companies, armed serves, under the auspices of the Red Cross Management Committee," April 25, 1948, Provincial Archives of Manitoba (hereafter cited as PAM), MG 10 B29, Box 22.

23   *Winnipeg Tribune*, April 30, 1948.

24   For example, *Winnipeg Tribune*, May 5, 1948.

25   *Winnipeg Free Press*, May 4, 1948.

26   *Winnipeg Free Press*, February 2, 1949.

27   *Winnipeg Free Press*, May 8, 1950.

28   In general, see J.M. Bumsted, "Developing a Canadian Disaster Relief Policy: The 1950 Manitoba Flood," *Canadian Historical Review* 48, no. 3 (1987): 347–73.

29   For the U.S. story, see Douglas Ramsey and Larry Skroch, *The Raging Red: The 1950 Red River Valley Flood* (Grand Forks, 1996).

30   *Call 320: A Documentary Record of the 1950 Manitoba Flood and Red Cross Activities in the Disaster* (Winnipeg, 1950).

31   Agreement, Province of Manitoba and Canadian Army, April 14, 1950, PAM, RG 11/A1/1.

32   Campbell to St. Laurent, May 7, 1950, PAM, RG 11/A1/1.

33   Press Release re Flood, May 7,1950, PAM, G45, Box 63.

34   A good summary of the "Fraser Valley Formula" is in the Manitoba Flood Relief Fund's memorandum for Jonathan Lewis, director, Commonwealth Gift Centre, London, May 19, 1950, PAM, G45, Box 62.

35   The Fund's papers are in PAM, G45, Box 62.

36   The report was prepared in great haste, wrote its authors, because of "the spirit of unrest and uncertainty in the province", J. B. Carswell and D. Bruce Shaw to D. C. Abbott and D. L. Campbell, June 6, 1950, PAM, RG11/A1/1.

37   Press release, premier's office, June 9, 1950, PAM G45, Box 63.

38   Red River Valley Board, *Report to the Hon. Douglas Campbell* (Winnipeg, December 15, 1950).

39   A. H. Rutherford and A. Baracos, *Damage to Houses Red River Valley Flood 1950* (Canada NRC Division of Building Research Technical Bulletin, 9: Ottawa, 1953).

40   Bumsted, "Developing a Canadian Disaster Policy," 368–70.

41   Greater Winnipeg Dyking Board, *Final Report on the Activities of Greater Winnipeg Dyking Board* (Winnipeg, 1951).

42   See, for example, Glenwood Crescent Association, *Riverside Owners "Appeal for Compensation" to a Special Committee of the City Council* (Winnipeg, November 1950).

43   G. L. McKenzie, *Report on Investigations into Measures for the Reduction of the Flood Hazard in the Greater Winnipeg Area*, 9 vols. (Ottawa, 1953).

44   See J.M. Bumsted, "The Manitoba Royal Commission on Flood Cost Benefit and the Origins of Cost-Benefit Analysis in Canada," *American Review of Canadian Studies* 32, no. 1 (Spring 2002): 97–121.

45   *Report of the Royal Commission on Flood Cost Benefit* (Winnipeg, 1958).

46   Duff Roblin, *Speaking for Myself: Politics and Other Pursuits* (Winnipeg: Great

Plains, 1999), 171–72.

47   Legislative Assembly of Manitoba, *Debates*, March 26 and 27, 1962.

48   Province of Manitoba, Department of Agriculture and Conservation, *The Red River Floodway* (Winnipeg, 1962).

49   John A. Hannigan and Rodney M. Kueneman, "Anticipating Flood Emergencies: A Case Study of a Canadian Disaster Subculture," in E. L. Quarantelli, ed., *Disasters: Theory and Research* (Beverly Hills, CA: Sage, 1978), 130–46.

50   See, for example, Manitoba Emergency Measures Organization, *Manitoba Flood Fighting Plan* (Winnipeg, 1972).

51   "General Agreement Respecting Flood Damage Reduction," 1976.

52   Manitoba Flood Disaster Assistance Board, *1979 Manitoba Flood: Recovery and Protection* (Winnipeg, 1979); Ian McLaurin and J. H. Wedel, *The Red River Flood of 1979* (Winnipeg, 1981).

53   Manitoba Water Commission, *Review of the Red River Floodway, Portage Diversion and Shellmouth Reservoir* (Winnipeg, 1980).

54   W. F. Rannie, "The Red River Flood Control System and Recent Flood Events," *Water Resources Bulletin* 16, no. 2 (April 1980): 207–14.

55   Laurence N. Ogrodnik, *Water Management in the Red River Valley: A History and Policy Review* (Winkler, 1984).

56   W. G. McKay, "The Unpredictable Red River," *The Manitoba Professional Engineer* (August 1997): 1–11.

57   *Winnipeg Free Press*, April 16, 1997.

58   Ibid., April 27, 1997.

59   Ibid., April 30, 1997.

60   Ibid., May 3, 1997.

61   International Red River Basin Task Force, *Red River Flood: Short Term Measures* (Ottawa and Washington, December 1997); *A Preliminary Assessment of Environmental Impacts Associated with the 1997 Red River Flood* (1998); Ernst & Young, *1997 Red River Flood Post Emergency Report, Part I* (Winnipeg, February 10, 1998); Manitoba Water Commission, *An Independent Review of the 1997 Red River Flood: Interim Report* (Winnipeg, March 31, 1998); Manitoba Water Commission, *An Independent Review of Actions Taken during the 1997 Red River Flood* (Winnipeg, June 1998).

62   Ombudsman Manitoba, News Release, July 16, 1999.

63   *Winnipeg Free Press*, October 27, 1999.

64   *Winnipeg Free Press*, September 11, 1999, quotes one voter in La Verendrye riding as saying that the Tories would not get his vote this year: "They screwed us around."

65   *Winnipeg Free Press*, September 12, 1999.

66   A new arena was finally approved, to be built on the downtown site of Eaton's Department Store, in 2001.

NOTES ON CONTRIBUTORS

David Breen is Professor of Western Canadian History at the University of British Columbia. His research interest is centred on the European settlement of the prairie West, particularly as it relates to land use and evolution of policies governing the development of natural resources. He is the author of *Alberta's Petroleum Industry and the Conservation Board* (1993) and *The Canadian Prairie West and the Ranching Frontier 1874–1924* (1983).

Patrick Brennan was born in Saskatchewan and received his Ph.D. from York University. He is currently an Associate Professor in History at the University of Calgary, where he specializes in Canadian military and political history with an associated interest in the prairie region. He is the author of *Representing the Nation's Business: Press-Government Relations in the Liberal Years, 1935–57* (1994).

J. M. Bumsted is a professor of history at the University of Manitoba and a fellow of St. John's College. He is the author of a number of works in Manitoba history, including *The Manitoba Flood of 1950* (1993) and *Floods of the Centuries: A History of Flooding in the Red River Valley of Manitoba* (1997). He is presently completing the last volume of a trilogy of works on the Red River Settlement.

Joe Cherwinski is Supervisor of the Canadian Studies Programme at Memorial University of Newfoundland. Joe Cherwinski's initial research was on western Canadian labour and the left. Most recently his interests have turned to the settlement period on the Prairies, with research on fringe religious groups on the one hand and the relationship between environment and social change on the other.

Hugh A. Dempsey is Chief Curator Emeritus of the Glenbow Museum in Calgary, where he filled various administrative roles, including those of Acting Director and Associate Director. He currently is an Adjunct Professor of History at the University of Calgary, a recipient of the Order of Canada, holds an honorary doctorate from the University of Calgary, and is an honorary chief of the Blood tribe. He is the author of eighteen books, including histories of Calgary, ranching, the Mounted Police, and biographies of Crowfoot, Red Crow, and Big Bear. He has been the editor of the quarterly magazine *Alberta History* since 1958.

Janice Dickin is Associate Dean (Research), Faculty of Communication and Culture, University of Calgary. Recently, her research interests have lain in the areas of life writing and in the contributions that new information technologies can make to qualitative scholarship. She is planning further exploration of the historiography of absence.

Clinton Evans, who holds as Ph.D. in History from the University of British Columbia, is a self-employed historical consultant. He has worked in the weed control industry, and has taught at Okanagan University College in Kelowna. He is the author of *The War on Weeds in the Prairie West: An Environmental History* (2002).

Dr. Lorry Felske is the Director of the Canadian Studies Program in the Faculty of Communication and Culture at the University of Calgary. He has done extensive research on the history of the coal mining industry and the associated communities in Alberta and southeastern British Columbia. Dr. Felske was the consulting historian for the Leitch Collieries Interpretative Site and for the Frank Slide Visitor's Centre in the Crowsnest Pass. He recently worked with Parks Canada on the National Historic Site designations for the coal mining structures and townsites in Coleman, Nordegg and East Coulee.

Max Foran is an Assistant Professor in the Faculty of Communications and Culture at the University of Calgary. The author of several books and articles on various aspects of urban development in western Canada, he has also published extensively on the beef cattle industry in Canada. His latest publication, *Trails and Trials: Markets and Land use in the Alberta Cattle Industry 1881–1948* was released by the University of Calgary Press in 2003.

David C. Jones is a Professor of History in the Faculty of Education at the University of Calgary. He has written or edited twenty-six books including the award-winning *Empire of Dust: Settling and Abandoning the Prairie Dry Belt* (1987) and *Feasting on Misfortune: Journeys of the Human Spirit in Alberta's Past* (1998). A noted speaker and lecturer, Dr. Jones was one of the first recipients of the President's Circle Award for Teaching Excellence at the University of Calgary.

Q